AUDREY PAVIA

Joanne Howl, D.V.M., Series Editor

Your
GERMAN
SHEPHERD'S
Life

Your Complete Guide to Raising Your Pet from Puppy to Companion

PRIMA PETS

An Imprint of Prima Publishing

Interior photos by Kent Lacin Media Services
Color insert photos © Isabelle Français
Chapter 6 illustrations by Pam Tanzey

Library of Congress Cataloging-in-Publication Data
Pavia, Audrey.
    Your German shepherd's life : your complete guide to raising your pet from puppy to companion / Audrey Pavia.
        p.   cm.
    ISBN 0-7615-2052-X
    1. German shepherd dog. I. Title
    SF429.G37P38   1999
    636.737'6—dc21   99-35890
                                                                                    CIP

99 00 01 02 HH 10 9 8 7 6 5 4 3 2 1
Printed in the United States of America

How to Order
Single copies may be ordered from Prima Publishing, P.O. Box 1260BK, Rocklin, CA 95677; telephone (916) 632-4400. Quantity discounts are also available. On your letterhead, include information concerning the intended use of the books and the number of books you wish to purchase.

Visit us online at www.primalifestyles.com

For Jackie,
my very first best friend.

Also Available from PRIMA PETS™

Your Cat's Life by Joanne Howl, D.V.M.

Your Chihuahua's Life by Kim Campbell Thornton

Your Dog's Life by Tracy Acosta, D.V.M.

Your German Shepherd's Life by Audrey Pavia

Your Golden Retriever's Life by Betsy Sikora Siino

Your Rottweiler's Life by Kim D.R. Dearth

Contents

Introduction

One of the most popular and recognizable of all pure-bred dogs is the German Shepherd. For reasons both tangible and intangible, the German Shepherd has captured the hearts and minds of dog lovers throughout the world.

If you own a German Shepherd—or want to—you are probably the kind of person who is drawn to a dog who is loyal, trustworthy, and faithful to the end. If so, you have picked the right breed, because all of these qualities belong to the German Shepherd.

An Overview of German Shepherd Ownership

Owning a German Shepherd—or any dog—requires a huge commitment in time, money, and effort. There may have been a day when having a dog around the house was no big deal. In the "old days," most dog owners had big yards or lived out in the country. Someone was always home to take care of the dog, morning, noon, and night. Dogs exercised themselves by running and playing outdoors, and seemed to just naturally get along with children, other pets, and family friends.

In today's world, however, things are very different. A great many people who choose to own dogs live in urban areas. They reside in condos or apartments, have very little living space, and oftentimes have no yard at all. They are single people who work away from home all day, or are working couples who leave early in the morning and don't come home until late at night.

Having a dog under these circumstances requires planning, commitment, and sacrifice. You have to really want a dog to make it work if this is your lifestyle. You must find a way to provide all the things your dog needs—companionship, exercise, socialization—regardless of how much effort it takes.

This is even more true when it comes to the German Shepherd. No lap dog, the German Shepherd is a big animal who requires a considerable amount of living space and regular exercise. He's also a dog who needs human company and doesn't do well during extended periods of isolation.

The German Shepherd is also a dog who needs to be trained, in large part because of his size, but also because he craves it. Hundreds of years of breeding have created in the German Shepherd a dog that is *meant* to be trained. A German Shepherd without training is a large, out-of-control, and unhappy dog.

German Shepherd owners who live in today's world must find ways to spend time with their dogs, to train them, and to exercise them. While all this work seemed to just happen in the days when life was simpler, in today's society, meeting the needs of a German Shepherd calls for considerable planning.

What It Means to Have a German Shepherd in Your Life

A wagging tail and sloppy kisses when you walk through the door at the end of a long day. A loyal confidante to tell your troubles to when you are feeling low. A quiet companion to sit by your side at pensive moments when you all you want to do is relax. A buddy to play with and jog with and go hiking with so you never have to do this stuff on your own.

All of these things are yours if you have a German Shepherd in your life. The truth of the matter is that you are never alone when you are with a German Shepherd. While you may not be able to converse in human verbiage with your canine friend, you will still communicate with your dog in quiet and subtle ways—and he with you. People who live with German Shepherds know that they are truly man's best friend.

Conversely, bringing a German Shepherd into your life means taking on tremendous responsibility. You must care for your dog and provide him with food, water, and shelter. You are his source for exercise and companionship, for safety and medical care, for love and guidance.

Having a German Shepherd in your life means sharing in a give-and-take relationship whose rewards are endless.

How Much Thought Have You Given to Having a German Shepherd?

Do you like to go out after work and partake in cocktail hour with your friends on a regular basis? Do you prefer to spend your weekends in museums or watching commercial sporting events on TV? Would you rather stay in a luxury hotel on your vacation rather than to go camping in the woods?

If you answered "yes" to these questions and you also think you want to own a German Shepherd, think again. Owning a German Shepherd means coming straight home from work at night to take your dog for a walk and provide him with company. Owning a German Shepherd means going to the park on weekends and playing fetch with him, or hanging out at the beach with your dog in tow. It also means spending at least some of your vacation time roughing it so your dog can come along and enjoy your company in the great outdoors.

Before you add a German Shepherd to your life, take a good look at your lifestyle and how you prefer to spend your time. If you enjoy being outdoors, are an active person, and don't mind being tied down by a dog who needs you, then you just might be ready for a German Shepherd. But if any of this sounds unpleasant to you, reconsider bringing a this dog into your life. A German Shepherd requires a tremendous commitment—one that should never be taken lightly.

Dog Ownership: The Many Sacrifices, the Many Joys

Owning a dog is not easy these days. It means spending time with your dog when you might rather be doing something else. It means getting up in the middle of the night to take your puppy outside for a bathroom break. It means paying veterinary bills, even when your pet is healthy. It means being responsible for another living creature when you've already got a million other responsibilities weighing heavy on your mind.

On the other hand, owning a dog today can be tremendously rewarding. It means having someone you can spend time with who won't judge you. It means that your children will have a friend who will love them no matter what. It means living with someone who will be happy to see you when you come home, even if you've only been gone for 10 minutes. And it means having a friend who will always be there for you when everyone else just can't be bothered.

Dog ownership is hard work—but the vast rewards of having a German Shepherd call you "master" make it all that hard work worthwhile.

1

So, You Want a German Shepherd

In This Chapter

- ❍ What Makes a German Shepherd Special?
- ❍ Keys to Your German Shepherd's Happiness
- ❍ Where to Find the Perfect German Shepherd for You

If you grew up watching television, a certain image no doubt pops into your mind whenever you hear the words German Shepherd. Most likely, you see a regal dog who saves lives, conquers evil, and does anything else asked of him. The legendary Rin-Tin-Tin embodies the essence of that idealized dog. His memorable image represents all the things we love about dogs: affection, bravery, and their undying devotion to us.

Of course, it's no accident that the dog who epitomizes this ideal is the German Shepherd. Shepherds are well known for their loyalty, courage, and intelligence. In fact, German Shepherds are so closely associated with these traits that they have become one of the most popular breeds in the world.

What Makes a German Shepherd Special?

Since you are reading this book, you probably count yourself among the millions of people who recognize that German Shepherds are very special dogs. Although Shepherds share much in common with other breeds, they embody certain characteristics that make them unique.

A Bit of History

Today's German Shepherd is a product of his past. The breed began hundreds of years ago, when farmers in the geographic region now known as Germany started to develop a special dog to herd their livestock. The farmers selected their best herding dogs and bred them with one another, and thus a specialized breed began to develop. By the late 1800s, this breed—now known as the German Shepherd Dog—had acquired a distinctive look, similar to what we see today.

Around that time, a German military officer named Max Emil Frederich von Stephanitz started a German Shepherd breed club in an attempt to help preserve and promote this excellent herding dog. The club succeeded, and to this day, von Stephanitz is considered the father of the German Shepherd breed.

Thanks to von Stephanitz's efforts, the German Shepherd soon gained recognition beyond the boundaries of Germany, not only for the breed's herding abilities, but also for its capabilities as a guard and police dog. The German Shepherd's eventual reputation for guarding and policing work makes sense, since the breed originally had been developed to herd and protect livestock.

By the early 1900s, the German Shepherd had become popular throughout Europe and even in the United States. In fact, after World War I, the British so admired the breed that they began calling it the Alsatian, so they wouldn't have to associate the dogs with their enemy, Germany.

Over the past century, the German Shepherd Dog has grown in popularity throughout the world, and the breed is today appreciated by dog lovers from Canada to Japan.

The Breed Standard

What makes the German Shepherd who he is? Where does his unique appearance come from? How was his amazing personality developed? The answers to these questions lie in the breed standard, a canine blueprint of sorts, developed by those who love and strive to preserve the German Shepherd breed.

A breed standard exists for every individual breed of dog recognized by the American Kennel Club (AKC), as well as the Canadian Kennel Club. Breed standards, which describe the physical characteristics and personality traits of an ideal example of the breed, guide those who breed and judge purebred dogs. The current AKC breed standard for the German Shepherd was most recently updated in 1994 by the German Shepherd Dog Club of America, Inc. It details the standard features of the breed sought by those who responsibly breed German Shepherds.

The breed standard starts by describing the general appearance of the German Shepherd, then carefully breaks down the different characteristics that make up the dog's overall appearance. The

What's the American Kennel Club?

Founded in 1884, the American Kennel Club (AKC) is a non-profit organization dedicated to the advancement of purebred dogs. Composed of over 500 dog clubs from across the nation, the AKC's objectives include maintaining a registry of purebred dogs, promoting responsible dog ownership, and sponsoring events, such as breed shows and field trials, that promote interest in and appreciation of the purebred dog.

To be eligible for AKC registry, a puppy must be the offspring of individually registered AKC parents, and the breeder must obtain the proper paperwork before the puppy's sale. Once registered, a dog is eligible to compete in AKC-sanctioned events and, if bred with another AKC registered dog, to have his/her offspring registered.

The AKC approves an official breed standard for each of the 147 breeds currently eligible for registration. The standard is written and maintained by each individual breed club. An attempt to describe the "perfect" dog of each breed, the breed standard is the model responsible breeders use in their efforts to produce better dogs. Judges of AKC-sponsored events and competitions use the breed standards as the basis of their evaluations.

Because of the AKC's emphasis on excellence and high standards, it is a common misconception that "AKC registered" or "AKC registrable" is synonymous with quality. However, while a registration certificate identifies a dog and its progenitors as purebreds, it does not necessarily guarantee the health or quality of a dog. Some breeders breed for show quality, but others breed for profit, with little concern for breed standards. Thus, a potential buyer should not view AKC registration as an indication of a dog's quality.

standard describes nearly every physical characteristic of the German Shepherd's body, one of the most important being his head. The German Shepherd's "noble and cleanly chiseled" head is one of the key features that sets him apart from other breeds.

The temperament characteristics form another important segment of the German Shepherd standard. The standard includes words like direct, fearless, self-confident, eager, and alert to describe the German Shepherd's wonderful personality.

These descriptions are more than just words. Just ask California police officer Jeff Azuar, who owned a police dog named Rondo—a dog who gave his life in the line of duty. It happened one day when Officer Azuar found himself pursuing a suspected hit-and-run driver. Azuar and several other police officers cornered the suspect in a culvert under a street, but couldn't get him to surrender. They needed Rondo's help to get the man out.

"After trying for quite a while to convince the man to come out, I had to send Rondo in after him," says Azuar. "We had no idea the man was armed." Rondo didn't hesitate—he obeyed Azuar's orders to approach the suspect. When Rondo reached the man, a struggle ensued. The man had a knife and Rondo was fatally injured. Rondo became a hero in his community and was honored with a funeral attended by 300 people and 40 police dogs.

Speaking of Temperament

Although the breed standard spells out certain requirements for the German Shepherd's temperament, a dog of this breed brings additional well-defined traits to the homes of those he lives with.

Because the German Shepherd was originally bred to be a herding dog—and is, in fact, classified in the American Kennel Club's Herding Group—the breed has a pretty high activity level. Shepherds like to go out and do things. Although a German Shepherd is sometimes content to just lay on the couch and veg out with his

Did You Know?

The wolf, from which dogs are descended, was the first animal to be domesticated.

owner in front of the television, he usually prefers running outside in the yard or at the park, playing Frisbee, or chasing a tennis ball.

The German Shepherd's tendency toward unconditional devotion to his owner further defines the breed's personality. Shepherds develop strong attachments to the people they live with, whether that's one person or an entire family.

> Loyal, protective, happy, and sensitive are words that easily describe the personality of this wonderful breed.

Take for example a German Shepherd named Helen. Helen's owners, Paul and Martha Walker of Prescott, Arizona, say that Helen's world completely revolves around their family. "There is nothing Helen would rather do than be with us," says Martha. "And that even includes eating! She wants to be with us all the time, doing whatever we are doing. She even takes turns spending time with everyone in the family. If the kids are playing a video game, she sits next to them and watches. If I'm outside in the yard gardening, she is there helping me. If Paul is out in the garage working on one of his projects, she wants to go out there and sit at his feet. On weekends when we are all home at the same time, she makes the rounds just to be sure she spends time with everyone!"

German Shepherds are not only known for being capable of great devotion. They are also exceptional guard dogs. Jack and Kara Ward of Illinois can attest to this firsthand. Their German Shepherd, Eldridge, gave a burglar quite a surprise one day when the criminal made the mistake of breaking into their home. "We were out one night having dinner and Eldridge was alone in the house," says Jack. "A burglar managed to jimmy a window open and get into the house. Boy, was he sorry. Eldridge must have come flying at him from out of nowhere. The guy left a trail of blood in the living room. Needless to say, he didn't take anything. He just tried to get out of there as fast as he could. When he was arrested a couple of days later, it was obvious that Eldridge had gotten him by the big bite mark on his arm. Which really shocked us because Eldridge is the sweetest dog in the world, and just loves strangers! He obviously knew the difference between someone who was welcome in the house and someone who was up to no good."

The skills of the German Shepherd are many. They are not only used throughout the world as guard and protection dogs, but are also frequently trained for duties that call for gentle sensibilities. Search-and-rescue work, where dogs are asked to look for lost people or victims of a disaster, is one such job. Animal-assisted therapy, which calls for visits to hospitals and nursing homes, is another.

Overall, the German Shepherd's temperament is one of the most heralded in the world of purebred dogs. Loyal, protective, happy, and sensitive are words that easily describe the personality of this wonderful breed.

Life Expectancy

As unpleasant as you might find the topic, you should probably consider the German Shepherd's life expectancy before you go out and get one of these amazing dogs.

German Shepherds live an average of 10 to 11 years. Because they are big dogs, Shepherds don't usually live as long as medium-size breeds, such as Dalmatians and smaller Golden Retrievers, who can live 12 or 13 years. The life expectancy of even smaller breeds, such as Pomeranians and Shih Tzus, can easily extend beyond that of German Shepherds, reaching ages of 14 years and sometimes older. However, German Shepherds do live longer than some of the giant breeds, like the Irish Wolfhound and Great Dane, which often pass away at the early age of six.

Keys to Your German Shepherd's Happiness

Every breed of dog has certain requirements that must be met in order for that breed to live an enjoyable, well-adjusted life. The German Shepherd is no exception. His size and activity requirements, along with his need for leadership and companionship, all factor into the components of what a German Shepherd needs in his everyday life.

How Much Space Does a German Shepherd Need?

As you probably know by now, German Shepherds are good-sized dogs, weighing anywhere from 60 to 100 pounds and measuring 22 to 26 inches at the shoulder. However, it's not so much the German Shepherd's physical size as it is his activity level that determines the amount of space he needs to live comfortably.

Because German Shepherds have been bred for centuries to herd livestock—a job that requires plenty of energy—the dog tends to be very active. This means they need lots of exercise in order to stay happy and healthy. An hour a day of good, strenuous activity is the minimum required for a healthy, adult German Shepherd.

A house with a yard is the best environment for a German Shepherd. The more room your dog has to move around, the more exercise he is likely to get—and the less likely he is to get in your way! Having access to a yard, however, does not alone ensure that your Shepherd will get the amount of exercise he needs. You must give him a reason to run around and exert himself, which means playing a game of fetch with him every day to make sure he gets sufficient exercise.

If you live in an apartment or condo, you can still provide your German Shepherd with the amount of exercise he needs. A long walk or jog, consisting of at least several miles a day, in addition to play sessions outdoors in a large, fenced area should do the trick. As a side bonus, you, too, will get plenty of exercise in the process of working out your dog.

Remember that your German Shepherd needs to get a solid amount of activity every single day. Don't mislead yourself by thinking you can fit a week's worth of your dog's exercise requirements into your weekend schedule. If your German Shepherd doesn't receive an adequate amount of exertion on a daily basis, he will likely become bored and neurotic, which might cause him to develop nuisance behaviors such as barking, chewing, and digging.

How Much Training?

Over the centuries, German Shepherds have been bred to follow the commands of their masters, whether farmers, soldiers, police officers, or Hollywood dog trainers. As a result, they naturally take to just about any kind of training.

Many reasons exist for at least giving your German Shepherd training in basic obedience. For one thing, as a big dog, your Shepherd needs to be under control at all times. Because of their size and exuberance for life, untrained German Shepherds can unwittingly hurt people by jumping up on them, dragging them when leashed, or even accidentally knocking them over. Boisterous German Shepherds pose a particular risk to children, the youngest of whom are dwarfed by the average adult Shepherd. Every

Did You Know?

The United States and France have the highest rates of dog ownership in the world, with almost one dog for every three families. Germany and Switzerland have the lowest rates, with just one dog for every ten families.

German Shepherd should have at least basic obedience training, so he'll know how to properly behave around humans.

Training your German Shepherd also helps to give your pet emotional security. Shepherds are highly social animals, as are all dogs. An instinct within your dog known as pack behavior harkens him back to the days when his ancient relatives were wild dogs living in social groups, or packs. Living in packs enabled the wild ancestors of the modern dog to hunt, reproduce, and survive by cooperating with their own species in a complicated hierarchy. Remember, this was long before kibble and dog breeders came on the scene!

Wolves and many other wild canids still live in packs, which has enabled behavioral scientists to observe and gain a better understanding of pack behavior. In their studies, these researchers have discovered that within each pack exists an individual leader, or alpha, whose job is to guide and to look out for the pack.

Because your German Shepherd's psyche instinctively places great emphasis on pack behavior, he needs to feel as if he is part of a pack. He also needs to feel someone is in charge of that pack. By teaching your dog basic obedience, you are telling him that you retain the alpha leadership position and, hence, have everything under control. Knowing this will give your German Shepherd great security in life. If he believes you are at the helm, he will feel free to kick back and relax while you run the show.

Conversely, if you don't train your German Shepherd, he may very well get the impression that no pack leader exists within your household. In that case, he may become insecure and fearful. Worse, he might try to take over the leadership position himself, which can result in aggressive and inappropriate behavior in your dog.

Another excellent reason for training German Shepherds is that they always love having a job to do, whether it's herding sheep, pursuing criminals, guarding property, or helping the handicapped.

A German Shepherd with a job is a happy German Shepherd. A German Shepherd who has received obedience training and is often required to execute what he has learned considers himself gainfully employed. (Training your German Shepherd is discussed in Chapter 6, Basic Training for German Shepherds.)

Can My German Shepherd Stay Home All Day Without Me?

Because German Shepherds are such people-oriented dogs, they are happiest when surrounded by the family they love. However, the constraints of modern life usually prohibit the average German Shepherd from being with his family 24 hours a day.

If you are a single person or are part of a two-adult working family, chances are any dog in your household will be left alone for long periods of time while you are away at work. This situation is not ideal for most breeds of dogs, particularly the German Shepherd.

The very qualities we love about the German Shepherd—devotion, affection, zeal—are the same qualities that make it hard for him to be alone all day without human companionship. Many dogs, regardless of breed, who are left on their own for long periods of time often experience separation anxiety or extreme boredom. These dogs seek relief from their discomfort by indulging in behaviors such as excessive barking and destructive chewing. German Shepherds are no exception to this rule.

Does that mean, if you are single or if you and your spouse both work, that you can't have a German Shepherd? Not necessarily, as long as you are willing and able to make some compromises. You can help your dog cope with long periods of solitude by following these simple guidelines:

Exercise before and after work.   One way to keep your dog from becoming bored or anxious in your absence is to tire him out before you leave for work. That means a strenuous game of ball in the backyard or a long jog through the neighborhood before you leave for the office. When you return—and you must return; never leave your pet alone overnight—your Shepherd will need another good session of exercise to work off some of the energy he's built up in your absence. Remember, he's been sitting home all day doing nothing!

Plenty of quality time.   In addition to lots of exercise before and after work, you should spend nearly all of your spare time with your German Shepherd. You should hang out with him during and after dinner, keep him nearby while you watch TV or read, and allow him to sleep in your bedroom at night.

Doggy day care.   Another option for German Shepherds whose owners work outside the home is doggy day care. You can arrange for daytime visitors or professional day care for your dog on the days you're away from home. For example, you can ask a neighbor to come in during the day to play with your dog, hire a professional dog walker or pet sitter to come to your house to exercise your dog, or take your dog to an official canine day-care center, where he can spend the day playing with other dogs in the company of his human sitters.

Surefire Ways to Make Your German Shepherd's Life Unpleasant

You'll find it fairly easy to please your German Shepherd, provided you know what he needs and are willing to give it to him. By the same token, certain things can make a German Shepherd pretty miserable and should be avoided at all costs.

You love your dog and want him to be happy, right? Guarding against the following no-nos, then, should be no problem.

Not enough companionship. German Shepherds are incredibly family-oriented dogs and suffer terribly in isolation. Leaving your dog home alone for extended periods of time will leave him feeling lonely and anxious. Locking him out in the backyard for hours on end will make him feel like an outcast. Chaining him outside all day and night so he can "guard the house" will devastate him.

Lack of exercise. Because German Shepherds were bred to herd livestock, they are full of energy and need a healthy outlet for it. Failing to give your German Shepherd at least an hour of strenuous activity per day will leave him with excess energy he won't know what to do with. Confining him for many hours on end will drive him crazy. Expecting your German Shepherd to be a couch potato, when his natural inclination is to run, is unfair and useless. He'll find a way to burn off that energy somehow, most likely in a way you'll consider destructive.

Inadequate training. Your German Shepherd needs guidance in his life, and he will look to you to provide it. If you fail to provide him the formal training he needs in order to understand his place in your home, you will end up with an unruly dog who cannot be controlled. An absence of training will make you and your dog unhappy. If he drags you when you're walking him, you won't take him on walks—and he won't get the exercise and attention he needs. If he behaves like a lunatic when company comes, you won't want him around—and he'll feel lonely and frustrated. Eventually, you may not want to be around him at all. When that happens, your German Shepherd is the one who suffers. (Training your German Shepherd is discussed in Chapter 6, Basic Training for German Shepherds.)

Disrespectful kids.   German Shepherds enjoy children who treat them with love and respect. They do not appreciate undisciplined kids who pull their tails, pinch their ears, and jump on their backs. Some Shepherds will suffer silently while being mistreated by overzealous children, but others may resort to running away and hiding, or worse, to biting in an attempt to defend themselves. It's important to teach your children to treat your German Shepherd with care and consideration, for the dog's safety and theirs.

Poor diet.   German Shepherds are athletic dogs who feel their best when they are fit and trim. Feeding your dog table scraps and/or poor quality dog food could lead to obesity, malnutrition, and susceptibility to health problems in your pet. (Your German Shepherd's nutritional care is discussed in Chapter 3, Food for Thought.)

Maybe a German Shepherd Isn't the Dog for Me

Before you go out and get yourself a German Shepherd, think long and hard about what you have read so far. If you're getting a sinking feeling that you won't be able to provide an appropriate environment for your dog—specifically, companionship, exercise, and training—then perhaps the German Shepherd is not the breed for you. Your lifestyle might be better suited to another, less active breed, or perhaps no dog at all right now. You will need to do some soul-searching to figure out whether dog owner-ship, particularly of a German Shepherd, is the right direction for you to take at this time.

Uh oh! What if you already have a German Shepherd in your household and have just now realized your lifestyle is ill suited for one? Should you take your dog to the pound right away? Of course not! Instead, rethink your situation and try to find a way to make it work. For example, if you come home after working all day and find that your German Shepherd has destroyed your living room, he obviously needs more exercise and companionship than you are providing. Hiring someone to help provide your German Shepherd with the company and workouts he needs should solve your problem.

If your German Shepherd is getting enough companionship and exercise but is sorely lacking in the training department, start taking him to obedience class once a week, so he can learn some manners. It doesn't matter how old your dog is, either. Although it's best to start training when the dog is young, any dog, especially a German Shepherd, can learn basic obedience at any age.

Whatever the problems you might be experiencing with your pet, don't give up too easily. German Shepherds are highly malleable dogs; with the right treatment, they can learn to behave as appropriately as they are supposed to. If you feel you need expert help in teaching your dog, don't hesitate to contact a dog trainer. Your veterinarian can recommend one.

Where to Find the Perfect German Shepherd for You

Believe it or not, the way in which you choose your German Shepherd plays a big role in determining the success of your relationship with your pet. The dog's age, where you acquire him, and the criteria you use to select which dog to take home all factor into the decision and its outcome.

Puppies Versus Older Dogs

Few things in life are as sweet and adorable as a puppy. Something about the way puppies exude love and joy captivates nearly everyone who comes into contact with them. However, although puppies are incredibly cute, they are also a lot of work.

> Although it's best to start training when the dog is young, any dog, especially a German Shepherd, can learn basic obedience at any age.

If you are considering getting a German Shepherd puppy, do so with the understanding that the dog's crucial early training will fall on you. You'll be responsible for socializing the puppy with other dogs, children, cats, and the world in general. Your puppy-training responsibilities also will encompass teaching him to eliminate outdoors and to follow basic house rules, as well as other assorted behaviors. (Training your German Shepherd is discussed in Chapter 6, Basic Training for German Shepherds.) All this takes plenty of dedication and work.

Of course, the good thing about having this responsibility is that it will enable you to mold your puppy into the adult dog you want him to be. Just as with human children, a young German Shepherd's socialization and training determine the kind of adult he will become. If you are dedicated to your puppy's early development, you will end up with a very nice adult dog. On the other hand, if you don't have enough time to spend with your puppy and, therefore, can't teach him what he needs to know, you may end up with a problem on your hands.

Along with time and training, patience tops the list of puppy requirements. Chewing on everything in sight is a natural puppy behavior mostly associated with teething—and it can drive you crazy. Puppies also seem to possess an unlimited supply of energy and can literally exhaust you with their mischievous antics.

If you want to avoid the effort and responsibility associated with puppies, consider getting an adult German Shepherd instead. Adopting an adult dog brings plenty of benefits. For one, you probably won't have to house-train him, because most adult dogs already know the rules regarding eliminating in the house. Plus, your adult dog will have already gone through the stages of destructive chewing and boundless, unbridled energy that all German Shepherd puppies experience.

The down side of getting an adult Shepherd rather than a puppy is that the dog's early training and socialization have already been completed—or not—and you'll be left with the results. If you acquire an adult dog who has received proper training and socialization as a pup, you should experience no significant problems. Otherwise, you'll have some work to do with your new dog to bring him up to par.

Buying from a Breeder

When the time comes to start looking around for a dog, whether you've decided on a puppy or an adult, consider buying a German Shepherd from a responsible breeder. Because they spend a lot of effort making sure the dogs they sell are healthy and well socialized, responsible breeders provide the best sources for German Shepherds. Dogs purchased from responsible breeders come with health guarantees and return policies (often for the lifetime of the dog), as well as built-in help whenever you need it.

One negative side of getting a German Shepherd from a breeder is that it will cost you more money than if you adopt a dog from an animal shelter or rescue group. It will not, however, cost you more than it would to buy a dog from a pet shop.

Finding a Good Breeder

Locating a responsible breeder from whom to buy your German Shepherd is probably the most important step in your dog-selection process. Begin by contacting your national German Shepherd Dog club and asking for a list of breeders in your area. Then, call the breeders closest to you and ask them the following questions:

❍ How many years have you been breeding German Shepherds? The more experience a person has in breeding German Shepherds, the more he or she will know about the breed.

❍ How many litters of German Shepherds have you bred? Responsible breeders do not usually breed more than one or two litters a year.

❍ Do you show your dogs at American Kennel Club, Canadian Kennel Club, or national and regional German Shepherd Dog club events? Breeders who show their dogs are committed to improving and preserving the German Shepherd breed.

❍ Which genetic examinations do you routinely obtain on your breeding stock? All dogs used for breeding should be certified as hip dysplasia–free by the Orthopedic Foundation for Animals (OFA) or PennHip to protect against hip dysplasia.

❍ What requirements do you have regarding prospective puppy buyers? Responsible breeders know exactly what kind of home they want their puppies to go to.

❍ At what age do your puppies go to their new homes? Puppies under the age of seven weeks should not be taken from their mothers.

❍ Do you require that pet German Shepherds be spayed or neutered? Responsible breeders require that all dogs sold as pets be altered.

❍ What guarantees do you give with your puppies? Responsible breeders include lifetime return and health guarantees (both illness and congenital defects) with each puppy sold.

Another aspect of buying a dog from a responsible breeder that some people find unpleasant is the screening process. In an effort to verify that you will be a good dog owner, a competent breeder will ask you a lot of questions about the kind of home you will provide for the puppy. Although some people resent the questioning, the screening process actually benefits both the dog and the buyer, because it helps ensure a good match.

The national German Shepherd Dog club in your country can provide you with a list of responsible German Shepherd breeders in your area. (Contact information for the national German Shepherd Dog club is provided in Appendix A.)

Buying from a Pet Shop

For many people, the most obvious place to buy a puppy is at a pet shop. Pet shops are convenient, and if you want a dog right away, you can certainly get one at a pet shop.

The problem with pet shops, however, is that you know virtually nothing about the dog you're buying. Most pet shops get their dogs from puppy mills, where dogs are kept like livestock and often do not receive basic socialization and health care. As a result, you could take home a puppy only to discover he is seriously ill or suffering from behavioral problems resulting from a lack of early socialization. Because these facilities give so little thought to the pedigrees of the dogs they use for breeding, puppy mills often produce puppies with genetically inherited diseases, which often show up later in the dog's life.

Expense presents another disadvantage to pet shops. A purebred puppy purchased from a pet shop can cost as much as three times that of a puppy purchased from a responsible breeder. Ironically, the puppy from the breeder will most often be healthier and better socialized than the pet-shop puppy, who costs a lot more!

Adopting from an Animal Shelter

You'll experience few feelings more gratifying than those that come from adopting a dog from an animal shelter. Knowing you have saved a dog's life will make you feel warm and fuzzy inside.

> The good thing about adopting a German Shepherd from a purebred rescue group is that you'll get help in determining whether the dog—and the breed, in general—is right for you.

Given the popularity of the breed, German Shepherds (usually adults) are often obtainable at local animal shelters, though you might have to wait for one to become available. Most shelters will allow you to put your name on a waiting list for a German Shepherd.

Dogs adopted from animal shelters often make wonderful pets, in large part because they are so grateful to you for giving them a home. Although they often need training and plenty of TLC, the effort usually pays off in the long run.

The drawback of adopting from a shelter is that you know little, if anything, about the dog's history. You can't be completely sure of the dog's personality—for example, how he interacts with children and other pets—or of any potential behavior problems he might have, until after you've taken him home and incorporated him into your life.

County and municipal animal shelters (i.e., the local pound) don't usually offer much in the way of help with difficult situations that might arise once your dog goes home with you. Many private shelters, however, do offer special training programs for dogs they adopt out. Dogs in these shelters receive basic obedience training and careful temperament screening to determine what kind of home would be best. As part of their services, these shelters often provide behavioral counseling to new owners who experience initial difficulties with the dogs they have adopted.

Of course, your adopted German Shepherd could very well present no behavioral problems and adjust nicely into your lifestyle. Whether the transition is smooth or bumpy, taking in a homeless dog may be well worth the effort because you will know you've saved a life.

Adopting from a Rescue Group

Nearly every American Kennel Club and Canadian Kennel Club recognized dog breed has a rescue program in place, sponsored by the breed's national club. The German Shepherd is no exception.

Purebred rescue groups are usually comprised of people who also breed and show dogs. These organized groups provide foster homes for dogs of a particular breed without a place to live. The groups also work to find suitable adoptive families for homeless purebred dogs. The adoption usually involves a screening process to ensure the dog and prospective new owner suit one another. The new owners often pay a moderate adoption fee, which helps offset the cost of caring for the dog in foster care.

The good thing about adopting a German Shepherd from a purebred rescue group is that you'll get help in determining whether the dog—and the breed in general—is right for you. You'll also receive ongoing assistance with the dog, should you need it. If the adoption doesn't work out or something else happens that prohibits you from keeping the dog, you have the option of returning the dog to the rescue group, in most cases throughout the life of the dog.

The only real handicap of adopting from a purebred rescue group comes if you've set your heart on a young puppy, since puppies rarely are available through purebred rescue. If you definitely want a puppy, don't expect to find one through a purebred rescue group.

For more information on adopting a German Shepherd from a purebred rescue group, contact your national German Shepherd Dog club, listed in Appendix A.

How Do I Choose the Pick of the Litter?

Once you've done your homework and selected a responsible breeder, you have to make a decision about which puppy to take home. Several factors should come into play when you look at a litter of puppies and try to decide which one is for you.

Expert Guidance

You're probably thinking that you and your family must go through the puppy selection process alone and somehow figure out which puppy is right for you. Not so! If you are getting a puppy from a responsible breeder, you can expect to receive plenty of help in making your choice.

No one in the world knows a litter of puppies better than his breeder (okay, and maybe the mother dog). The breeder, who was probably present when the puppies were born, has spent every day since watching and caring for them. Not only that, the breeder is an expert on the German Shepherd breed. Consequently, the breeder can provide you with a lot of advice on which puppy is best for you.

By the time you are ready to choose a puppy, the breeder will already have obtained information from you about the kind of dog you are looking for. Do you want a mellow companion for the kids? A dog you can do lots of hiking and camping with? A potential competitor in fun dog sports, such as flyball? The breeder has the ability to assess the personality of every puppy in a litter and then decide which puppy has the temperament best suited for your needs.

Of course, another reason you won't be alone in picking out a puppy is that the breeder probably plans to keep at least one of the puppies in the litter! Responsible breeders breed dogs for the show ring, and if the litter includes a great show prospect, you can bet the breeder intends to keep him!

Signs of Good Health

Although you can depend on your breeder to give you lots of guidance in deciding which puppy to take home, you should look out for certain factors in any puppy. One of those considerations is good health. First, visually examine the puppies and the mother for the following healthy characteristics:

- ○ Clean coat with healthy-looking hair
- ○ Clear eyes and nose, free of any discharge
- ○ Clean ears, free of dark, waxy buildup
- ○ Pink, healthy-looking gums, not pale
- ○ Firm and muscular body
- ○ Flat abdomen, no pot belly
- ○ Clean rectal area showing no signs of diarrhea

If the puppies in the litter possess all of these attributes, they are probably healthy. Remember, when one puppy looks sick, the entire litter could be infected with the same organism. However, working with a truly responsible breeder means you'll see no signs of illness in any of the dogs.

Don't forget to verify that your breeder has certified the puppy's parents with the Orthopedic Foundation for Animals (OFA) or PennHip. Dogs certified as "Excellent" or "Good" by OFA are most likely to produce healthy offspring. This certification guarantees the parents are free of hip dysplasia, a problem that plagues German Shepherds and can be passed down through the genes.

Evaluating Temperament

Your breeder will guide you in judging the temperament of the puppy you are considering for purchase. For added insurance, you can give the puppy a temperament test of your own to make sure he'll make a good pet. You'll need to bring a few objects with you to perform the test: an unused chew toy or clean sock, a metal dog bowl, and a tennis ball. To check the puppy's temperament, follow these steps:

Step 1. Gauge the puppy's friendliness with the entire litter present. He should be happy to see you and should come to you when you sit down on the floor and call him. If he ignores you, it's not a good sign.

Step 2. Take the chew toy or sock and drag it along the ground. The puppy should show an interest in it and even chase it. Most likely, all the puppies in the litter will end up running after it! This is good. Puppies that show no interest in the sock or toy, don't have much drive to play and may prove harder to train.

Step 3. Take the puppy away from his littermates into an area with a hard floor. Ask the breeder or a member of your family to play with the puppy. When the puppy is deeply involved in play, drop a metal dog bowl on the floor, about four feet away

A Boy or a Girl?

Should you get a male or female German Shepherd? Does gender really make a difference in the kind of pet your German Shepherd will be?

The answer you get to these questions depends on whom you ask. Some people swear that male German Shepherds make the most loyal and devoted companions. Other people believe that females are the most sensitive and giving pets.

In actuality, your German Shepherd should be spayed or neutered, which levels the playing field. Hormonal urges and instincts drive all unaltered dogs, whether male or female, which affects their ability to make good pets. If you spay or neuter your German Shepherd, you'll have a wonderful pet, regardless of the dog's gender.

from him, so that it makes a loud noise. The puppy should seem startled by the sound but should either investigate the noise or go back to playing once encouraged. If the puppy acts so terrified by the racket that he refuses to resume playing, he is too sensitive to make a good pet.

Step 4. With the puppy still in a room without his littermates, gently roll the tennis ball past him to see if he chases it, picks it up in his mouth, and brings it back to you when you call him. If he does, he'll be a great dog to play fetch with! If he doesn't, don't count on him being the type to return sticks or other objects when he grows up.

Step 5. Play with the puppy away from his littermates for a few minutes. Then, place him on his back on the floor with your hand on his chest, gently but firmly holding him down. The puppy should wiggle and cry a little bit, showing that he doesn't like the restraint, but should eventually relax. If he doesn't struggle at all, he's very passive, which isn't a good trait in a pet. If he growls and threatens you while he's fighting to break loose, he's got a dominant personality and may spell trouble as a pet.

Step 6. This last step makes many people uncomfortable, but it is necessary to determine how the puppy will react as an adult if he is ever accidentally stepped on or hurt in some other way. This is especially important if you have children, since kids can easily step on a dog's tail accidentally, or trip and fall on a dog who is lying on the floor. You want to make sure this puppy isn't the type to attack you or your child should such an accident occur.

The unpleasant part of this step is that you must deliberately pinch the puppy's paw to gauge his reaction. Before you do this, request the breeder's permission. If the breeder is familiar with puppy temperament testing, he or she should have no problem with allowing you to do this.

Start by playing with the puppy for a couple of minutes. Then grab the puppy's paw and give it a firm pinch in between the toenails, on the webbing of his paw. If you pinched him as hard as you should have, the puppy will yelp. After the puppy yelps, attempt to resume playing with him or try to reach out and pet him. If he forgives you quickly and starts to play or allows himself to be petted, he will make a good pet, especially around kids. If the puppy runs away and refuses to let you touch him or play with him, or worse, if he becomes aggressive and tries to bite you in retaliation, this is not the puppy for you.

2

Welcome Home!

In This Chapter

❍ Preparing for Your German Shepherd's Arrival
❍ German Shepherd–Proofing Your House and Yard
❍ Which Supplies Do You Really Need?
❍ The First Night with Your German Shepherd Puppy

You've decided to add a German Shepherd to your family, and you've found the puppy or adult dog you want. You've worked out all the details with the breeder, rescue group, or animal shelter. Now you're ready for your new dog to come home.

But before your new four-footed friend puts one paw on your property, you need to make some advance preparations. Acquiring a new dog means adding a huge responsibility to your life, and naturally requires some arrangements and adjustments before you bring your dog home.

Preparing for Your German Shepherd's Arrival

You probably already realize that you'll need certain equipment on hand before you bring your German Shepherd home. However, you may not have thought about the other preparations necessary to ready your home and your family for a new dog. A German Shepherd is a big responsibility and will strongly affect your household on a day-to-day basis.

It's important to realize that your German Shepherd will be more than a pet—she'll become a member of the family. Just like any other family member, she must abide by certain rules. By the same token, the people in your family also must follow some new rules now that a dog lives in your house.

"When Baron came to live with us, our whole routine changed," says Carol Matson of St. Louis, Missouri. "We had certain rules that we all followed, but the addition of Baron to the family meant adding more rules and changing some of the rules we already had. Having a dog in the house made everything different."

Setting Boundaries

Your entire family is excited about the impending arrival of your new German Shepherd. But certain decisions must be made before she makes her grand entrance. Before the big day arrives, sit down to a family meeting (or, if you live alone, set aside some time) to address the following details:

○ Will you allow your German Shepherd to have the run of the whole house? Think about whether you want your dog to access all the rooms of your house or to be restricted to specific areas. If you'd prefer that she stay out of certain rooms, use baby gates or closed doors to keep her out. Eventually you can train your Shepherd not to enter these rooms, but for now use physical barricades.

○ Where will you confine your dog in the beginning? When you first bring home a new pet, whether she's a puppy or an adult dog, it's best to initially confine her to a small area of your home, allowing her to gradually get used to the rest of the house over a period of weeks. Your dog will feel more secure in a smaller area, and restricting her stomping grounds reduces the chances of her destroying things or soiling the rug while you're away from home. Until you're certain your dog is not destructive, keep her confined in this area whenever you're unable to supervise her.

> Come up with a list of things your dog is not allowed to do, and make sure everyone in the family understands those rules.

○ What house rules will you expect your German Shepherd to obey? Come up with a list of things your dog is not allowed to do, and make sure everyone in the family understands those rules. (Mandatory rules for German Shepherd behavior are discussed in Chapter 6, Basic Training for German Shepherds.) You'll need to teach these edicts to your dog. German Shepherds learn quickly, so you shouldn't encounter any problems communicating these rules to your dog, as long as you're consistent. For example, if your dog isn't allowed on the couch, then she must never be allowed on the couch. If you and other family members give your dog mixed messages about these rules by not consistently enforcing them, the dog will learn to disregard them.

What Do You Mean It's My Turn?

Before your new dog comes home, decide who in the family will perform which jobs and when. Keep in mind that children aren't qualified to take on the sole responsibility for a dog. It's your job as a parent to make sure the child's dog-related chores get done—and to do them yourself, if the child won't or can't do them.

Establish a job schedule for the following dog-care responsibilities:

○ **Exercising.** Determine who will exercise the dog on a daily basis. This includes walks and play sessions.

○ **Feeding.** Appoint someone to feed the dog and to make sure she has fresh water.

○ **Clean-up.** Figure out who gets the fun job of cleaning up the dog's waste from the backyard.

○ **Bathroom breaks.** Decide who will get up in the morning to let the dog out so she can relieve herself. Also decide whose job it will be to make sure the dog goes out again at night before bedtime.

○ **Baths.** Pick a water-lover to take on the job of bathing your German Shepherd every month or so.

○ Where will your German Shepherd sleep? Keep in mind that wherever your dog sleeps at first will be the same place she'll sleep for the rest of her life with you. So if a year from now you don't want a 100-pound dog sleeping in your bed, don't allow that cute eight-week-old puppy to snuggle with you at night!

○ Who will perform each dog-related chore? Caring for a dog is serious work. If you live alone, obviously you'll be responsible for all of the work. However, if you have children over the age of seven and/or a spouse, you can certainly get some help! The details of who will do what for the dog should be worked out before the dog comes home.

❍ What dog-related safety rules must everyone in the home follow? Each member of your family must understand that an open front door or backyard gate could mean the escape and subsequent loss of your dog. Likewise, things like poisonous substances and other hazards must be kept out of your dog's reach, along with stuff she might eat, like kids' toys, jewelry, socks, and other items. Establish a list of safety rules for your dog that all family members must follow.

❍ How will you schedule your dog's activities? With the help of everyone in the family, create a schedule for the dog. Figure out when she'll eat, go out for potty breaks, and be played with or taken on walks. Dogs like routine, so having set times for these events will help your German Shepherd feel secure.

German Shepherd–Proofing Your House and Yard

Having a German Shepherd puppy around the house is a lot like having a toddler in your midst. Both types of youngsters are innocent, curious, and likely to get into everything. Add to that the fact that the four-footed version also has sharp teeth, powerful jaws, and a burning desire to chew on everything in sight and you can see why you'll need to do some dog-proofing before you bring home the little tyke.

House-Proofing

Because your German Shepherd thinks like a dog and not like a human, she's incapable of placing judgments on the various items within your home. A priceless Ming vase and an empty mayonnaise jar look pretty much the same to her. She'll make no distinctions between your expensive designer shoes and the old, beat-up slippers you bought from the five and dime store 15 years ago. In other words, your German Shepherd is just as likely to chew or break your valued possessions as she is the stuff you don't care about. That's why it's up to you to keep the good things out of her reach.

The same goes for hazardous items. If it smells good, your German Shepherd will probably eat it. The "it" may be some leftover stew you spilled on the kitchen floor—in which case you won't mind if she cleans it up. On the other hand, it could be the highly toxic antifreeze you spilled on the driveway—and if she drinks that, she could die within 24 hours. It's up to you to know what's healthy and what's not, and to keep your dog from the stuff that will harm her.

To safeguard your puppy (or older dog) from potentially harmful things in your home—and to safeguard your home from your pet—follow these basic guidelines for dog-proofing your house:

Chewables.   Remove from your Shepherd's range any and every object she could possibly chew or swallow. (This is especially important if your new dog is a puppy, since puppies are notorious chewers.) The list should include shoes, socks, plastic army men, compact disks, nylon panty hose, sewing needles, jewelry, books, magazines, rags, and anything potentially hazardous to your dog's digestive system that might be lying around the house.

Next, get down on the floor to check for any telephone or electrical wires that might be within reach of your dog. If you discover any wayward wires, move them to a safer place, where your dog can't chew on them. Also, encourage everyone in your family to keep drawers and closet doors closed to prevent your dog from getting herself into trouble with the contents.

Replace some of the objects you remove from your dog's reach with safe chew toys. Teach your dog to limit her gnawing to only these toys.

Breakables. Keep in mind that puppies and even older dogs can be rambunctious creatures. Although you should discourage your German Shepherd from running and playing inside the house as a matter of course, your dog may still bang into the furniture now and then. In fact, sometimes all it takes is a wagging tail to send a precious knick-knack falling to the ground. Keep valuable breakables high off the ground so they won't end up as casualties.

Toxic materials. Keep kitchen and bathroom cleaners, along with vitamins and medications, securely stored away. If your German Shepherd learns how to open the floor-level cabinets with her paws and nose—as many German Shepherds do—you'll need to put child latches on the cabinets. As a precaution, you should also make sure the lids on hazardous products are screwed on tight. Keep cabinet doors and drawers closed at all times to keep your dog from gaining access to these poisonous materials.

Your garage is probably another place where you store hazardous materials, and these, too, should be kept away from your dog. Antifreeze poses a particular danger to dogs, because of its sweet smell and taste combined with its extreme toxicity. Store all antifreeze and other poisonous products in a place where your dog can't get them. Also make sure that there are no antifreeze leaks on your garage floor or driveway for your dog to lap up.

Trash cans. Dogs are notorious for finding their way into garbage cans, where they can snack on whatever morsels humans have tossed away. This can be a dangerous habit for your dog to develop, because throwaways like chicken bones and spoiled food can harm your dog's health. Put your trash cans in a location where your German Shepherd can't get to them and/or cover all garbage cans with snug lids that an inquisitive nose can't pry open.

Yard-Proofing

Your German Shepherd will likely spend a lot of time outside in the back yard. It's imperative that you make this part of your home safe for her and safe *from* her. Take the following precautions to dog-proof your yard:

Security.   Before you put your German Shepherd outside for the first time, walk around the perimeter of your yard to make sure there aren't any gaps in the fencing through which your dog might escape. Better yet, take your dog with you, since she'll be the one most likely to spot potential escape routes. Keep an eye out for things your dog could climb on to gain access to the top of the fence. Also make sure the bottom of your fence is secured deep within the soil, since your dog could easily dig under and out if the fence has only a shallow foundation.

Poisonous plants.   Do a little research to find out which plants are harmful to dogs. You can usually obtain this information from a number of places, including nurseries, veterinarians, and poison centers (especially the ASPCA's National Animal Poison Control center at (800) 548-2423). Carefully scour your property to determine whether any of these species are growing in your yard or garden areas. If you find any, get rid of them before you let your dog run free in the yard without your supervision.

Gardens.   Most dogs love to dig, and German Shepherds are no exception. Consider protecting your garden from your dog's dig-

Common Household Hazards

- Household cleaners, laundry detergents, bleach, furniture polish
- Medication
- Suntan lotion
- Poisons (such as ant poison)
- Mouse traps
- Human trash (poultry bones, spoiled food)
- Pins, needles, buttons, other sewing accessories
- Ribbons or string that can get lodged in the throat or intestine
- Plastic
- Rubber bands, paper clips, twist ties, thumb tacks
- Shoe polish
- Alcohol
- Cigarettes and other tobacco products
- Matches and lighters
- Antifreeze, motor oil, brake fluid
- Windshield-washer fluid
- Paint and paint remover
- Nails, screws, saws, etc.

ging urges by putting a wire fence around flowerbeds and vegetable plants. You can also place decorative stones over larger areas of bare soil, so she can't try to tunnel her way to China.

Which Supplies Do You *Really* Need?

You'll need to get a number of items for your dog before you bring her home for good. But don't worry, shopping for your new dog can be fun! You'll find all kinds of neat dog stuff out there.

The best places to do your shopping are pet supply stores (the bigger the store, the larger the selection) and pet supply catalogs.

Common Poisonous Plants

Your garden might look picture perfect, but it could hold many hazards for your German Shepherd. A number of common garden plants are toxic to dogs. Most of these dog-unfriendly plants will only make your dog sick, but some can actually kill her. If you have any of the following plants in your yard, re-move them or find a way to keep your dog from gaining access to them:

American yew	China berry	Lily-of-the-valley
Angel's trumpet	Coriara	Lupine
Arrowgrass	Delphinium	Mountain laurel
Azalea	Elderberry	Oleander
Bird of paradise	English holly	Philodendron
Bittersweet	Dumb cane	Rhododendron
Black-eyed Susan	English ivy	Rhubarb
Black locust tree	Foxglove	Toadstools
Boxwood	Hemlock	Wandering Jew
Buttercup	Jack-in-the-pulpit	Bulbs
Castor bean	Kalanchoe	Yews

For a comprehensive list of toxic plants typically found in your region of the country, contact your local agricultural extension office.

If you plan to shop by mail, order a few weeks before your dog is scheduled to arrive to ensure all your doggy items are there when you'll need them.

Dinnerware for Your Dog

Your dog needs her own bowls for her water and her food. Rather than using two of yours from the kitchen cabinet, get her bowls of her own. She'll appreciate it, and you won't have to worry about running out of dishes for your dinner parties!

A huge variety of bowls made especially for dogs are available on the market. When you select bowls for your dog's food and water, look for ones that are deep enough to contain the food or water without spilling when your dog drinks or eats. If your dog is a puppy, make sure the bowls are big enough to hold the food and water but not so deep that the puppy can't reach her head all the way down to the bottom.

Select bowls that are weighted at the bottom or designed so the base is wider than the top. This will prevent the bowls from tipping over easily. Also, get separate bowls for food and water, rather than a two-in-one dish. Separate bowls are a lot easier for you to care for, and your dog will be less likely to foul her water with food by accidentally dropping bits of kibble into the water bowl.

Dog bowls typically are made from one of three kinds of material: ceramic, metal, or plastic. Ceramic is usually the best, because it's harder to tip over and easy to clean. Metal bowls are fine as long as they are designed not to tip over. Although plastic bowls are the least expensive of the three, some dogs are allergic to them and can develop blemishes on the chin.

Collars and Leashes

All dogs need a collar and a leash. The moment you take possession of your dog, she should start wearing a collar with identification tags, and she should keep them on at all times. You should bring both the collar and the leash with you when you pick up your dog.

The correct size and type of collar for your dog depends on her age. If your new German

Shepherd is a young puppy, buy a standard buckle collar to begin with. Buckle collars are available in flat and rolled leather as well as in nylon.

Nylon collars come in a variety of colors and patterns and are less expensive than leather. Leather collars, on the other hand, have a quality look to them, and the rolled type are less likely to damage and mat the coat on your dog's neck.

If your German Shepherd is an adult dog and you plan to take her to obedience classes (as well you should), you will probably need a metal choke collar for her training. However, you might want to check with your trainer before purchasing a training collar, because some trainers prefer using other types of collars. (Your dog should wear a choke chain only when she is being trained or when she's on a leash under supervision. Unsupervised dogs should never wear choke chains, because the collars can get caught on objects and cause strangulation.)

The moment you take possession of your dog, she should start wearing a collar with identification tags, and she should keep them on at all times.

If your German Shepherd is a puppy, you'll need to buy more than one collar before she reaches adulthood, replacing the collar as her neck size changes. Start with a small, puppy-sized collar and check it every week to make sure it hasn't grown too tight. You should be able to fit two fingers between the collar and your dog's neck. Don't forget: Your young pup will grow rapidly, and her collar will need periodic adjusting.

You'll probably want to buy a leash that matches the collar— for aesthetic purposes. Your dog won't care, but you'll want to look good walking her down the street! It goes without saying that you don't need to match a leash with a choke collar. Any leash will work with one of those.

For a puppy, get a four-foot-long leash; get a six-foot-long leash for an adult dog. Because German Shepherds are big, strong dogs, select a heavier leash to give you more control.

You may also want to consider getting a retractable leash that can extend as far as 20 feet. Retractable leashes come in handy when you and your dog are at the beach or in the park, and you want to give her more room to roam but still keep her under control.

Bedding and Shelter

You've already decided where your dog will sleep. Now it's time to break out the wallet and buy a bed for her to lie on.

Because German Shepherds are big dogs, they need big beds. Pet supply providers offer a wide variety of beds suitable for German Shepherds, including airline crates, baskets with cushions, and big pillows that go directly on the floor.

If your new dog is a young puppy who isn't yet housebroken, consider buying an airline crate for her first bed. A crate serves many useful functions in your dog's life, including helping you to house-train her.(House-training is discussed in Chapter 6, Basic Training for German Shepherds.)

If your new German Shepherd is already house-trained, you can get her any kind of bed you want. Some beds are filled with cedar, which reputedly helps to repel fleas. Other beds contain fiberfill or different types of washable stuffing. Whichever type of bed you choose, make sure it's big enough for your German Shepherd to stretch out on and soft enough to keep her hips and elbows from pressing into the hard floor.

"Mandy loves the big bed cushion we bought her when she was an older puppy," says Jeanne Morris of Memphis, Tennessee. "It has a fake sheepskin cover and is rather plush. Mandy will lie down on it at night and stretch out in total luxury. It's pretty obvious that she really loves that bed!"

For German Shepherds who will be spending considerable time outdoors, you may want to purchase one of the many types of doghouses on the market. Or you can build your own. Whether you buy or make the doghouse, make sure it's completely waterproof. If you live in a cold climate, your dog's house should also be insulated. Place the doghouse in a sheltered part of your yard, preferably under a tree or patio where it will be out of the sun, with the entrance facing away from the direction the winter wind usually blows. Provide a cushion or other soft bedding for the floor of the doghouse.

Crates are Great

If your new German Shepherd is a puppy, you will need to purchase a crate. You'll use the crate as a tool for house-training your puppy and to confine your pup when you can't supervise her. She'll use it as a bed as well as a home away from home when you travel with her. You can choose from a plastic and wire airline crate or an all-metal crate .

Although you may be tempted to buy a crate that will be big enough to serve as her bed once your German Shepherd's fully grown, you'll need to start out with a much smaller crate in order to effectively house-train your puppy. Get one that is large enough for her to comfortably stand up and turn around in but not too much bigger, or she won't mind going to the bathroom inside of it.

At first, your puppy should sleep on newspapers and a towel in the crate. This makes it easier for you to clean up any possible accidents. Once your pup learns to eliminate outside and not inside her crate, you can buy her a washable crate pad or cushion to sleep on.

The Joy of Toys

Probably the most fun items to buy for your German Shepherd will be her toys. All dogs love to play, and your job is to find the toys best suited to your particular dog's personality.

If your new German Shepherd is a puppy, put chew toys at the top of your shopping list. Your puppy needs strong, durable chew toys to help exercise her growing jaws and get her through the teething stage without her destroying items in your house. Adult dogs, too, appreciate chew toys because some dogs never outgrow the desire to chew.

Casper is an example of an adult dog who still likes to chew. "I don't know what it is about him, but he started chewing on things when he was a pup and just kept doing it into adulthood," says owner Kevin Roberts of Pueblo, Colorado. "We kept waiting for him to grow out of it, but he never did. So we just keep him in a supply of hard plastic chew bones and that seems to keep him happy."

Nylon bones, rubber gizmos, and even pig's ears are just some of the chewable dog toys available at your local pet supply store or through canine mail-order catalogs. It might take a little trial and error to find the type of chew toy that appeals most to your adult dog, but with teething puppies, just about anything will do!

Other toys to consider for your German Shepherd include rubber balls, flying

Did You Know?

The average cost per year for owning and maintaining a dog in the United States is $1,220.

How Much Is This Going to Cost?

The basic supplies for your new dog can come with a hefty price tag depending on size and quality, and often it's a price you'll be paying more than once. Remember to factor in these costs when making the decision to get a dog. Prices likely will vary depending on where you live, but the following should give you a good idea of what to expect.

Item	Low Price	High Price
Crate	$20.00	$200.00
Food and Water Bowls	3.00	60.00
Collar	4.00	40.00
Leash	4.00	50.00
ID Tag	3.00	15.00
Pet Stain/Odor Remover	4.00	10.00
Brush	4.00	20.00
Toys	1.00	40.00
Food (8 lb. bag)	4.00	9.00
Bed	10.00	200.00
TOTAL	$57.00	$644.00

discs, and rope toys. These items will provide you and your dog with hours of fun as you toss and your dog retrieves (hopefully!).

Some dogs also love squeaky toys, which let out a squeal every time the dog chomps down on the toy. Few things are funnier than observing a dog deliberately squeaking a squeaky toy! But take care when buying canine squeaky toys. Make sure to select a toy that is sturdy enough to withstand the powerful jaws of a German Shepherd. You don't want to bring home something your dog can easily tear up and swallow.

Other Essentials

Other beneficial items to consider buying for your dog include the following:

- ❍ **Baby gates.** These will allow you to separate your German Shepherd from those areas of the house that are off limits to her.
- ❍ **Shampoo and conditioner.** Your dog will need periodic baths to stay clean and smelling nice. Buy a quality shampoo and conditioner made just for dogs. (If your Shepherd is a puppy, make sure the shampoo is labeled as safe for use on pups.)
- ❍ **Grooming tools.** Pick up a pair of large-size canine nail clippers for trimming your dog's toenails. You'll also need a flea comb, a vented metal pin brush, and a shedding blade for brushing your German Shepherd's coat. If you plan to brush your dog's teeth—which vets recommend to prevent damaging tartar from forming on your dog's teeth and gums—purchase a toothbrush and toothpaste made especially for dogs from your pet supply store. If your dog is a puppy, now is a good time to get her used to the tooth-brushing routine!
- ❍ **Poop-scooping tools.** You may want to invest in a tool to help you dispose of your dog's waste. Poop scoops provide a convenient way to clean up your dog's excrement. They come in hand-held varieties, as well as in longer types that save you from having to bend over. Of course, there are other simpler tools for picking up poop, like good old plastic bags. Keep a box of those handy at all times.

The First Night with Your German Shepherd Puppy

To give you a sense of what your puppy will go through on her first night in your home, consider this: For her entire life until

May I See Some I.D., Please?

○ **Identification (ID) tags.** An ID tag, the most popular method of identifying dogs, should appear at the top of your to-get list. Your dog should wear a collar with an ID tag attached at all times, without exception. You can choose from several different varieties of tags, from imprinted plastic or metal tabs to metal tubes with the information rolled up inside on a piece of paper. Whichever kind you select, make sure it fastens securely to your dog's collar and contains at least your address and telephone number.

In addition to the tag with your address and phone number, your dog should also wear a rabies vaccination tag. Not only is it the law in most areas, it also will inform animal control officials, should they find your dog, that she has been inoculated against rabies.

○ **Tattoo.** A tattoo is a great way to provide permanent identification for your dog. Many local dog clubs offer tattoo clinics in which a small tattoo is placed on the dog's skin, usually on the inner thigh. Veterinarians often provide this service, too. Many German Shepherd owners tattoo their pets with their registration number or with a number designated by a tattoo registry service. A registration number tattoo enables the finder of the dog to trace the dog's owner through the registering organization. (Dogs registered with lost-and-found services should also wear identification tags bearing the toll-free phone number of the service.) Other owners use their own social security number or driver's license number as their dog's identification tattoo, because both numbers can be traced, with the help of government agencies, to the dog's owner.

Should you decide to have your dog tattooed, wait until she is fully-grown before having the number applied to her skin. If you tattoo your dog when she's too young, the number may become distorted as she ages and her skin stretches.

○ **Microchip.** The newest form of canine identification is the microchip. With this method of identification, a tiny microchip that can be read using a special scanner is implanted under your pet's skin. Many animal shelters around the country now use these scanners and will check any pet that comes through their doors to determine whether the animal has been fitted with a microchip. If the scanner detects a microchip, the dog's identification number, which is embedded on the chip, will appear on a digital read-out. Shelter workers can then locate the dog's owner using this digital code, which has been registered with a microchip identification company.

now, she's known only her mother, her siblings, and a few humans she's met, including you. On the day you bring her to your house, she loses nearly everything she's ever known.

Of course, she gains you! And a whole new family! Unfortunately, your puppy won't realize this great exchange right away. At first, all she'll notice is that she misses her mom and littermates.

When you first bring your new puppy home, she will gladly, exuberantly, and eagerly explore her new surroundings. The reality of missing her canine family won't hit her until it's time for bed. Not long after you put the puppy in her crate and tell her "good night," you are bound to hear some crying. If your puppy is very upset about being away from her mom and littermates, she'll cry consistently all through the night.

You can do several things to help your puppy feel more comfortable and to keep her from crying into the wee hours. But beware: Your heart will break when you hear your puppy's mournful cries, and you'll want to rescue her and put her in bed with you to comfort her. However, you don't want to teach your puppy that every time she cries, you'll come running and release her from the crate. If she learns to associate crying with freedom, she'll soon cry every time you put her in the crate.

Instead of giving into her complaints, try these techniques to help relieve your puppy's distress and keep her crying to a minimum:

Don't change her diet. On your puppy's first day in your home, feed her the same food she received at the breeder's house. If you change her diet too quickly, an upset stomach and a bout of diarrhea are likely to result, and the puppy will be miserable all night.

Tire her out. Before you put your puppy to bed that first night, spend some time playing with her in the room where she will sleep. This will not only wear her out and make her ready for bedtime, it will also help her feel more comfortable in the room.

Keep her near you. If your long-term plan is to allow your dog to sleep in your bedroom with you (in her own bed), then you can put the puppy's crate in your room that first night and leave it there indefinitely. (However, if you plan to have your dog sleep in another area of the house, start things off right by putting your pup's crate in that area from the very beginning.) By allowing your puppy to sleep in the same room with you, your presence will alleviate much of her separation anxiety. Keeping her nearby also will enable you to hear her whimpers in the middle of the night when she needs to go to the bathroom.

Of course, it may be hard at first to tell whether your puppy is crying because she's lonely or she wants out or she has to go potty. When she starts to whine, immediately take her outside to go to the bathroom. If she doesn't go within five minutes, she was probably crying because she wanted out of the crate. Put her back in and ignore her cries. If she continues crying for another 20 minutes or so, take her out to go potty again. You may soon discover that your pup is crying simply because she wants to come out. If that's the case, you'll have to ignore her cries and just offer her a bathroom break every couple of hours. Eventually, she'll learn that she must be quiet and sleep when she's in the crate.

Give her comfort items. If your puppy will be sleeping in her crate in another part of the house away from you, give her something to comfort her and make her feel less alone. Ideally, offer her an item from her birth home: a piece of the blanket she slept on or a toy she used to play with. If you can't get an item from the puppy's previous home, the next best thing is an item of clothing from your dirty clothes hamper. Your scent will be all over it, and although the two of you haven't yet had time to completely bond, it will reassure her that someone she knows is nearby. (Make sure your pup doesn't try to eat any of these comfort items since they may cause an intestinal blockage if swallowed.)

Another way to help your puppy cope with her first night alone is to provide her with a radio tuned to a talk radio station. This works for some puppies, while others take no comfort in it. It's certainly worth a try, in case your puppy is one of those who feels better when hearing human voices.

Making an Older German Shepherd Feel Welcome

If you have adopted an adult German Shepherd, your early experience with her will differ from the experience of bringing home a puppy. Adult dogs are usually more secure than puppies on their first night away from home (whether "home" was a shelter, foster home, or breeder's house). However, your new pet will still go through a transition period. You can help your adult Shepherd to feel at home in her new digs by following these guidelines:

Keep things mellow You might feel compelled to invite everyone in the neighborhood over to meet your new dog the day she comes home. After all, you're excited she's come to live with you! Unfortunately, inviting hordes of people over to greet your new German Shepherd is the last thing you should do. Remember, your dog is in new and strange surroundings with people she hardly knows, including you. Give her a chance to acclimate to her new home and her new owner before you start introducing her to a lot of strangers.

Don't change her diet   Just as with puppies, older dogs need to be given the same food they were eating at their previous home. Introducing a new food can cause digestive problems and leave your adult dog with a bad case of diarrhea on the first night in your house.

Teach her where to sleep   You should have already determined where in your home your dog will sleep. If you're the generous type and want your new dog to cozy up to you on your bed (and you'd better have a pretty big bed to accommodate a German Shepherd), your dog will probably have a pretty comfortable first night. If you plan to let your dog sleep in your room but on her own bed or in another part of the house, set up the dog's bed in a corner and hang out there with her to let her know this is the place she must sleep. You would be wise to use a baby gate

> If your puppy will be sleeping in her crate in another part of the house away from you, give her something to comfort her and make her feel less alone.

or closed door to confine the dog to this room, at least at first, so she's sure to get the idea that this is the room where she must stay at night.

Give her comforting objects   Just as with puppies, adult dogs take comfort in sleeping with an item that reminds them of their previous home or of you. A toy or the dog's bedding will retain the scents of the place where the dog used to live and help her with the transition from her old home to her new one. If you are unable to provide her with an item from her previous home, give her an article of clothing from your hamper, so that your scent reminds her of your presence during the night, unless she has a tendency to chew up and swallow some items.

3

Food for Thought

In This Chapter

- ○ Choosing the Best Food for Your German Shepherd
- ○ Preparing Your German Shepherd's Meals Yourself
- ○ What's All the Fuss About Supplements?

If you've spent any time around dogs, you've seen it: desperate eyes staring with such intensity at every morsel you savor that you feel as if your dog is going to telepathically will the food out of your hand and into his mouth. When it comes to food, most dogs—German Shepherds included—are masters at the game of begging. No sooner does food appear in a room than so does the always hungry and pity-inspiring pooch.

Should you give in to your German Shepherd's pleading gazes and persistent wants, and allow him to eat whatever his heart desires? Or should you more selectively control his dining habits?

Why Good Nutrition Matters

The old, but astute, saying, "You are what you eat," applies not only to humans but to dogs as well.

In order to ensure that your German Shepherd lives a long and healthy life, you need to provide him with good nutrition. You may wonder why this is so important. After all, the species subsisted on less-than-quality diets for centuries and somehow managed to thrive. Indeed, dogs are hardy creatures and can live for several years on below-standard diets. In fact, stray dogs in many impoverished countries live solely on scraps found in garbage cans.

However, although some dogs manage to subsist on bad food for a fair amount of time, these dogs do not live long, healthy lives. An inadequate diet can result in a variety of health problems and in the untimely death of the dog. For a lengthy, illness-free life, dogs need good nutrition designed for their specific needs.

Every dog requires certain nutrients in order to keep his body working properly. One of the most important functions of the proteins, fats, and carbohydrates found in food is that they serve as energy sources for your German Shepherd's body. Everything your dog does, including sleep, utilizes energy derived from the calories provided by food. In addition to providing energy-generating calories, food is the primary source of the vitamins and minerals your dog needs for his physical development and well-being. Your German Shepherd requires pretty much the same vitamins and minerals you do, although in different quantities.

Your dog will receive most of his essential vitamins and minerals from his food, provided he's eating a balanced diet. Quality commercial dog foods will satisfy the bulk of your dog's nutritional needs. However, some dogs, such as those that are fed home-prepared meals, typically require vitamin and mineral supplements. If a nutritional supplement is required, give it in small doses each day to allow the dog's body time to eliminate any excess.

Choosing the Best Food for Your German Shepherd

What exactly constitutes good nutrition for a dog? Will table scraps with an occasional bowl of kibble provide the nutrients your dog needs? Will a daily feeding of canned dog food from the grocery store meet your dog's nutritional needs?

Believe it or not, dog food is a somewhat controversial topic. For many years, veterinarians recommended feeding dogs a diet of commercial dog food purchased at the grocery store. However, premium dog food brands—available only from veterinarians or pet supply stores—have gained in popularity within the last 10 years or so. Lately, with the increased interest in homeopathic health care and holistic living in general, some veterinarians have been telling owners to actually prepare their dogs' food at home.

Which one of these options should you choose when it comes to feeding your German Shepherd? Read on to learn the facts on each feeding method, so you can make an educated decision that suits both you and your dog.

Premium Foods Versus Grocery Store Brands

One of the most prevalent controversies regarding dog food centers on whether premium dog food brands are better than grocery store brands. Before the 1970s, grocery stores and rural feed

Did You Know?

Greyhounds have the best eyesight of any breed of dog.

marts were pretty much the only places where dog owners could buy food for their pets. Pet stores also carried dog food, but they offered the same few brands found in the grocery store.

In the 1970s, dog food companies began producing what they called premium brands, which were higher in price and sold only in pet stores and through veterinarians. The manufacturers touted these brands as being of higher quality than their grocery store cousins. Although most brands in both categories meet the nutritional standards set by the National Research Council (NRC), the premium brands typically utilize higher quality ingredients. As a result, many dog owners perceive that the quality of the premium brands exceeds that of the less-expensive grocery store brands.

> The primary differences between premium brands and grocery store brands are the type and consistency of ingredients and the amount of each included in the food.

The primary differences between premium brands and grocery store brands are the type and consistency of ingredients and the amount of each included in the food. While many grocery store brands list vegetable products, such as ground corn and cereal grains, high on the label (by law, each ingredient included in a pet food must be listed in order of weight), premium brands list a higher quantity of meat-protein ingredients. Premium brands often contain actual meat rather than the meat meals (such as poultry by-product meal) often found in grocery store brands.

The media and some manufacturers of less-expensive products have challenged these assertions, claiming that grocery store and premium foods are of equal value. Nevertheless, most veterinarians still recommend feeding premium dog foods rather than cheaper grocery store brands.

Can Your Dog Go Veggie?

The number of people adopting vegetarian diets in the United States has grown over the last two decades. Many people go vegetarian for health reasons; a good many animal lovers take on this lifestyle for reasons of conscience.

If you are a vegetarian, you may wonder whether your dog can live on the same kind of diet. While cats are true carnivores and, therefore, cannot subsist on a vegetarian diet, dogs are actually omnivorous—that is, they eat a variety of vegetable and animal proteins—and so can do well on purely vegetarian fare.

A number of commercial vegetarian dog foods are sold on the market (usually available in health food stores). These diets are balanced and meet standard nutritional guidelines that have been established for dogs by the AAFCO (Association of Animal Feed Control Officials). They contain the amount of protein, amino acids, and vitamins all dogs need in their diets.

Cost Differences Between Foods

Because premium dog food brands contain higher quality and supposedly more consistent ingredients, these brands naturally are higher in price than grocery store brands. However, price differences exist within each category. For example, canned grocery store brands can vary in price as much as 25 cents or more per can. The reason for this price difference is complex and includes factors like brand recognition and other retail elements—basically, the price is determined by what the market will allow. The quality of ingredients within the product are also an important factor contributing to the cost variances between brands.

The same holds true for premium foods. Other factors can also play a part in cost differences. For example, brands sold as "all natural"—meaning they contain no artificial colors or preservatives—are sometimes higher in price than their not-so-natural counterparts. The reason for this is that it's more difficult to produce an all-natural product than one that contains man-made chemicals.

Bulk also contributes to price variances in premium and grocery store brands. The manufacturers of many premium brands state that you don't need to feed your dog as much of a premium brand as you would a grocery store brand. In other words, you get more pound for your dollar, figuratively speaking, with a premium brand. Your dog needs less premium food to feel full and to receive his daily dose of nutrition. So, although you pay more for the premium food, you feed less of it. (Premium food manufacturers justifiably boast the added bonus that dogs who eat premium brands produce less waste, since the food is more effectively digested.)

> When it comes to dog food, generally speaking, you get what you pay for. The higher quality products will cost you more than the lower quality ones will.

Also, when it comes to dog food, generally speaking, you get what you pay for. The higher quality products will cost you more than the lower quality ones will. Not only do veterinarians recommend you feed your dog a high-quality pet food, your dog will be happier and healthier if you spring for the best stuff you can get.

Another contributor to cost differences is whether the food is canned, semi-moist, or dry. The canned version of just about any dog food is more expensive than its semi-moist or dry counterparts. Given this reality, it costs more to feed canned food than the other two kinds. It costs a bit less to feed semi-moist than to feed dry food. (Semi-moist is not available in all brands of dog food.) Dry food is the least expensive. Many dog owners prefer feeding dry food not only because it costs less, but also because it is more convenient than canned food. For example, it's a lot easier to pour your dog a bowl of kibble than it is to open a can and scoop out the food. On the other hand, nearly every dog alive prefers canned food to dry. There is something about canned food that makes it much more palatable than kibble. From a health and nutrition standpoint, dry food is reported to be just as good for your dog, despite his preferences for the wet stuff.

All-Natural Foods

In the 1980s, the popular trend of natural products—food, skin care, clothing, you name it—spread to the pet-food market. As a result, a large number of commercially prepared all-natural dog foods are available to pet owners today.

What is the difference between a premium dog food and an all-natural dog food? Plenty, if you ask the manufacturers of the all-natural products! All-natural dog foods are void of certain ingredients that many people deem undesirable, specifically preservatives like butylated hydroxyanisole (BHA) and food dyes like FD&C Red No. 40, which are known to cause cancer in laboratory animals. Although science has yet to prove that these ingredients are detrimental specifically to dogs that ingest them as part of their regular meals, many owners prefer not to feed their dogs food containing these chemicals.

All-natural dog foods come in both canned and dry varieties. They tend to cost more than other "non-natural" premium brands, but many owners feel the peace of mind that comes with feeding natural foods is worth the expense.

Did You Know?

Veterinarians estimate that between 30 percent and 50 percent of today's dog population is overweight.

Preparing Your German Shepherd's Meals Yourself

Many people consider their dogs to be members of the family, so it's not surprising that many dog owners also prepare their pets' meals at home—just like they would for their spouses or children!

Why make your dog's dinner when you can easily go out and just buy it? Proponents of home-prepared meals for dogs believe that fresh, natural ingredients free of the processing that goes into any canned or dried dog food are simply healthier for the dog. In fact, anecdotes abound of dogs who have lived far beyond the life expectancies for their breeds or who have rebounded from general poor health after being fed home-prepared meals over an extended period. So, if you have the time and inclination, you may want to consider preparing your dog's food.

Making your dog's dinner at home does require knowledge and a bit of research. In order to ensure your dog receives all the essential nutrients, you must provide the right combination of ingredients. A number of resources exist to help dog owners know exactly what to feed their pets, including your dog's veterinarian and books focusing on natural diets for dogs. When preparing meals for your German Shepherd, your best strategy is to follow prescribed recipes by canine nutritionists.

When a German Shepherd named Talus developed a severe food allergy, his veterinarian suggested that Talus' owner, Katherine Roth of Morris Plains, New Jersey, prepare the dog's food at home instead of giving him commercial dog food. "My vet gave me all the information I needed to prepare Talus' meals myself," says Katherine. "He also gave me advice on what supplements to add to make sure Talus was getting a balanced diet."

Some points you will need to consider when making your pet's food at home include:

○ **Give variety.** The greater the variety of ingredients you provide your dog, the healthier he will be.
○ **Opt for convenience.** Use recipes that are most convenient for you to make, given your lifestyle. This will help make at-home food preparation easier on you.
○ **Introduce gradually.** Don't spring home-prepared meals on your dog overnight. Introduce the new food gradually so your dog's body and palate have time to adjust to the idea.
○ **Go organic.** Use organically grown meat and produce whenever possible. These ingredients are free of pesticide residue and other additives believed by many to be harmful to your dog's health. As long as you are preparing your dog's meals yourself, you may as well go all out when it comes to good health!

How Often and How Much Do I Feed My German Shepherd?

Not all dogs eat the same amount of food every day. Tiny breeds, such as the Chihuahua, obviously consume a lot less chow than their larger-breed counterparts, such as the German Shepherd. But even within each breed, the proper amount of food varies from dog to dog, depending on the age, size, activity level, and personal preferences of the individual dog.

The Importance of a Feeding Routine

Before you figure out how much food your dog needs to eat, you should determine an appropriate feeding routine. A schedule for

Feeding Goliath

A Dietary Note About Large Breeds

Recently, much concern has developed among breeders and veterinarians about the proper feeding of German Shepherd puppies and puppies of other large breeds. Research shows that accelerated growth—possibly caused by higher-calorie puppy food—plays a contributing role in orthopedic problems, such as hip dysplasia and osteochondritis dissecans, a defect of developing cartilage that causes chronic lameness.

Consequently, some German Shepherd breeders recommend a specially formulated food for large- or giant-breed puppies that holds a puppy to a slower growth rate. Don't be alarmed: This type of large-breed puppy food will not stunt your dog's growth—it will just control it to a healthier rate. Your Shepherd will grow just as big as he's supposed to; it will just take a little longer for him to get there.

Other breeders wean their puppies on adult-maintenance food and recommend that the owners continue to feed the adult food to their German Shepherd or other large-breed puppy until the dog reaches old age and requires a senior formula. Consult your veterinarian and breeder to help determine the best type of food for your dog.

If you decide to feed your pup a "regular" puppy food, make sure your veterinarian carefully monitors your dog's growth. You will need to switch him to an adult-maintenance food at a younger age than you would a smaller breed.

feeding is important, because it not only will help give your dog a sense of security (he'll find comfort in knowing when he'll eat every day), it also will encourage a hearty appetite in your dog.

Max, a German Shepherd owned by Tom and Rebecca Southard of Jacksonville, Florida, has been eating his breakfast and dinner at virtually the same time every day for the six years he has been alive. "We've been diligent about keeping Max on the same feeding schedule, and we've never had a problem getting him to eat," says Rebecca. At 6:30 every evening, he is standing by his food bowl, waiting for his dinner!"

Most experts recommend that you feed your German Shepherd two smaller meals twice a day—once in the morning and once in the evening. The reason for this is that German Shepherds and other large breeds are prone to a dangerous condition called bloat, the likelihood of which may be reduced by eating two smaller meals instead of one large meal. (Bloat is discussed in Chapter 5, Common Health Concerns.) A good rule of thumb is to feed your dog right after you get up in the morning and again about the same time you eat your dinner. Avoid feeding your dog right after exercising. Also, try not to feed him just before you go to sleep, since eating often induces bowel movements—not a bodily function you want your dog to experience in the middle of the night when he can't get outside to relieve himself.

Try to feed your dog at about the same times each day. If you keep to a regular schedule, your German Shepherd will come to expect his meals at specified times and most likely will eat everything you give him.

Puppy Feeding Schedules and Amounts

German Shepherd puppies grow in leaps and bounds and have very different nutritional needs than their adult counterparts. If your German Shepherd is a puppy, you'll need to provide him with a completely different dietary program than you would if he were fully grown.

Most puppies begin eating solid food at around four to five weeks of age. They start to eat solids while still nursing and gradually switch to all solid foods by six to eight weeks of age. Since puppies usually go to new homes when they are about eight weeks old, your pup most likely will be completely weaned and eating solid food by the time he comes to live with you.

Between the ages of eight weeks and five months, your puppy will experience his greatest need for energy. During this period, he also will grow to about half of his adult body weight, which means he will need lots of good, quality food to support his growth.

When your puppy is very young, you should feed him four times a day. The amount you feed depends on the food you give him. Your puppy should eat a dog food formulation designed especially for puppies. If you feed a commercial dog food, read the label and determine how much food to give your pup daily, based on the manufacturer's recommendation. If you prepare your puppy's meals yourself, check with your veterinarian to find out exactly how much you should give your new dog.

Take care not to overfeed your puppy. Although some puppy owners like to provide "free-choice" feedings to their puppies—where food is accessible to the pup at all times—most experts recommend against this, especially for large breeds such as the German Shepherd. Obesity in puppies can result in impaired bone development and health problems later in life, particularly in bigger dogs.

> Between the ages of eight weeks and five months, your puppy will experience his greatest need for energy.

As your puppy matures, gradually reduce the number of feedings. By adulthood (one year), he should receive two servings per day.

When you first get your new German Shepherd puppy, feed him the same food he was getting at his previous home, so you don't upset his delicate digestive system. If you want to change his food to another brand, make the change gradually over a period of a week by mixing the new food with the old food in increasing amounts. Making the change in increments will keep your puppy from developing an upset stomach and a bad case of diarrhea.

Feeding Your Adult German Shepherd

When your German Shepherd reaches one year of age, he is officially an adult dog. By then his growth will have slowed considerably, and you no longer need to feed him like you would feed a puppy. At that point, he should switch to a dog food formula designed specifically for full-grown dogs.

If you feed your German Shepherd a commercial dog food, follow the feeding guidelines on the label and do not give your dog more or less than is indicated at first. (Many dog owners have a tendency to overfeed their dogs, which results in obesity. Being overweight is as harmful to dogs as it is to humans.) As time goes by, you can determine whether your dog requires more or less food than the manufacturer recommends. Use the quality of your dog's coat (it should be thick and shiny) and his weight (he shouldn't be too heavy or too thin) as a guide for measuring how well your dog is doing on his current food intake. If you aren't sure if your dog is doing well on the recommended ration, ask your veterinarian for help.

If your German Shepherd starts to become overweight, talk to your veterinarian about increasing your dog's exercise and switching him to a lower-calorie diet. Your veterinarian may recommend

Did You Know?

Houston topped the 1998 list of cities with the highest number of postal workers bitten by dogs, with Chicago a close second.

The Importance of Water

Water is important to every living creature, and your German Shepherd is no exception.

Water makes up around 65 percent of your adult dog's body and even more of your puppy's constitution. Dogs need water to help their cells function properly and to aid in proper digestion. Basically, dogs need water to live. Without water, a dog will die within only a few days.

The water in your dog's body needs to be replenished on a regular basis, since it is routinely lost through respiration, digestion, and urination. On hot days or when exercising heavily, your dog needs even more water to keep his body running smoothly.

To keep your German Shepherd at optimum health, provide him with constant access to plenty of cool, fresh water.

that you reduce your dog's food ration or put him on one of the many lower-calorie commercial diets available at pet supply stores. If your pet's weight problem is a stubborn one, your vet may suggest you feed your dog an even lower-calorie prescription diet available only through veterinarians.

Some German Shepherds actually need more food than the amount recommended on the label of commercial dog foods, but those dogs usually are very active. If your dog regularly engages in rigorous activities, you may find he'll need more food to keep up his energy level and to maintain a normal body weight. If you are unsure whether your dog fits into this category, discuss the matter with your veterinarian.

When your German Shepherd reaches his senior years—which are around the age of six or seven for this breed—you may need to change his diet. Since older dogs tend to become overweight and to experience reduced organ function, special senior diets for dogs often provide a good choice for older dogs, especially those who are carrying too much weight. Most of these foods are lower in calories than regular maintenance diets, have a lower protein content, and also contain higher amounts of the B vitamins.

Remember that whenever you want to change your dog's diet, you must do it gradually over a week's time. Never switch foods abruptly, since this can cause problems with his digestive system, resulting in diarrhea and general discomfort for your dog. Instead, add the new food to the old food in increasing amounts each day until your dog is ultimately dining only on his new rations.

In the rare event that your German Shepherd suddenly refuses to eat, contact your veterinarian. A lack of appetite can be a sign of serious illness.

Is It Okay to Share My Food?

The dog who wouldn't prefer your dinner to his dog food hasn't been born. Let's face it: Human food smells and tastes better than dog food, not only to us humans but to the dogs too!

It would be nice to just give our dogs the same thing we eat, whenever we dine. In fact, our prehistoric ancestors probably did just that, which is how the dog ended up being domesticated some 10,000 years ago! However, in this day and age, we recognize that table food (food that people eat) alone doesn't provide dogs with the nutrients they need. They actually require food specifically designed for the canine metabolism in order to thrive and stay with us for a long time.

So, given the dog's specialized nutritional needs and requirement for dog food, is it ever okay to give your dog table scraps?

Toxic Treats: Dangerous Foods for Dogs

Most dogs will eat just about anything offered to them, which isn't always a good thing. A number of popular human foods are detrimental to your dog's health and shouldn't be fed at all. These include:

○ Chocolate. Dogs love the taste, but chocolate in large quantities can harm them. A chemical found in chocolate called theobromine, along with a familiar substance called caffeine, can affect your dog's heart.

○ Onions. Onions provide a flavor that dogs enjoy, but too much of them can cause hemolytic anemia, which is a destruction of the red blood cells.

○ Garlic. Garlic contains levels of toxins that can harm your dog's blood if it is fed in high quantities. It's okay to give it to your dog now and then in tiny amounts, but don't give him too much, too often.

The answer is yes, as long as you do so only in moderation. An occasional sliver of roast beef or a chunk of baked potato will not harm your dog. But don't overdo it. Only give table scraps occasionally, meaning not every day. As a good rule of thumb, make sure the amount of table scraps and treats you feed your dog does not comprise more than 10 percent of his overall diet. Also, avoid feeding very rich, high fat foods containing things like butter, cream, and a lot of oil. These food substances can wreak havoc with your dog's digestive system.

Although your dog will enjoy an occasional treat from the table (fed to him in his bowl, so he doesn't become an obnoxious beggar), there is another reason not to make it a regular habit: Too much people food will ruin his appetite for dog food. Stories abound of dogs who become so spoiled dining on table scraps that they refuse to eat anything else.

If you want to give your dog treats, feed him the healthiest stuff you can. Some of the best dog treats you can give are commercially produced goodies like dog biscuits, bite-sized semi-moist morsels, and other assorted treats. Many of the same dog food companies that produce premium-brand dog foods also offer premium-quality dog snacks, which are a healthier option than leftover people food.

Just as with anything, feed treats only in moderation. In fact, you may want to consider using treats only as a training tool. Once your German Shepherd makes the association between treats and obedient behavior, you'll have a very biddable dog on your hands.

What's All the Fuss About Supplements?

Many people take vitamin supplements to ensure they receive all the nutrients they need. But what about your dog? Should he, too, receive vitamin and mineral supplements?

Veterinarians and nutritionists have argued over this question for some time now. Some experts believe dogs should receive supplements; others are avidly against it.

The reason for the controversy is this: Commercial dog foods are designed to provide balanced nutrition for dogs. Those experts who argue against owner supplementation believe that dogs fed a quality commercial dog food are already receiving the nutrients they need. They contend that adding supplements to this carefully designed diet will throw it out of balance and cause potential health problems—specifically, vitamin toxicity, which can result when excess amounts of fat-soluble vitamins build up in the dog's body. Other problems, such as interference with absorption and availability of other nutrients within the body, can also result.

On the other side of the argument are those experts who believe that many of the vitamins originally present inside the ingredients used in commercial dog food are destroyed by the processing that goes into making these products. Despite the fact that commercial dog food manufacturers add some supplements to the food after processing to make up for this, advocates of supplementing insist that the loss of nutrients is greater than what is added.

When it comes to the subject of supplementation, your veterinarian is the best person to advise you regarding your puppy or adult dog. Most veterinarians recommend that dogs and puppies who eat a balanced, commercially prepared diet do not require supplements. The exception are dogs suffering from specific health problems, which require more of a certain vitamin or mineral than can be found in commercial diets.

One situation in which experts agree on supplementation is when a dog receives a home-prepared diet. If you make your dog's food, rather than buy it in a pet supply store, you need to add a vitamin and mineral supplement to ensure your dog gets all the nutrients he needs.

Medical Care Every German Shepherd Needs

In This Chapter

○ Going to the Veterinarian
○ Preventive Medicine
○ Spaying and Neutering
○ Sick Calls and Emergencies

German Shepherds are hardy dogs, and you can plan on having yours around for quite a while—providing you hold up your end of the responsible ownership bargain.

A big part of being a good dog owner is providing your pet with preventive health care. Like humans, German Shepherds need regular medical checkups and other types of preventive care in order to live a long and wonderful life.

Going to the Veterinarian

Your dog adores you above and beyond all others. But when it comes to your German Shepherd's health, your dog's best friend is her veterinarian.

Many people think of taking their dog to the vet only in an emergency, such as a fractured limb or a serious illness. However, although your vet is certainly available in situations of dire need, emergencies comprise but a fraction of the services your veterinarian can perform for your dog. Along with regular inoculations, dental care, and spay/neuter surgery, your veterinarian can provide you with advice on what to feed your dog, how to keep fleas and ticks at bay, and how to find a trainer or behaviorist who can help you deal with your dog's behavior.

Selecting the Right Vet

Given the significant role the veterinarian plays in your dog's life, it's important for you to choose the right professional to administer her health care. Although you could open up the phone-book and choose the first veterinarian on the list, you should employ better ways to pick this most important person in your German Shepherd's life.

If you purchased a German Shepherd puppy from a breeder in your area, you can begin your quest for a veterinarian by asking the breeder for a referral. Responsible breeders are a great source for names of good veterinarians.

If you did not purchase your dog from a breeder or if your dog's breeder lives far away, try asking your dog-owning friends and neighbors for names of good veterinarians. Even if you're new to the area, it's easy to get referrals to a few veterinary hospitals—just take your German Shepherd for a walk in the park and ask the dog owners you meet who they use for veterinary care. Most dog owners are happy to share the name of a veterinarian they like who has treated their dog. You might also ask local humane societies and pet supply stores for recommendations.

Once you're armed with a name or two, scope out each hospital. Most veterinarians work in hospital environments in which one or more other doctors are on staff. Some practitioners work solo in their own clinics. Your aim is to find a clean and well-organized practice that is accommodating to clients, provides excellent health care, and is conveniently located so you can easily get to it when needed.

Start by paying a visit to the clinic. (Make arrangements in advance since hospitals are usually very busy.) Talk to the office staff and inform them you are considering using them for your dog's regular veterinary care. Ask them for a tour of the facilities, specifically the examining rooms and the back office area, where dogs are kept when convalescing or recovering from surgery. Tell the staff you also would like to meet the attending veterinarian; if the clinic has more than one vet, you might want to meet with all or some of them.

While you are visiting, gather some more information about the clinic. Ask for a fee schedule for various services, including vaccinations, exams, and spay/neuter surgeries. If the prices are very high, find out exactly what you are getting for your money. If you are not happy with the answer, you may want to investigate other clinics in the area. However,

Did You Know?

Tests conducted at the Institute for the Study of Animal Problems in Washington, DC, revealed that dogs and cats, like humans, are either right- or left-handed.

realize that when it comes to the quality of veterinary care, you often get what you pay for. Be willing to pay for the best veterinary care you can afford.

Ask about the clinic's hours of operation. Make sure these hours are compatible with your schedule. Most clinics offer weekend hours to accommodate clients who work full time during the week.

Find out if the clinic is a member of the American Animal Hospital Association (AAHA). Members of this organization adhere to strict standards for medical procedures and hospital management. You may also want to contact your state's veterinary medical board. The board can verify that the hospital's vets are licensed to practice and can tell you if any formal disciplinary action has ever been taken against them.

Another important question to ask is whether or not the clinic provides 24-hour emergency care. If not, the veterinary practice should refer you to a nearby round-the-clock emergency hospital that you can depend on in the event your dog needs care during off-hours. If the clinic you are considering refers patients to an emergency hospital, also pay a visit to that facility. The staff at the emergency clinic should answer your questions and give you a tour of the facility.

> The veterinarian should handle your dog well, spend adequate time with you and your pet, and answer all your questions.

If you like what you learn about the veterinary clinic during your visit, probe a little more deeply into the medical expertise of the veterinarian(s) who staff the clinic. Find out if the staff veterinarian(s) specialize in any particular health-care areas. Ask if the clinic consults with other veterinarians, such as veterinary colleges or outside specialists, in the

Finding a Specialist

Just as with human medicine, the veterinary profession features specialists whose training and experience extend beyond fundamental veterinary education and who focus on a specific area of veterinary medicine.

A time may come when you will want to consider taking your German Shepherd to a veterinary specialist. If your dog suffers from a disease or condition, your primary veterinarian may recommend a specialist in that specific field of medicine, or you could take your pet directly to someone who concentrates in that particular field.

Fields of veterinary specialty include anesthesiology, behavior, dentistry, dermatology (skin care), emergency and critical care, internal medicine, nutrition, oncology (cancer), ophthalmology (eye problems), preventive medicine, radiology (x-rays, diagnostics), surgery (of any kind), and toxicology (poison). You can find a specialist in your area by contacting the American Veterinary Medical Association, listed in Appendix A.

event your dog develops a serious condition that might exceed the expertise of the staff veterinarians.

Once you decide which veterinarian you would like to use on a regular basis, make an appointment for your puppy or adult German Shepherd. If you've just acquired your dog, schedule an exam right away to determine your dog's general health. If you've had your dog for a while and he has seen a veterinarian within the last year, you can wait to make an appointment until it's time for your dog's next yearly examination and vaccines.

During your dog's initial exam with the veterinarian, take the opportunity to get to know your dog's new best friend. The veterinarian should handle your dog well, spend adequate time with you and your pet, and answer all your questions.

Your German Shepherd's First Visit

The nature of your pet's first exam will depend on whether your dog is a puppy or a full-grown adult. Your German Shepherd puppy will receive a more detailed exam than will a healthy adult dog who just needs a well-care examination and annual vaccines.

When you visit the veterinarian for your dog's first checkup, you should bring with you a few things, in addition to your pet. Make sure to bring in your dog's health care records, which the breeder and/or previous owner (if applicable) should have supplied when you acquired your Shepherd. (Responsible breeders always provide health care records to those who purchase dogs from them.) You also need to supply a recent (less than 12 hours old) stool sample, so the veterinarian can determine whether your dog is infected with internal parasites. Since most puppies are born with worms in their intestinal tracts, your veterinarian will probably need to prescribe a deworming medication if you have a puppy.

Regardless of your German Shepherd's age, during the initial visit the veterinarian will examine your dog for congenital defects and infectious diseases. The veterinarian will weigh your dog to establish a baseline weight from which to compare in the future and will examine your dog's coat for fleas and ticks. The vet will also check the condition of your German Shepherd's heart, lungs, and other organs; look into his eyes and ears; and inspect his mouth and teeth.

The examining veterinarian will discuss your dog's vaccination records and tell you whether your pet needs any inoculations. He or she will tell you which shots the dog will require in the future and when. If you live in an area where heartworm poses a problem—and it does in most areas of the country—your veterinarian will discuss putting

Questions to Ask Your Vet

○ How do you handle after-hours emergencies? Are you affiliated with a nearby animal emergency center?

○ Do you provide 24-hour coverage for hospitalized animals? If not, how often are overnight patients checked?

○ What are the average fees for checkups, spaying and neutering, and vaccinations?

○ Does the veterinarian specialize in any areas, such as allergies, dentistry, ophthalmology, orthopedics, or surgery? A veterinarian can't just claim to be a specialist. He must go through additional training to become a board-certified expert in these disciplines.

○ Does the veterinarian make house calls? Under what circumstances?

○ Who provides care when the veterinarian is not available?

your dog on a heartworm prevention program (Heartworm prevention is discussed in Chapter 5, Common Health Concerns.)

If your German Shepherd is a young puppy around eight weeks of age, the breeder most likely took care of the pup's initial inoculations against diseases like distemper, parainfluenza, parvovirus, and hepatitis before you brought him home. (The records from the breeder should indicate this.) The veterinarian will then discuss a vaccination plan for your puppy and will let you know when the puppy is due to receive its second set of shots.

For a German Shepherd puppy, that first exam is a good time to talk to the veterinarian about spaying or neutering your pet. Some veterinarians have begun to safely perform this surgery on pups as young as eight weeks old, although most veterinarians prefer to wait until the dog is six months old. Find out your veterinarian's age preference for this surgery and plan to make an appointment for when the time is right.

What Your Vet Might Ask You

During your dog's first visit to the veterinarian, the doctor will attempt to get to know both you and your pet. Expect him or her to ask you the following questions:

❍ When is the last time your dog was examined by a veterinarian?

❍ Which inoculations has your dog received?

❍ Is your dog spayed or neutered?

❍ What are you feeding your dog?

❍ Have you noticed any possible signs of illness, such as diarrhea, poor appetite, sneezing, or depression?

❍ How well does your dog move? Does he run and play with ease and comfort?

If your dog is fully grown but has not yet been spayed or neutered, talk to the veterinarian about setting up a time right away to have this important surgery performed.

Preventive Medicine

When it comes to keeping your German Shepherd healthy, preventive medicine is the key. A powerful ally in the fight against potential disease, your veterinarian will help you set up a program to keep your dog in good physical health.

Annual Visits

Humans receive yearly physical checkups, so why shouldn't dogs? Well, they should! Your veterinarian will probably recommend that your pet come in once a year for a thorough going over to determine his general overall health and to receive his annual boosters.

Annual exams are important. Not only do they give you a chance to touch base with your dog's veterinarian and update him or her on how your dog is doing, they also give the veterinarian a chance to catch any potential health problems in your dog before they progress too far.

When you bring your dog in for his annual exam, you can expect your veterinarian to check for certain things. The doctor will probably weigh your dog to determine whether his weight is consistent from one year to the next. The veterinarian will use a stethoscope to listen to the dog's heart and lungs. He or she will palpate, or feel, major organs through your dog's skin to ensure they are of normal size and free of tumors. The vet will also examine your dog's anal area for signs of diarrhea, parasites, and possible anal sac infections.

Using a special instrument, the veterinarian will look into your dog's ears and eyes to determine their health. The doctor will also check the dog's mouth to determine the health of the gums and whether the dog's teeth need cleaning.

The veterinarian will question you about your dog's general health in an attempt to find out whether your dog is exhibiting any early signs of illness. Based on the information you provide and the examination, the veterinarian will proceed accordingly, ordering further tests or simply giving your dog a clean bill of health.

Vaccinations

Dogs have been on the planet for a long time, which means they are subject to a host of infectious organisms that have often evolved to prey specifically on the canine. In order to protect dogs from these terrible diseases, veterinary medicine has developed a number of vaccines designed to boost the canine immune system against invading bacteria and viruses.

You may wonder whether you really need to have your German Shepherd vaccinated. After all, the dogs you see running around the park look pretty healthy. Your next door neighbor's pooch is always full of vim and vigor and doesn't seem affected by any illness. In fact, you've never even heard of anyone's dog coming down with any of those scary-sounding diseases like parvovirus, rabies, and distemper that supposedly plague dogs. When all the dogs around your pet seem perfectly healthy, is it really possible a contagious disease could infect your Shepherd?

The answer to that question is a resounding yes. Organisms that can make dogs terribly and often fatally ill are present in the environment. The reason these diseases are not widely visible in your community is the fact that most pet dogs are regularly vaccinated. If you take a chance by not inoculating your dog against them, you are inviting trouble.

It is imperative that your dog receives his vaccinations on a regular basis, with the vaccination schedule dependent upon his age and a determination of his needs by your veterinarian. Young puppies need a series of shots, beginning early in their lives, to help protect them against illnesses that are particularly dangerous to young dogs. Adult dogs usually receive most of their inoculations on a yearly basis. Some vaccines can be administered every two or three years.

Your veterinarian will tell you which vaccines your dog needs and how often, based on the dog's age, your geographical location, and other factors. To assure the maximum protection for your German Shepherd, stick by the schedule your veterinarian establishes.

Sample Vaccination Schedule

This chart shows a typical vaccination schedule. Contact your vet as soon as you bring your puppy home to schedule his first checkup and to set up the perfect vaccination schedule for your pet.

8 Weeks: Distemper, hepatitis, leptospirosis, parainfluenza, and parvo (DHLPP), usually combined in one injection.

12 Weeks: DHLPP, possibly Lyme disease and bordetella

16 Weeks: DHLPP, rabies, Lyme disease (if begun at 12 weeks)

20 Weeks: Parvo booster for pups considered at high risk

1 Year after last vaccination: DHLPP, bordetella and Lyme if previously given, rabies

Vaccination schedules are an area of great debate in the veterinary community, so it is critical that you discuss this issue with your vet and set up a schedule that makes sense for your dog.

Puppies Before puppies reach the age of eight weeks, they should receive inoculations against distemper, parainfluenza, and parvovirus. These inoculations usually prevent the inoculated dog from contracting these serious illnesses, which can easily kill a puppy. If you got your puppy from a responsible breeder, the dog should have already received these vaccines before he came to your home. The breeder should have provided you with a written record of these vaccines, which you can share with your veterinarian.

Between the ages of 8 and 12 weeks of age, your puppy should receive his first DHLPP inoculation, which is an all-in-one vaccination meant to ward off distemper, hepatitis, leptospirosis, parainfluenza, and parvovirus. When your puppy reaches 16 weeks of age, he will need his first rabies vaccination. Also at 16 weeks, the puppy will get another DHLPP injection, which will complete the puppy series of shots. (Your veterinarian may alter this schedule depending on your pup's needs.)

Adults Booster shots given periodically during your dog's adulthood will reinforce the inoculations given to your puppy during his formative years. Most vets recommend a DHLPP booster every year. Your German Shepherd must receive a rabies booster one year after receiving his initial rabies vaccine, and then every one, two, or three years after that, depending on where you live.

Your veterinarian may recommend that your German Shepherd receive other inoculations as well. Whether your dog needs shots to protect against such illnesses as coronavirus, bordetella (kennel cough), or Lyme disease is determined by your geographical location and other factors. For example, if you live in the Northeast your vet may recommend inoculation against Lyme disease, which is rampant in that part of the country. If your dog is exposed to many other dogs on a regular basis, your vet may suggest inoculation against kennel cough, which is highly contagious. If your veterinarian suggests that your dog receive any inoculations beyond DHLPP and rabies, ask him or her to explain the reasons to you so you'll understand why the shots are needed in your particular situation.

Dental Care

Dental care comprises an important part of preventive health management for your German Shepherd. The health of your dog's teeth is a very important component and can not only affect his ability to eat, but also impacts his general well-being.

What's All the Fuss About Natural Medicine?

Natural living is not just a trend for humans: Many dog owners have embraced the natural lifestyle for their pets as well. A major component of this is homeopathy.

Homeopathy consists of a system of medical treatments based on the theory that certain illnesses can be cured with small doses of substances that in large doses would produce symptoms like those of the disease. Administering small doses of these stimulate the body to defend itself against the disease.

Homeopathy is a very old practice that pre-dates modern medicine. You can find homeopathic practitioners among the ranks of both human and veterinary medical professionals.

A number of traditional veterinarians also practice homeopathy as an alternative treatment to several different illnesses. Many dog owners prefer to take their pets to veterinarians who practice both conventional and homeopathic medicine, which gives them the option of using either type of medicine in a given situation. For example, you might allow your vet to treat your dog with antibiotics for an infection (the traditional approach) but homeopathically for allergies.

The benefit of homeopathic treatment is that the remedies used rarely produce side effects, which is not usually the case with drugs prescribed through traditional medicine. The down side of homeopathy is that it is not widely accepted within the veterinary community, probably because very little scientific research exists to back up homeopathic practices. Consequently, homeopathic practitioners must prescribe treatment without the benefit of scientific data to indicate the best dosages and treatment plans. Also, dog owners sometimes find it difficult to locate homeopathic veterinarians, because these practitioners are much less common than traditional veterinarians. You can locate a homeopathic veterinarian by contacting the American Holistic Veterinary Medical Association (See Appendix A).

In order to understand the importance of keeping your German Shepherd's teeth healthy, you need to know a little bit about your dog's dentition.

The anatomy of canine choppers is surprisingly similar to that of your teeth! Each tooth has a crown and a root, and is covered with enamel for protection against wear.

Puppies are born without teeth (actually, the teeth are there but are hidden below the gum line). In the puppy's first six weeks of life, 28 "baby teeth" gradually erupt from the gum. As with human children, the puppy slowly loses these baby teeth, which are replaced by permanent teeth. This process can start when the puppy is as young as eight weeks old and continues until most dogs are six months of age. German Shepherd puppies tend to lose their baby teeth earlier than smaller dogs. (If you notice that your young German Shepherd has more than one tooth occupying the same spot at the same time, and the baby tooth is not loose and about to fall out, a visit to your veterinarian is warranted.)

Once your dog's adult teeth are in place, they need regular dental care, just like your human teeth do. The main reason for both human and canine dental care is essentially the same: to prevent periodontal (gum) disease.

Dogs are prone to gum disease just as humans are, for nearly the same reasons. The buildup of tartar, a combination of minerals excreted by the salivary glands, bacteria, and other elements, results in infection, which weakens the ligament and bone that holds the tooth into the gum. If tartar accumulates on your dog's teeth unchecked, gingivitis and, ultimately, tooth loss result.

In addition to lost teeth (and terrible breath, another symptom of diseased gums), very bad periodontal disease can create a systemic infection that spreads via your dog's bloodstream throughout his body. Such infections are life threatening.

The most effective way to keep your dog from developing periodontal disease is to have his teeth professionally cleaned on a regular basis. Your veterinarian can perform this procedure on your dog in the clinic.

Veterinary Dental Care   How will you know if your dog needs his teeth cleaned? If you take your dog to the veterinarian for annual physical examinations and boosters, the doctor will tell you during the visit whether your dog's teeth need cleaning. The annual exam includes a review of your dog's teeth.

In order for your veterinarian to check the condition of your dog's teeth and gums, he or she will open your dog's mouth and evaluate the amount of tartar present on your dog's teeth. If your veterinarian sees a buildup of tartar, or inflammation at the gum line, he or she will recommend that you schedule a teeth cleaning for your pet as soon as possible.

In order to adequately clean your German Shepherd's teeth, the veterinarian needs to reach the tartar located beneath the gum line. The only way to effectively perform this procedure is to render your dog unconscious with a safe anesthetic. Your dog will receive this anesthetic to put him in a state of deep sleep while the veterinarian thoroughly cleans each tooth above and below the gum line. If the vet detects any abscesses or seriously infected teeth during the cleaning, he or she will treat the problem with medications and, in some cases, by surgery.

Your dog will most likely recover rapidly from the anesthetic and can go home the same day that he gets his teeth cleaned. If the doctor found a substantial gum infection during the procedure, he may prescribe an oral antibiotic to give your dog for a week or so after the cleaning. If your veterinarian detects a serious

Did You Know?

Your German Shepherd has 42 teeth in his mouth, the same amount as all other breeds of dogs.

infection before the cleaning is performed, he or she may recommend an oral antibiotic before the procedure as well.

Most dogs need their teeth cleaned only once every two years or so. Some dogs have a greater propensity for tartar buildup, however, and need cleanings as often as every year.

At-Home Dental Care   Although regular cleanings by your veterinarian are a must, tooth care at home is also important. You can reduce the number of times your German Shepherd needs to have his teeth cleaned by the veterinarian as well as reduce the amount of damage to his teeth and gums by bacteria by practicing dental hygiene on your dog in between veterinary visits.

You can help keep your dog's teeth clean and healthy at home in two ways: by providing something for your dog to chew on and by brushing your dog's teeth on a regular basis.

Your German Shepherd's wild ancestors kept their teeth clean and healthy by gnawing on the bones of their prey. The action of stripping meat from bones and chewing through the actual bone matter to get at the marrow inside did wonders for keeping tartar from building up on these wild canids' teeth. You can provide your German Shepherd with a similar and safer dental workout by giving him chew toys designed specifically for this purpose.

The other way to help keep your German Shepherd's teeth clean is to brush them at least three times a week. While the idea of brushing your dog's teeth may sound silly, it really isn't if you think about it. Humans brush twice a day to keep tartar from building up on their teeth. Why shouldn't this same course of action do the same for dogs?

In order to brush your dog's teeth effectively, you'll need to use a canine toothbrush. You can use a human-style brush with a shorter handle or the rubber type that fits over your finger like a cap and features tiny nubs that help remove the plaque as you rub. You'll find both types of brushes at a pet supply store. Another option is to use a piece of gauze wrapped around your index finger.

You'll also need toothpaste made especially for dogs, since you can't use regular toothpaste. Most dogs dislike the taste of human toothpaste and much prefer the meat flavors of canine pastes. Unlike humans, dogs do not spit after brushing. Therefore, any toothpaste that goes in your dog's mouth ends up in his stomach. Canine toothpaste is meant to be swallowed; human toothpaste is not.

You should experience little difficulty brushing your German Shepherd's teeth provided your dog is trained and easy to control. To get started, tell your dog to sit and then kneel or bend down next to him. Put a little toothpaste on your dog's toothbrush and lift the lip on the side of his mouth, exposing the teeth. Begin brushing in a circular motion and work your way down along the entire row of teeth. Move to the other side of your dog's mouth and complete the process on the rest of his teeth. Don't forget those small choppers in the very front!

If you begin the teeth-cleaning process while your German Shepherd is a puppy, teaching him early on to sit still while you brush every one of his teeth, you'll have a much easier time of it when he grows up. If your German Shepherd is already full-grown and has a hard time sitting for the brushing, first practice some obedience training with him on a regular basis. (Obedience training is discussed in Chapter 6, Basic

Did You Know?

A dog's heart beats between 60 and 120 times per minute, compared with 60 to 80 times per minute for humans.

Teeth Cleaning Sans Anesthesia

In order to avoid the worry and expense that comes with putting a dog under anesthesia for a teeth cleaning, some owners take their dogs to groomers and non-veterinary dental hygienists for cleanings.

However, most veterinarians recommend against dental cleaning without anesthesia by non-veterinary professionals—because it is difficult, if not impossible, to clean below the gum line on a dog that is fully awake. (Dental cleaning without anesthesia is also against the law in many states.) Scaling below the gum line is uncomfortable for most dogs, and they won't tolerate it. Because most harmful tartar is located below the gum line, a cleaning that does not include this area of the dog's teeth is ineffective.

Another reason veterinarians do not recommend this type of cleaning is that when it is performed in the absence of veterinary supervision, teeth cleaning can spread infections of the gum to a dog's blood stream.

Some dogs cannot undergo anesthesia for health reasons. In those cases, cursory cleaning can be done without anesthesia but only under the supervision of a veterinarian.

Training for German Shepherds.) Also, do the brushing a little at a time, so your dog won't have to sit still for so long.

Spaying and Neutering

Your German Shepherd is a beautiful animal with decades of careful breeding behind him. Given this reality, it may have occurred to you that you should breed your dog to help carry on his purebred line.

Although it's true that your German Shepherd is a very special animal, it is not true that you should breed him. Why not breed your pet? There are a number of very good reasons.

Breeding and Overpopulation—Just the Facts

The first and most important reason to not breed either a male or female German Shepherd is because there are already too many dogs in the world and too few homes for them. "But my dog is purebred," you may be thinking. "There are always homes for purebreds." This common belief is simply untrue. Purebred dogs account for approximately 25 percent of the population of animal shelters around the country. Many of those purebreds are subsequently euthanized, simply because no one wants them.

> **P**urebred dogs account for approximately 25 percent of the population of animal shelters around the country.

Breeding your German Shepherd will contribute to the vast pet overpopulation problem that has plagued the United States for the past several decades. Adding more dogs to the number of pets already in need of good homes will only aggravate the problem. Even if you plan to find homes for all of your dog's puppies, you will still contribute to the problem because your puppies will get homes that orphaned dogs could have had.

Health and Behavioral Concerns

Having a litter of puppies around the house might sound like a whole lot of fun, but, in reality, a lot of health risks are associated with keeping a female dog's reproductive system intact and with allowing her to give birth.

Research has shown that unspayed female dogs are at greater risk of developing mammary cancer, ovarian cancer, pyometra, and other serious illnesses later in their lives. The birth process itself can also endanger your dog's life. While most dogs experience no trouble giving birth, some need emergency cesarean sections, while others suffer serious and sometimes fatal complications. The puppies don't always make it, either.

Your female dog's health isn't the only issue to consider when weighing the benefits of spay surgery. The hormones that go along with the urge to breed can make your dog act a bit crazy during the times she is in estrus. Female dogs in heat often look for ways to escape their homes and yards so they can find a mate. They also attract roaming male dogs to your property. Some research has shown that unspayed females are also more likely to bite than their unspayed counterparts, and female dogs in estrus can ruin your furniture by bleeding on it.

Male dogs left intact are prone to fewer specific health problems than are unspayed female dogs (although testicular cancer poses some concern), but they are inclined to a lot more behavioral problems if they are not neutered. The hormones surging through the bodies of male dogs encourage them to constantly seek out a female dog. This means they are always trying to find a way to escape, so they can roam around the neighborhood in search of a female in heat. Those same hormones also encourage aggression in the male dog. Unneutered males are more likely to bite humans and fight with other dogs than are neutered males. Conversely, neutered male dogs tend to be more affectionate and attentive to their owners, undoubtedly because they no longer have breeding on their minds.

Other problems that can occur in unneutered male dogs include repeated urine-marking (often, inside the house), difficulty in training, and frequent howling and barking out of frustration at not being allowed to find a mate.

Spay/Neuter Surgery

It's important to your dog's health and behavior that you have him or her spayed or neutered. But what exactly does this surgery entail?

Spaying is the lay term for ovariohysterectomy, the surgical procedure for disabling a female dog's reproductive system. The spay surgery consists of removing the dog's ovaries and uterus. The dog is given a general anesthetic, and the surgery is performed in a short amount of time. Recovery is relatively quick, with dissolvable sutures often used, which means the stitches are absorbed by the dog's body rather than removed by the vet. A dog can undergo spaying at any time in her life, starting at eight weeks of age. Spaying before the dog's first heat, which usually occurs between six months and one year of age, provides the greatest health benefits. Most veterinarians will recommend spaying your dog at six months of age, since this is the most conventional time to perform the procedure.

Neutering is performed on male dogs, and is technically called orchiectomy, or castration. In this minor surgery, the vet removes the dog's testicles from the scrotum. The dog is given a general anesthetic for the procedure, and recovery is fast and easy. A male dog can undergo neutering surgery any time after the age of eight weeks. It is best to neuter your dog by the age of six months to prevent the development of certain hormone-related behaviors, such as excessive urine marking and aggression.

Improving the Breed

Another reason not to breed your dog is that, if done correctly, purebred dog breeding is a difficult, expensive, and complicated hobby. Responsible breeders spend years studying their breed of choice, show the dogs they breed to ensure the dogs' quality before letting them reproduce, and are very knowledgeable on the science of dog breeding. They are also willing to spend

Breeding Myths

All kinds of urban legends abound on the subject of breeding dogs. Most of them can be easily dispelled:

❍ **Myth: Breeding purebred dogs is a good way to make money.** Truth: If done responsibly and with the welfare of the dogs in mind, dog breeding is not the way to earn extra cash. Pregnant females need prenatal veterinary care, which will cost you. Complications during the birthing process can also require an emergency visit to the veterinarian for a cesarean or other operation. Once the puppies are born, you may need to supplement them if the mother dog can't provide enough milk, which means spending money for special milk substitute for the pups. When the pups are six weeks old, they all will need their first set of inoculations. Since German Shepherds are known for having large litters of as many as 10 to 12 puppies, this trip to the vet can set you back quite a bit. Once you've spent all this money on your litter, you may then have trouble finding enough people to buy the pups and may end up giving some away. The end result: You'll be lucky to break even.

❍ **Myth: Since everyone wants a purebred dog, you'll have no trouble finding homes for your dog's puppies.** Truth: It is almost as difficult to find homes for purebred dogs as it is to find homes for their mixed-breed cousins. Although many people find purebreds very attractive and are more likely to open their homes to a dog of pure breeding, the fact remains that animal shelters are full of purebred dogs who, despite their pure lineage, can't find a home.

❍ **Myth: Every dog should be bred at least once to ensure that he or she is emotionally well adjusted.** Truth: The idea that a dog needs to experience motherhood or fatherhood at least one time before being spayed or neutered is a complete falsehood. Dogs that have been allowed to breed before being altered exhibit no personality differences from those that haven't. In fact, dogs who are spayed or neutered before they are old enough to conceive actually make better pets, because sex hormones haven't yet influenced their behavior.

Myths About Spaying and Neutering

Some people are nervous about spaying or neutering their dog because they've heard bad things about the process. The following rumors are false:

○ **Myth: Spaying or neutering a dog causes the animal to get fat.**
Truth: People tend to associate spaying and neutering with a gain in their dog's weight. In reality, it is not the surgery that causes a dog to become obese, but simply the dog's entry into adulthood that precipitated the problem. Puppies are much more active than adult dogs, and when a dog becomes an adult, it naturally slows down. Weight gain results when a dog receives too much food or the wrong kind of food and/or too little regular exercise. The truth is that rather than harming a dog's health by causing it to become fat, spaying and neutering actually help a dog's health by reducing the risk for a number of diseases, including cancer.

○ **Myth: Spaying or neutering makes a dog lazy and boring.**
Truth: Because spay and neuter surgeries are usually performed around the time a dog undergoes the transition from puppyhood to adulthood, many people associate a mellowing of their dog's personality with the surgery rather than with the dog's increased age. In reality, spaying or neutering makes a dog a better pet, because it takes the animal's mind off of mating and allows the animal to focus all of his or her attention on its owner instead.

○ **Myth: Spaying or neutering a dog robs the animal of its femininity or masculinity.**
Truth: The notion that a dog will lack its femininity or masculinity if spayed or neutered is a classic example of the tendency of human beings to project their own feelings onto their pets. Dogs don't have a conscious sense of their gender the way humans do. Your dog is no more likely to miss his or her reproductive organs than you would miss a portion of fingernail you just clipped off.

money—not to make money—on their hobby. Responsible dog breeding is not a profit-making venture.

Although your pet German Shepherd is undoubtedly a beautiful and dignified creature, that does not mean he is suitable for breeding. The only individual dogs within any breed that should reproduce are those that will improve the breed by contributing special characteristics and good health to the gene pool. To determine the quality of a dog, a qualified dog judge must evaluate the animal in a dog-show ring, and an expert also must carefully appraise the dog both physically and genealogically for genetic disease. How do you know your dog is not one of the animals destined to improve the breed? Because breeders keep those dogs for themselves or sell them specifically as show animals. If your German Shepherd was sold or given to you as a pet, that means his job in life is to serve as a companion—not as a breeding animal.

Sick Calls and Emergencies

We all dread the idea of having to some day rush our pets to the hospital for an emergency. Although most dog owners are fortunate in never having to encounter a scary emergency with their dogs, enough find themselves in emergency situations that it's important to know what to do if and when such a situation arises.

When to Call the Vet

It's not always easy to know exactly whether a call or trip to the veterinarian is appropriate. If your dog seems a little under the weather, should you quickly rush him to the hospital? If not, how long should you wait and what should you do before calling your veterinarian for help?

Fortunately, you can look for a number of signs that will tell you whether your dog needs the veterinarian in any medical situation. As a rule of thumb, if your dog experiences any of the following symptoms, you have an emergency on your hands that warrants an immediate visit to the veterinarian:

○ Bleeding. Your dog is bleeding heavily from any place on his body.
○ Severe stomach pain. Your dog's stomach is distended, and he is retching and salivating.
○ Can't stand up. Your dog tries to stand but cannot rise or stay up.
○ Straining. Your dog strains to go to the bathroom, and nothing or very little comes out.
○ Bloody urine. Your dog eliminates blood or bloodstained urine.
○ Injury. Your dog has been hit by a car, fallen from a high place, or bears a wound that is deep or exposes the bone.
○ Labored breathing. Your dog pants heavily, experiences raspy breathing, or coughs a lot.
○ Severe pain. Your dog appears to feel severe pain in any part of his body.
○ Possible poisoning. You saw or believe you saw your dog eat a toxic substance or plant.
○ Disorientation. Your dog seems disoriented, confused, or inexplicably aggressive.
○ Swelling around the face and head. Your dog may be having an allergic reaction that may restrict his breathing if not taken care of right away.
○ Bites. Another animal has bitten your dog.
○ Fever. Your dog has a rectal body temperature of 105 degrees Fahrenheit or higher.

How to Take Your Dog's Temperature

This is one of those indignities that your German Shepherd won't enjoy, but it doesn't take long, and you can reward her with a treat afterward. It can be helpful to have an assistant to hold the dog so that she won't squirm. Lubricate a digital rectal thermometer using petroleum jelly or a water-based lubricant. Gently insert it into the rectum, where it should remain for one minute. The normal canine temperature ranges from 100 to 102.5 degrees Fahrenheit. Call your veterinarian if your dog's temperature is approaching 105 degrees Fahrenheit.

Other signs of illness do not require an emergency trip to the veterinarian but do warrant an immediate phone call. These include:

- Diarrhea. Your dog has constant or intermittent diarrhea over a 24-hour period.
- Vomiting. Your dog has vomited his food or stomach juices for a 24-hour period.
- No appetite. Your dog turns up his nose at food he normally eats with relish.
- Fever. Your dog's rectal body temperature exceeds 103 degrees Fahrenheit (105 or higher is an emergency).
- Swelling. A swollen area appears on your dog's body and is hot to the touch.
- Eye pain. Your dog's eye is teary, held partially or completely closed, is swollen, or has a cloudy surface.
- Itchiness. Your dog scratches and/or bites incessantly at his skin, ears, or other parts of his body.

First-Aid Kit

An important part of keeping your dog healthy includes keeping a good first-aid kit on hand. In an emergency situation, you should contact your veterinarian immediately. What follows are items that you should always have on hand should the unexpected occur.

- ○ Your vet's phone number
- ○ The National Animal Poison Control Center's hotline number: (888) 426-4435
- ○ Aspirin (for pain and swelling—should only be used on the advice of a veterinarian)
- ○ Antihistamine (for allergic reactions; ask your vet which brand and dosage are best)
- ○ Tweezers (for removal of splinters, ticks, or other objects lodged in your dog's skin)
- ○ Antiseptic scrub (to clean wounds)
- ○ Cotton balls (for use in wiping eyes, ears, and wounds)
- ○ Sterile saline eye wash (to rinse foreign objects from eyes)
- ○ Sterile gauze roll and pads of various lengths
- ○ Scissors (to cut the gauze and matted hair around wounds)
- ○ Rectal thermometer (for taking your dog's temperature)
- ○ Lubricant jelly or liquid (for lubricating the thermometer; use a water-based brand rather than petroleum jelly, which can irritate the rectal lining)
- ○ Antibiotic ointment (for minor wounds)
- ○ Canine first aid book
- ○ Needlenose pliers
- ○ Styptic powder (in case nails are cut too short)

How to Administer Medication and Pills

If your dog contracts an illness or condition that requires regular medication, you're the one who will have to give it to him! Make sure to give the medication as often as the veterinarian recommends it, for as long as the veterinarian suggests, and in the proper dosage.

Most oral doggy medicines come in one of two forms: liquid or pills, both of which you can administer a couple of different ways. On the other hand, if your vet asks you to give your dog eye or ears drops, your methods are somewhat limited.

Giving Pills

If you're lucky, the pills your veterinarian gave you will taste good and your dog will eat them right from your hand. Chances are, however, that you will have to either coerce your dog into accepting the pill or hide it in the dog's food, if your veterinarian says it's okay to do so.

If the vet prescribes the type of medication that must be given directly to the dog without food, you will need to pop the pill directly into your dog's mouth. There is a fast, easy way to do this that won't result in a wrestling match!

First, tell your dog to sit (this is where obedience training can really come in handy). Kneel or bend down in front of your dog and grasp the top of her muzzle with one hand, pointing it skyward, while you gently pry open her mouth with the other hand (the one holding the pill). Put the pill inside your dog's mouth on her tongue as far back as you can reach and then close her mouth. Hold her jaws closed with nose pointed up with one hand while you rub her throat with the other hand. Wait until you see your dog swallow before you let go of her nose. Keep an eye on your dog for a few minutes afterward to make sure she doesn't spit the pill back up.

If your veterinarian says it's okay to disguise the pill in your dog's food, you are in luck! Do this by placing the pill at the bottom of your dog's empty food bowl and grinding it into a powder with the back of a spoon. Then mix some canned dog food or other moist edibles into the bowl, making sure to evenly distribute the pill throughout to minimize the taste.

Another trick is to roll the pill up in a slice of cheese or other tasty treat that your dog never refuses. Most dogs are so eager to gulp down the food, they don't even notice the pill hidden inside.

Giving Liquids

If your veterinarian prescribes a liquid medication for your German Shepherd, you can give it to your dog either directly by eyedropper or syringe, or you can mix it into her food. Ask your veterinarian which method he or she prefers you use.

To give your dog liquid medications directly from a dropper or syringe, tell her to sit. Fill the dropper or syringe with the correct dose of medication and hold the dropper in your hand. Kneel or bend down next to your dog and grasp her muzzle with your free hand, pointing her nose to the sky. Insert the dropper or syringe in between her lips, on the side of her mouth, toward the back. Slowly squeeze the liquid into your dog's mouth. She should swallow the liquid as it enters her mouth.

> Another trick is to roll the pill up in a slice of cheese or other tasty treat that your dog never refuses. Most dogs are so eager to gulp down the food, they don't even notice the pill hidden inside.

If your veterinarian says it's okay to give your dog her liquid medication mixed with her meals, use canned dog food or another moist food and stir in the liquid thoroughly. Make sure the food is cool or at room temperature. Mixing the liquid medication with a heated food may reduce the medication's potency.

Giving Ear and Eye Drops

If your dog has been diagnosed with an ear infection or eye problem, chances are your veterinarian will ask you to administer medication in the form of drops at home.

Most dogs are more tolerant of ear drops than they are of eye drops, so you shouldn't experience too much trouble putting ear drops in your German Shepherd's rather large listening devices. To perform this task, ask your dog to sit. Ear drops in hand, kneel or bend down next to her and grasp the affected ear. Pull back the earflap and put the drops directly into her ear canal. Let go of the flap and rub the base of the ear for a minute to evenly distribute the drops. If your veterinarian instructed you to put drops in both ears, perform the same procedure for the other one. Expect your dog to shake her head and possibly paw at her ear after you put in the drops.

Eye drops are more difficult to administer than are ear drops, so it is best to enlist the help of a second person. Ask your dog to sit and have your helper kneel or bend beside her, holding her head steady with nose pointed upward. Hold the dog's eye open with one hand and squeeze the drops in one at a time. Be prepared for her to try to pull away when she feels the drops hitting her eye. This is where your helper can really come in handy, by holding your dog's head firmly in his or her grasp.

If you have no one to help you put drops in your German Shepherd's eyes, you will need to restrain your dog on your own. This means kneeling or bending down behind her to prevent her from backing away from you. Hold her muzzle with one hand and place the drops in with your other hand. Do this as quickly as you can, so your dog has little time to figure out what is going on!

Leaving a List for the Dog Sitter

If you plan to go away for an extended period of time, and someone—a friend, relative, professional dog sitter, or boarding facility—will care for your dog in your absence, leave a list of vital health information on your dog for reference. This list should include the following:

❍ An accounting of all medications your dog is currently receiving, along with instructions on dosage and administration

❍ Information on any specific medical conditions your dog has

❍ The type of food your dog eats, when she eats it, and how much she is given

❍ How much exercise your dog gets, where she gets it, and when

❍ Phone number of your veterinarian and local emergency hospital and number where you can be reached

❍ Any special care or other items of importance the caretaker should know

Costs

The obligations of dog ownership include caring for your pet when she gets sick. In addition to the time and effort involved, this also involves money. Veterinary care is not cheap, and a major illness or injury in your dog can set you back as much as several thousand dollars.

If you think of your German Shepherd as a member of your family, you shouldn't hesitate to provide your dog with the best veterinary care you can afford. However, it doesn't hurt to prepare for potential medical costs.

Although veterinary care is less expensive than human medical care, many people find it surprising just how much veterinary care does cost. It is not unusual to hear pet owners grumbling about the cost of veterinary care, complaining to all who will listen about how they just spent $200 to get their dog's teeth cleaned or $100 just for an annual exam and inoculations. To many pet owners, these sums seem disproportionately large. But if you look at all that is involved in providing medical care for animals, the prices you are paying may cease to surprise you. Comparing human and animal medicine is a good way to understand why veterinary medicine is so expensive.

When you go to visit your family physician, you usually see your doctor in an office located within a medical building. Aside from an examining table, a sink, and a few contraptions, such as a blood pressure machine and lamp, the doctor's office contains little in the way of medical equipment. If you need surgery or extensive testing that requires x-rays or sonograms, you go to a laboratory that is separate from your doctor's practice.

Veterinarians, on the other hand, rarely have the luxury of referring patients to surgery centers or diagnostic labs for analysis. The equipment required for operations, x-rays, sonograms, and a host of other tests must be purchased or leased by the veterinarian and kept on premises. That means renting a bigger office than that of your medical doctor, as well as a considerable investment in very expensive equipment.

While your family physician employs a nurse and a couple of clerical workers in his or her office, veterinarians must employ a staff of veterinary technicians and other hospital workers to aid in caring for the sick animals that stay in the veterinarian's care. This results in a higher overhead than the average physician incurs.

In order to offset the costs of large office space, expensive medical equipment, and bigger staffs, veterinarians must charge amounts that will allow their businesses to run effectively.

Some people believe that because veterinary fees are what they are, veterinarians must be getting rich in the process. In most cases, that is not true. The majority of veterinarians spend the first five to ten years of their professional lives paying off exorbitant student loans, since the four years of specialized schooling required to become a veterinarian costs an average of $100,000. Once veterinarians leave school and start working, their salaries rarely reach the heights that human doctors' do. The average small animal veterinarian, who owns his or her own practice and has been working as a veterinarian for ten years, earns a yearly salary of about $70,000, the maximum amount most private-practice veterinarians can earn.

How to Discuss Finances with Your Vet

However justifiable the cost of veterinary medicine, it remains hard for many dog owners to pay for unexpected veterinary care. Regular checkups, vaccinations, and teeth cleanings will set you back a few hundred dollars every year, which is a manageable amount for most dog owners—especially those who plan ahead by saving for that expected annual exam. But if a dog becomes seriously ill, the cost of veterinary care can escalate beyond the means of many people.

No dog owner wants to deny their pet medical care during a crisis because he or she can't afford it. However, many people are faced with this very real dilemma. Although veterinarians are in

Did You Know?

Shelters in the United States take in nearly 11 million cats and dogs each year. Nearly 75 percent of those animals have to be euthanized.

the business of providing care to sick animals, they are also human beings who know and understand the emotional bond—and financial constraints—of most families who own pets.

If you are faced with a situation in which your dog is seriously ill and the veterinary costs for curing her are well beyond your means, don't hesitate to speak with your veterinarian about the problem. Explain the difficulties you are having and find out if the veterinarian can offer you a payment plan that enables you to gradually pay off your dog's medical bills. Most veterinary hospitals accept credit cards. Your veterinarian may agree to bill part of your expenses to your card now and some later in an effort to help you make the payments.

It's important to express money concerns to your veterinarian for another reason: The procedures the veterinarian recommends for your dog may depend on how much you can afford to spend. Your veterinarian will always first suggest the best, most effective option for your pet. However, if money is a big concern, your veterinarian may be able to offer alternative, less expensive treatments, but keep in mind that these less expensive treatments may not be as effective.

Savings Plans and Insurance Plans: How They Can Help

Just as you would protect your family by saving money and purchasing medical insurance in case something unforeseen should befall one of you, you should consider a savings plan and medical insurance for your dog. How likely is it that your German Shepherd will ever require major medical care for an illness or injury? According to statistics, 50 percent of pets in American households need veterinary attention as a result of a serious illness or injury at some time in their lives.

Savings   One of the wisest moves you can make when you first get your German Shepherd is to start a savings plan for your dog. It sounds silly—after all, your pooch won't attend an Ivy League university or throw a big wedding when he grows up. However, he just might get sick at some point in his life, and if he does, you'll be glad you were wise enough to save for a rainy day. Nothing is more painful than having to make a life-or-death decision about a sick pet based on whether you can afford to pay for the medical care.

Think of it this way: If you sock away $10 a week in a savings plan when you first get your German Shepherd puppy, by the time your dog is three years old, you will have saved nearly $1,500.

If your dog becomes ill at any point in his life, you will have the money you saved to fall back on to pay his bills. You can pull from your savings plan every year to pay for your dog's annual exam, vaccinations, and occasional teeth cleanings. If your dog lives to a ripe old age without ever getting seriously ill, you will have a nice sum of money you can use to take a vacation or buy that boat you've always wanted!

Insurance   Believe it or not, you can actually purchase medical insurance for your dog. A medical insurance policy can help you pay your veterinary bills should your German Shepherd become seriously ill or injured.

Pet medical insurance works a lot like traditional human medical coverage. You pay a premium each year, and your pet is covered in case he becomes sick or

Did You Know?

In 1957, Laika became the first dog in space, riding aboard the Soviet satellite Sputnik 2.

How to Make an Insurance Claim

It's your responsibility as a policyholder to make the best use of your insurance plan. Take these steps to get the most for your money:

1. Designate a file for pet insurance forms.

2. Always take a claim form with you to the veterinarian's office. Many companies require a veterinarian's signature.

3. Make copies of receipts. A receipt must accompany every claim form. Some companies require only copies; others require originals. Keep a copy for your records.

4. Make copies of completed claim forms. If a question or payment issue arises, a copy to review on your end of the phone line will be reassuring.

5. Note an acceptable payment period on your calendar. Reimbursement may slip your mind, and it may be delayed in cases where a problem is encountered and you forget to inquire about the payment's status.

6. Mark claims paid and date received. Leave a paper trail that's easy to understand. Looking back a year later, you'll be glad for the notations.

© 1999 Solveig Fredrickson

hurt. As with human medical coverage, certain restrictions exist within pet insurance policies.

For example, a typical bare-minimum policy for a German Shepherd can cost you around $50 per year, possibly less if you plan to cover more than one pet. The policy would probably include a deductible of around $40 per incident, with a $1,000 limit for each illness or injury. Policies like this often have a $5,000 limit for the entire policy.

Typical policies pay 80 percent of the first $200 of your pet's veterinary bill and 100 percent of the amount exceeding $200, up to the per-incident limit. Coverage usually includes office visits,

10 Questions to Ask Every Provider

Before choosing a pet insurance or membership plan, be sure to get straight-forward answers to all your questions. If it makes you more comfortable, get the answers in writing.

1. Does your policy follow fee/benefits schedules? If so, please send me your detailed coverage limits. In the meantime, please give me examples of coverage limits for three common canine procedures so I can compare them to my current veterinary charges.

2. Does your policy cover basic wellness care, or does it cover only accidents and illnesses? Do you offer a wellness care endorsement that I can purchase on top of my basic plan for an additional fee? What other endorsements do you offer, and how much do they cost?

3. Under your policy's rules, can I continue taking my dog to his current veterinarian, or do I need to switch to another veterinarian?

4. Does your policy cover hereditary conditions, congenital conditions, or pre-existing conditions? Please explain each coverage or exclusion as it pertains specifically to my dog. Is there a feature where pre-existing conditions will be covered if my dog's pre-existing condition requires no treatment after a specified period? What is that period?

5. What happens to my premium and to my dog's policy if your company goes out of business? What guarantees do I have that I won't be throwing my money away?

6. How quickly do you pay claims?

7. What is your policy's deductible? Does the deductible apply per incident or annually? How does the deductible differ per plan?

8. Does the policy have payment limits over a year's period or during my pet's lifetime? How do the payment limits differ per plan?

9. What is the A.M. Best Co. rating of your insurance underwriter, and what does that rating mean?

10. Is there a cancellation period after I receive my policy or membership? How long do I have to review all my materials once I receive them, and what is the cancellation procedure?

injections, prescriptions, laboratory testing, x-rays, surgery, and hospitalization.

The typical pet medical policy excludes preventive medical care. However, some HMO-type plans do allow you to purchase well-care examinations, vaccinations, teeth cleaning, and parasite control coverage.

The benefits of insuring your German Shepherd are obvious. If your dog encounters illness or injury, you will receive help in paying the veterinary bills. Also, because most pet insurance companies provide an identification tag for your dog's collar that states the dog is medically insured and by whom, your German Shepherd is more likely to receive veterinary treatment if she ever became lost and subsequently injured.

The down side to buying insurance for your pet is that the coverage is limited, and you will be required to pay premiums every year for a policy that you may never need to use—if you're lucky.

The decision of whether to buy insurance for your German Shepherd is a personal one. Some people find that pet insurance gives them peace of mind that makes it worth the cost of the premiums, even if they never use the policy. Others would rather take their chances and deal with whatever problems may come if and when they happen. This decision is ultimately up to you.

Common Health Concerns

In This Chapter

○ Parasites Inside and Out
○ Illnesses and Emergencies
○ Obesity

A host of diseases, conditions, and parasites plague the canine species, just as they do humans. As a conscientious dog owner, you can do plenty to keep these ailments at bay. Understanding the specific health problems to which your dog is susceptible will enable you to recognize problems before they get out of hand.

Parasites Inside and Out

Parasites present a problem for most animals, from lizards to cows. Dogs, of course, are no exception and are prone to some particularly unpleasant creatures that like to attach themselves—literally—to the canine body. The most common and troublesome of these parasites are fleas, ticks, and worms.

Parasites are organisms that survive by feeding off of the bodies of other animals that serve as hosts to the parasites. Although some organisms exist inside and outside of hosts without causing any harm—sometimes even helping the host, such as bacteria that live in the digestive systems of all mammals, where they break down food—many parasites harm the hosts they invade.

In small numbers, most parasites will merely make your dog uncomfortable. But if those numbers go unchecked or are combined with certain diseases or other conditions, parasites can present a very dangerous threat to your dog's health.

Recognizing when your German Shepherd is suffering from a parasitic infestation and/or infection is important. You can help sustain your pet's good health by learning how to identify the symptoms that indicate your dog has parasites and how to eliminate these organisms from his body.

Internal Parasites

Dogs and other mammals must cope with a host of particularly ugly parasites—the type that lives inside the body. Internal parasites find their way into the dog's system and feed on the dog's blood, sometimes to the point of actually killing the animal.

A number of different kinds of internal parasites can affect dogs. The most common are worms that settle into and damage particular areas of the body. These worms rob the dog of nutrients, drain the dog's bodily fluids, cause failure of vital organs by interfering with their function, and wreak other assorted havoc in the dog's body. Therefore, it's important to keep these parasites in check.

Roundworms   If you take good care of your dog, you should never experience a problem with a parasite like roundworms—right? Actually, since nearly all puppies are born with roundworms, it's virtually impossible for your dog to avoid getting them sometime in his life.

Roundworms, also known as ascarids, live in a dog's intestines, where they feed off the animal's bodily fluids. Adults can measure anywhere from one to seven inches in length. Roundworms can cause the most damage in puppies, especially if the infection goes untreated.

Roundworm eggs can be transferred to a puppy through the placenta, mother's milk, or from the environment. The eggs then move to the puppy's intestines, where they eventually hatch. The larvae that hatch from these eggs migrate to the puppy's lungs, then enter the windpipe and move up to the throat, where the puppy swallows them. The larvae then return to the puppy's intestines where they grow to adulthood.

Pregnant females and other dogs or puppies contract roundworms by ingesting soil that contains the eggs, which pass to the soil from an infected dog's feces. They may also get them by eating infected mice or birds.

Roundworms do little harm to adult dogs, because few of the larvae make it back to an adult dog's intestine to complete the cycle. In puppies, however, roundworms can actually lead to death if the infection is severe.

Puppies severely infected with roundworm have round pot-bellies and poor-looking coats. Other symptoms include diarrhea, an underweight appearance, vomiting, and, sometimes, white strand-like worms in the stool.

Since roundworms are prevalent in puppies—and can do considerable damage to their fragile bodies—it's important for your vet to examine your German Shepherd puppy as soon as you get your dog. If you purchased your puppy from a responsible breeder, he or she most likely dewormed the puppy before you acquired him. (Three and six weeks of age are the best times to deworm a puppy.) Check with your breeder to make sure your puppy was dewormed.

If your puppy was not dewormed at a young age or you are unsure whether he was dewormed, talk to your veterinarian about deworming him as soon as possible. If you suspect your adult German Shepherd has roundworms (usually evident in the stool), contact your veterinarian for treatment.

The usual prescription for roundworms is a chemical agent that is administered by mouth to the puppy or dog. Your veterinarian will determine which dewormer is best for your pet, based on the animal's age, condition, and other factors.

Hookworms   One of the nastiest internal parasites that affect dogs is the hookworm. These parasites can cause serious internal damage and, in puppies with severe infections, can even cause death. Hookworms present more of a problem in warm, humid climates than in dry, arid climates.

Hookworms are small worms shaped like hooks—hence the name. They measure around one-quarter to one-half an inch in length. Hookworms thrive by attaching themselves to the wall of the small intestine, where they drain blood from the dog.

Hookworm eggs hatch inside the dog's intestine, and the larvae pass through the dog's feces. Other dogs become infected with hookworms by coming into contact with the larvae in feces or in contaminated soil.

Collecting a Fecal Sample

When you take your dog out to eliminate, bring along a plastic sandwich bag and a container in which to store the sample. A clean plastic dish with a lid, such as an empty margarine tub, is ideal.

Place the plastic bag over your hand, pick up the sample, and place it in the container. It should be collected no more than 12 hours before your dog is examined by the veterinarian. Refrigerate it until you can get to the veterinary clinic.

Hookworms typically infect puppies at around three weeks old, when the eggs are transmitted to the pups through the mother dogs' milk. Once inside the puppies' intestines, the larvae hatch and feed.

Hookworms can cause severe anemia, especially in puppies. In young pups, the primary symptom of hookworm is bloody or black diarrhea. In adult dogs, the signs of hookworm infection include vomiting, diarrhea, weight loss, and anemia. Adult dogs with very serious hookworm infections can exhibit the same symptoms as those of an infected puppy: bloody diarrhea and severe anemia.

Because most adult dogs develop immunity to hookworms, severe infections with this parasite are unusual in mature German Shepherds. However, adult dogs with weak immune systems (caused by malnutrition, stress, and other factors) can encounter difficulty in fighting off hookworms. Young puppies are most susceptible to this parasite, since their immunities are not yet fully developed.

Your veterinarian will diagnose hookworms in your dog by examining the stool for eggs. Treatment for hookworm infections consist of deworming drugs that kill the parasite inside the dog's body. If your veterinarian finds evidence of a hookworm infection in your German Shepherd puppy, he or she will deworm your pet right away.

In some dogs, hookworms also reside within the animal's tissue and not just in the intestines. In those cases, an infestation is difficult to treat, because the deworming medication kills only those parasites in the dog's intestines and does not affect parasites lodged in tissue.

Tapeworms   Most people have heard of tapeworms. These parasites, which attach themselves to the small intestines, rarely cause serious problems in dogs.

Tapeworms, which are flat and ribbon-like, range in length from around one inch to several feet. A tapeworm attaches to the wall of the intestines with a part of its body called a scolex, which is basically the worm's head. Using hooks to fasten themselves, tapeworms absorb nutrients from the dog's intestines through the surface of their bodies.

Each tapeworm reproduces by producing and fertilizing its own eggs, which are contained in packets in segments of the worm's body. These segments detach from the parasite's body and pass into the environment through the dog's feces. The worm segments often cling to the fur near the rectal area of dogs infected with tapeworms.

The primary cause of tapeworm infection is fleas. Fleas eat the eggs of tapeworms and, in turn, the dog swallows the fleas. (If you've ever seen a dog biting at a flea, it's easy to understand how this happens.) The tapeworm eggs then hatch in the dog's body and infest the small intestine.

Dogs can also acquire tapeworms by eating raw meat. Don't allow your dog to eat animals he has killed or found dead, since tapeworm eggs could contaminate the flesh.

A sure sign of tapeworm infection is the presence of worm segments clinging to your dog's fur just below the tail, around the anus. Also, if your dog has a serious flea infestation, he almost certainly also has tapeworms. Your veterinarian should examine your dog's stool for tapeworm eggs to confirm the diagnosis and prescribe treatment.

If your dog has tapeworms, your veterinarian will prescribe a deworming agent that you will need to give your pet on a periodic basis.

Heartworm   One of the most dangerous parasites affecting dogs is the heartworm. If not prevented and controlled, this aggressive organism can easily kill a dog. Heartworm poses a big problem in areas where mosquitoes are common.

Heartworms are long, spaghetti-like worms ranging in size from four to 12 inches long. They are transmitted to the dog's body by mosquitoes, which spread the organism from one dog to another through the insect's saliva, and inhabit the pulmonary artery and the right ventricle of the dog's heart.

> Heartworm poses a big problem in areas where mosquitoes are common.

Heartworms start out in a dog as larvae deposited in the skin by an infected mosquito. The larvae then migrate into the bloodstream and make their way to the dog's heart and pulmonary artery, where they mature into adults. This entire cycle takes about six months to complete.

Once the worms find their way to the animal's heart and pulmonary artery, they reproduce (providing both sexes are present, as is usually the case). The live offspring, called microfilaria, are released into the dog's bloodstream, where they are ingested by mosquitoes. They mature inside the mosquito and are spread when the mosquito bites other dogs.

Heartworms are extremely dangerous to dogs, because their presence can cause clotting of the arteries, liver failure, and heart failure. In the early stages of infection, dogs show few symptoms. However, after a while, infected dogs start to experience difficulty breathing and lose weight. If the heartworm goes untreated, the dog will most likely die from congestive heart failure.

Treating heartworm is risky, because the treatment can cause the dead or dying worms to be shed into the lungs. If this happens, the dog will develop breathing problems and could die. Although dogs with heartworm can be successfully treated, prevention provides a much safer option for dogs.

To keep your dog from ever getting heartworm, your veterinarian will recommend placing your dog on a heartworm preventive pill, given once a month, starting around six months of age. Your dog may need to receive this pill for the rest of his life in order to keep heartworm at bay.

If your German Shepherd is an adult dog and has not been on a heartworm preventive since puppyhood, your veterinarian will most likely want to test your dog for heartworm infection before starting him on a preventive program. The reason for this is that when dogs with existing infections receive certain heartworm preventives, complications can arise from the dead bodies of the heartworms that have been living in the dog. Since the worms are often hard to detect, your dog may require x-rays and repeated blood tests to determine whether he has heartworm.

Mosquitoes, which are very difficult to control, spread heartworm. If you live in an area of the country that has mosquitoes year-round, you might want to keep your dog indoors during the time of day when mosquitoes do most of their feeding (in the late afternoon and early evening) to help prevent heartworm infection.

Coccidia   A coccid is a common protozoan (single-cell) parasite that poses a problem primarily for puppies. A coccidia infestation (coccidiosis) in a puppy or, in rare cases, an adult dog can result in diarrhea and illness. It is commonly found in dogs that live in overcrowded and unsanitary conditions, such as puppy mills and some pet shops.

Coccidia reside in the dog's intestinal tract and may irritate it. Infested dogs eliminate (in their feces) tiny sacks, called cysts, spreading the coccidia to other dogs that come into contact with the feces and inadvertently ingest the egg sacks.

Puppies are more likely to develop coccidiosis and the resulting disease than are adult dogs. Pups pick up coccidia from their mothers or from living in a dirty environment.

Symptoms of coccidia usually include blood-streaked stool or diarrhea, loss of appetite, dehydration, muscle weakness, and anemia. A severe infection in a young puppy can ultimately lead to death.

Coccidia is preventable. To stop this organism from taking hold, keep your dog's environment clean and sanitary, frequently removing his waste. In addition, never board your dog any place that is crowded and unclean.

Did You Know?

The earliest fossil evidence of dogs dates back to 10,000 B.C.

Getting rid of coccidia requires treatment by a veterinarian, who will prescribe a drug to kill protozoa. The dog will be treated for a period of a week or more. The vet may also prescribe a remedy to control diarrhea.

Giardia   The protozoan giardia causes health problems not only for dogs but also for humans and many other mammals as well. This parasitic organism is found in quite a few untreated freshwater sources, which increases the risk of infestation for German Shepherd owners who like to hike and camp with their dogs.

Giardia inhabit the small intestine, causing diarrhea and, in severe infestations, subsequent dehydration and weight loss. The diarrhea resulting from giardia infections usually contains both mucus and blood.

> Even crystal-clear rivers, streams, and lakes in pristine wilderness areas can be sources of giardia infection. Try to keep your German Shepherd from drinking from these water sources when you are hiking or camping.

Dogs contract giardia by drinking water that has been contaminated with the eggs of the organism. Contamination occurs when water is fouled with the waste of other animals and is not treated. Even crystal-clear rivers, streams, and lakes in pristine wilderness areas can be sources of giardia infection. Try to keep your German Shepherd from drinking from these water sources when you are hiking or camping. Before allowing your pet to drink fresh water, first either boil the water (make sure to let it cool) or treat it with a special chemical meant to kill giardia and other protozoa.

Giardia is most damaging to puppies. However, it's important to control these protozoa in all dogs, because evidence suggests humans can also contract the species that affect canines by drinking contaminated water.

Dogs that suffer from giardia infections must receive treatment with an anti-protozoal medication designed to kill the organisms. Your veterinarian will prescribe this drug and may also give you something to control your dog's diarrhea.

External Parasites

At some point in your life as a German Shepherd owner, you will probably have to deal with the nuisance of external parasites. These organisms feed on the blood of dogs and other animals.

While external parasites don't typically threaten canine lives—unless they are present in very large numbers—they can make your dog's life miserable and can spread disease.

Four common external parasites prey on dogs: fleas, ticks, skin mites, and ringworm. Each organism requires very different controls and treatment.

Fleas   Probably the best known of all canine parasites is the flea. Despite its small size, this obnoxious pest has a way of making itself most apparent.

Fleas are tiny black or brown insects that feed on the blood of mammals. Some 2,000 different species of fleas exist, each of which prefers different hosts. The flea species that causes the most grief to dogs, ironically, is called the cat flea.

Fleas have a complicated life cycle, which is one of the reasons they are so hard to control. The adult flea spends part of its life on the dog, feasting on your pet's blood. Male and female fleas often mate on the dog, and the female often lays eggs there. However, most of the eggs that are laid on the dog don't stay there for very long; they quickly fall off and land in the environment, where they hatch. The flea larvae feed on organic matter in the environment, including the blood-containing feces of adult fleas, which also falls off the dog and into the environment, making it accessible to the larvae. The larvae eventually spin cocoons and emerge as adult fleas, which jump back onto the dog using their very powerful legs. The cycle then begins again.

Adult fleas can live as long as a year under the right conditions. Fleas prefer warm, humid climates. In most of North America, they are most bothersome during the summer and fall.

Aside from being annoying, fleas can cause a host of problems for your dog. Young puppies or adult dogs that are in poor health and become heavily infested with fleas can actually develop anemia. Fleas can also spread tapeworms to your dogs.

The most common problem that results from fleas is flea allergy dermatitis. This skin condition, which results when a dog becomes allergic to a protein contained in the fleas' saliva, can cause intense itching and subsequent hair loss and secondary bacterial infection.

Fleas are difficult to treat, because they spend a good portion of their life cycle in the environment, rather than on the dog, where you could more easily target them. In order to keep fleas under control, you need to treat both your dog and your dog's environment.

Recent developments in canine parasite control have led to the creation of new products that work especially well in keeping down flea numbers. These medications are available only through your veterinarian. One such product includes a pill (or liquid) that interferes with the fleas' ability to reproduce, which you give to your dog on a monthly basis. Once a flea bites a dog treated with this chemical, the flea can no longer complete the reproductive cycle.

Another new flea stopper you can buy from your vet is a liquid product that is applied directly to the dog's skin and kills fleas that bite the dog. Over a six-week-period, this chemical eliminates all adult fleas in the dog's environment.

More traditional flea-control methods are also available. Since it is imperative to attack fleas in the environment as well as on the dog if using traditional methods, you'll need to use products like flea sprays and dips on your pet in conjunction with environmental treatments like foggers and yard sprays. Flea collars alone do not sufficiently protect your dog from fleas.

You can help keep fleas under control by frequently washing your dog's bedding, combing him regularly with a flea comb, and bathing him with a flea shampoo once a month or so during flea season.

Ask your veterinarian to help you design a flea-control program that will work best for you and your German Shepherd.

Ticks   Ticks are ugly external parasites that are hard to completely avoid. Sooner or later, your German Shepherd is bound to pick up a tick somewhere.

Ticks are small, brown or black arachnids that are related to the spider. They obtain nourishment by attaching themselves to the skin of dogs and other mammals and sucking blood from the host. Two species of ticks prey primarily on the dog: the American dog tick and the brown dog tick. These ticks must feed three times on a dog before they can reproduce. Ticks mate on the dog and lay eggs in the dog's environment. Tick larvae eventually develop into nymphs and finally adult ticks. Adult ticks wait on the stalks of plants and grasses until a dog walks by. When the dog brushes on the plant, the tick crawls onto the dog.

Dogs that host large numbers of ticks can develop anemia from the blood loss. Ticks also spread infectious diseases, such as Lyme disease, Rocky Mountain spotted fever, canine hepatozoonosis, and canine ehrlichiosis.

To remove a tick, grasp it firmly yet gently as close to your dog's skin as possible using tweezers or a special tick remover. Do not use your fingers unless absolutely necessary (for example, if you are hiking in a remote area and have left tweezers out of your first aid kit) because the tick could spread disease to you. Pull back with a steady motion until the critter disengages. Never try to harm the tick while it is still attached, such as by placing a hot match on its rear end, as this will only anger it and could cause it to spew disease-laden saliva into your dog. Once the tick is free, flush it down the toilet or drop it in alcohol to kill it. Apply rubbing alcohol to the site of the tick bite and an ice pack if the area swells. Watch for signs of illness that could emerge in the days and weeks to follow, particularly a stiff walk and lethargy, which could indicate Lyme disease. Report such symptons to the vet right away.

Since part of the tick's life cycle occurs in the dog's environment, if your dog continually gets ticks, wash his bedding and treat it with a product designed to kill ticks on dogs. As a preventive measure, cut down weeds, tall grass, and other foliage where your dog spends time, since ticks prefer this type of habitat.

Scabies   A tiny arachnid called a mite can give your German Shepherd plenty of grief. Several different kinds of skin mites can attack your dog. One mite, called the *Sarcoptes scabei*, causes a disease known as canine scabies.

Scabies is a contagious skin disease that causes intense itching. The mite that causes it burrows into the epidermis layer of the dog's skin, where it lays its eggs. Although the mite is microscopic, the itching and reddened, crusty skin that results from the infection is very visible. The hair in the area where mites are concentrated falls off, and the scratching and biting that the dog does to its skin makes the area look and feel even worse. Scabies are most likely to affect the edges of your dog's ears and his face, elbows, front legs, and underside.

Scabies spread easily to other dogs through direct contact or by touching infected bedding. Humans also can get mites from their dogs, which results in itching, usually around the waist. Mites can't reproduce on humans, however, and will normally die off on their own in a few weeks.

It's important to treat scabies as soon as it is diagnosed. Your veterinarian can help you determine whether your dog is actually plagued with the *Sarcoptes scabei* mite that causes the disease by performing a skin scraping and examining the tissue under a microscope.

Scabies treatment consists of killing the offending mite. Your vet will recommend that you bathe your German Shepherd in an insecticidal dip, or the vet will give your dog an oral medication. If your vet prescribed a dip, you will need to repeat the treatment every 10 days for about a month until all the eggs have hatched and all the mites have been killed. With an oral treatment, you will have to give three to four doses two weeks apart.

Your veterinarian may also prescribe cortisone to relieve the itching until the mites are completely gone.

Ringworm   Unlike most other common external parasites that trouble dogs, neither an insect, an arachnid, nor a worm (contrary to what the name suggests) cause ringworm. Rather, ringworm is actually a fungus, and it can infect dogs, cats, and humans.

The organism that causes most ringworm infections in dogs is called *Microsporum canis.* The name "ringworm" comes from the fact that the organism often causes a ring-like blemish on the skin that measures about two inches in diameter.

The circular blemish is usually a reddish color, and hair loss occurs at the infected site.

Quite contagious, ringworm usually spreads from dog to dog or from dog to human (usually to children, who are most susceptible to it) by direct contact with the reproductive spores of the fungus. These spores exist in soil or on the skin of infected hosts. The fungus enters the outer layers of the dog's skin, where it lives on the keratin protein found there.

Although ringworm is not particularly itchy or irritating, it looks rather unpleasant. If the fungus is located on a dog's toenail, it can cause the nail to become deformed when it grows out.

Veterinarians diagnose ringworm by examining hairs plucked from suspicious lesions or growing a culture for seven to ten days.

Most ringworm infections are of short duration, typically lasting from four to 12 weeks before dissipating on their own, with no treatment. However, because ringworm is so contagious, you should take your dog to a veterinarian right away if you suspect ringworm. A prescription drug may be necessary to fight off the parasite to prevent other family members—human and animal—from becoming infected.

Illnesses and Emergencies

German Shepherds are fairly resilient creatures that get sick or hurt infrequently. Nevertheless, illness and injury can occur in dogs, no matter how well we take care of and watch over them.

Knowing how to recognize and handle certain symptoms and situations can make a huge difference in your dog's welfare. Fast and accurate diagnosis and response can mean the difference between a dog who recovers soon and one who doesn't recover at all.

The following illnesses and emergencies comprise the most common medical problems dog owners run into during their pets' lives. Learn the details of each potential malady, so you can take the right action quickly if your dog needs help.

Bites and Stings

German Shepherds love the outdoors, where they can play, run, and investigate the world around them. Of course, this canine love of nature comes with associated hazards, including run-ins with insects and other small but threatening creatures.

Wasps, bees, ants, and spiders can give your German Shepherd plenty to yelp about, should your dog end up tangling with certain of these species. In certain areas of the country, dogs face such other menacing critters as scorpions, centipedes, snakes, and tarantulas.

Most creatures that sting and bite dogs only do so out of self-defense. If your dog harasses a snake or corners a bee, the animal is going to retaliate as a way of protecting itself. Knowing this tidbit of animal behavior can help you train your dog to leave wildlife alone. Not only is this an Earth-friendly attitude to have, but it's also a good way to keep your dog out of trouble.

Insects and Arachnids   When it comes to dogs, the most common culprits of bites and stings are insects and arachnids. Insects, such as bees and wasps, will sting to protect themselves and also their hives. Ants will sting or bite to protect their colonies. Arachnids, including certain spiders and scorpions, will bite or sting to protect themselves and their nests.

In most cases, your dog will experience little more than pain from insect and arachnid bites and stings.

However, some types of these crawling and flying pests can endanger your dog's life.

When a dog receives a bug bite or sting, he'll usually feel obvious discomfort. If the bite or sting is located on the leg, the dog will probably limp or hold his leg up in the air. If the sting or bite is elsewhere on the body, the dog will lick, scratch, or chew at the area. The area itself will most likely redden and swell.

The first step in handling a bite or sting is to identify the creature that delivered it. A wasp, bee, or ant sting will probably cause no harm to your dog, unless he experiences an allergic reaction to the sting. If, after being stung, your dog begins to exhibit facial swelling or has trouble breathing, rush him to a veterinary clinic immediately.

Wasps and ants do not leave behind a stinger, so all you need to do to treat the area is to apply a paste made of baking soda and water to the spot where the sting occurred. If a bee stings your dog, the insect will usually leave a stinger in your pet's skin. Use a tweezers to grab the stinger at the point of entry, then gently and steadily pull it out. Do not grasp the bigger end of the stinger with your fingers or with a tweezers to pull it out, because squeezing the stinger will inject more toxins into the skin and cause the dog more pain. If a tweezers is not available, use your fingernail or a pocket knife to gently scrape the stinger out of the skin, taking care not to let the stinger break off. Most stingers are not embedded deeply and can be removed in this way.

If you determine that an arachnid—for example, a spider or scorpion—has bitten or stung your dog, it's important to figure out exactly which animal delivered the blow. Certain spider species, such as the black widow and the brown recluse, and certain related arachnids, such as the tarantula, can cause severe illness with their bites. If one of these creepy crawlies bites your dog, take him to an emergency clinic immediately. Scorpions use the stingers at the end of their tails to sting their prey as well as to defend themselves. Scorpion stings are very painful, produce localized swelling, and sometimes cause serious, life-threatening illness. Dogs that are stung by these animals must receive medical attention from a veterinarian.

If your pet is stung by a harmless variety of insect or arachnid, you can help soothe your dog's pain by applying a baking soda paste to the area. If significant swelling develops, apply ice packs to the affected area. (Be sure to wrap the ice in a towel first so as not to damage your dog's skin with cold.) You can treat bites that result in itching with calamine lotion purchased at your local drug store.

Snakes   Fortunately, most snake species in the United States are relatively harmless. Most snakes will bite if harassed by a dog, but the majority of those bites are not poisonous.

However, two types of snakes will deliver venomous bites to dogs that vex them: pit vipers (rattlesnakes, copperheads, and cottonmouth moccasins) and coral snakes.

Your first duty as a German Shepherd owner is to find out whether any of these types of snakes are found in the area where you live. Contact your local wildlife services agency and inquire as to which poisonous snakes are common to the part of the country where you live.

Your next job is to teach your dog to stay away from all snakes. If you enjoy hiking with your German Shepherd, keep him on a leash at all times and

Did You Know?

Dogs see color less vividly than humans but are not actually color-blind.

strongly reprimand him if he shows any interest in any type of snake you see on the trail. Some people in areas where poisonous snakes are common even go so far as to take their dogs to special anti-snake training classes to make sure their dogs develop a strong aversion to any kind of snake they may run across on trails or even in their own yards. (If you are interested in doing this, contact a local dog obedience club in your area. You can obtain a list of obedience clubs from the American Kennel Club.)

If your dog is bitten by a snake despite your training efforts, you must first identify the species of snake that delivered the bite. If you have learned how to recognize the poisonous snakes in your area and if you witnessed the bite, you should be able to identify the species with little difficulty.

On the other hand, if you weren't present when the snake bit your dog, but you suspect your pet received a bite from a poisonous snake, examine the area of the wound. You will probably notice swelling at the site of the bite, along with pain at the touch. Your dog will probably act anxious and wobbly.

Most snake bites occur on the leg and head, and will feature impressions on both sides of the skin. Harmless snakes will leave tooth impressions in the dog's skin that are in the shape of a U on one side and a U-shape with a V-shape inside it on the other. Non-poisonous snakes do not leave the two distinctive, round puncture marks at the top of the bite that are characteristic of poisonous snakes.

Poisonous snakes will leave a U-shaped bite on both sides of the skin, along with two round puncture marks appearing close together at the base of the U-shape. The two puncture marks, the telltale signs of the fangs of a poisonous snake, indicate the snake has injected venom into the dog.

First-Aid Kit Essentials

- ❍ Your veterinarian's phone number
- ❍ An after-hours emergency clinic's phone number
- ❍ The National Animal Poison Control Center's hotline number: (888) 426-4435
- ❍ Rectal thermometer
- ❍ Tweezers
- ❍ Scissors
- ❍ Penlight flashlight
- ❍ Rubbing alcohol
- ❍ Hydrogen peroxide (three percent)

- ❍ Syrup of ipecac and activated charcoal liquid or tablets (poisoning antidotes)
- ❍ Rectal thermometer
- ❍ Eye dropper
- ❍ Nonstick wound pads, gauze squares, and roll cotton to control bleeding, elastic bandage
- ❍ Adhesive tape
- ❍ Needlenose pliers
- ❍ Styptic powder (in case nails are cut too short)

If you are absolutely sure your dog was bitten by a non-poisonous snake, you don't need to do much. The bite will cause your dog little pain and will heal on its own. Just keep an eye on the wound to make sure it doesn't become infected. For several days following the bite, look for signs of reddening and swelling in the affected area.

If a poisonous snake bites your dog, the situation is very different and you need to take action immediately. First, do whatever you can to keep your dog quiet. He may be in great pain and hard to subdue. However, it's important for you to keep your dog as still as possible, since movement will only encourage the venom to travel more quickly throughout the dog's circulatory system.

Cover your dog with a blanket or whatever you can find to keep him warm, and rush him to a veterinarian immediately.

Veterinarians who live in areas that are highly populated with poisonous snakes usually keep anti-venom on hand to treat snake-bitten dogs.

Vomiting

Just as with humans, vomiting can signal something as simple as an upset stomach from eating a food that was not quite right or a symptom of a serious illness like cancer—or just about anything in between.

Occasional vomiting—especially if you've been feeding your dog table scraps or recently changed his diet—is nothing to worry about in adult dogs. Chances are he swallowed something that disagreed with him or has an upset stomach from some other minor and temporary problem. However, if the vomiting continues for more than 24 hours and/or is accompanied by diarrhea, blood, fever, pain, weakness, or other health problems, it may indicate a serious ailment. If your dog is a puppy and vomits at all, it could mean a problem.

If you see your dog vomit, pay close attention to him for the next day to determine whether he repeats the vomiting. Also check for blood in the vomit and watch the dog for diarrhea. If any of these symptoms appear, call your veterinarian immediately.

If your dog experiences only occasional vomiting as a result of eating foods that disagree with him, stop feeding table scraps and limit your dog's diet to the same brand and kind of dog food each meal. Don't give him toys that he can easily chew up and swallow, and keep a close watch on what he's eating.

If your dog throws up a few times within a several hour period, withhold his food and provide him with plenty of water. The next day give him boiled white-meat chicken and white rice. If he keeps this down, continue to feed this to him for the next two days. Then add a small amount of his regular dog food to his diet and gradually increase the dog food until he returns to his regular diet. If your dog doesn't respond to this bland diet and continues to vomit after 24 hours, contact your veterinarian.

Some causes for vomiting include eating rich and different food, ingesting bones or other inappropriate items, motion sickness, internal parasites, bacterial infection, kidney failure, and cancer.

If you notice that your dog is retching but produces no vomit, take him to the veterinarian. This could signal bloat, which is fatal if left untreated.

Diarrhea

Much like vomiting, diarrhea can indicate a sign of anything from minor gastrointestinal upset to serious illness. The nature of the diarrhea can help you determine whether the situation is serious or not.

Occasional diarrhea is usually of no great concern, especially if it comes on the heels of a change in diet. Abrupt changes to a dog's food often result in loose stool. However, if the diarrhea lasts more than 24 hours, is tinged with blood, and/or is accompanied by fever, pain, weakness, or other health problems, your dog could have a significant illness.

As soon as you notice that your dog has diarrhea, immediately withhold his regular dog food, while continuing to offer him plenty of fresh water. The next day, feed him a bland diet of boiled white-meat chicken and white rice. Feed this for a couple of days, keeping an eye out to determine whether the diarrhea continues. The bland diet should help his system return to normal. If it does, you can gradually add your dog's regular dog food to the bland food over a period of days until he is back on his normal diet. If he doesn't respond to the bland diet and continues to have diarrhea, call your veterinarian.

Diarrhea can result from an abrupt change in diet or from eating rich foods. Swallowing bones, garbage, or other non-edible items also can cause diarrhea, as can internal parasites, bacterial infection, kidney failure, and cancer.

Choking

In many ways, German Shepherds resemble small children. For example, they both sometimes put the wrong things in their mouths, placing themselves at risk for choking.

A dog chokes when something blocks his airway and prohibits him from breathing normally. Choking poses a life and death situation that cannot wait for veterinary intervention. If your dog chokes, you will need to handle the situation yourself, right then and there.

Choking most often occurs when a dog tries to chew on and then swallows an object that doesn't belong in his mouth. Choking is a bigger problem with puppies than with adult dogs, since teething puppies are much more likely to chew on inappropriate items.

You can tell if your German Shepherd is choking by his behavior. A choking dog will experience difficulty breathing, probably rub his face on the ground, make choking sounds, rub at his mouth with his paw, and might have a blue tongue.

If your German Shepherd is doing one or all of these things, assume he is choking and take action quickly. Open your dog's mouth as wide as you can and try to locate the obstruction. If you can see the foreign object, try to dislodge it with tweezers or needle-nose pliers. Only use your fingers if you absolutely have to and be aware that you could be bitten. Be careful not to mistake your dog's larynx for an obstruction. If this doesn't work, you'll have to give your dog the Heimlich maneuver, a method that forces air out of the lungs and simultaneously pushes out the offending object. To administer the Heimlich procedure on your dog, wrap your arms around his torso behind the rib cage. Apply pressure in a sharp, quick motion. Take care not to use too much pressure; apply just enough force to push the air out of your dog's lungs. Continue doing this until the object comes out.

> In many ways, German Shepherds resemble small children. For example, they both sometimes put the wrong things in their mouths, placing themselves at risk for choking.

When trying to dislodge the item, avoid the temptation to pick your dog up by the hind legs and turn him upside down. Although you might safely do this with a smaller dog, German Shepherds are too large for this method, and it can damage your dog's joints and ligaments.

Once you remove the item from your dog's throat, take him to a veterinarian for examination as soon as you can. Even a successfully removed object can cause damage to a dog's airway.

If you are unable to remove the item from your dog's airway, immediately take him to a veterinarian. It takes less than a minute after a dog stops breathing for the animal to go into cardiac arrest.

Bleeding

Dogs can bleed for any number of reasons, although wounds—whether internal or external—are the most common cause of bleeding

A bleeding dog can present a frightening sight, especially if you don't know what to do to stop the flow of blood. Knowing how to identify the cause of bleeding and knowing the basics of controlling blood flow can help tremendously, if you are ever faced with an emergency situation.

External Bleeding   Open wounds, in which the skin is broken, cause external bleeding. German Shepherds manage to get open wounds in any number of ways, including bites from other animals, broken limbs, punctures from sharp objects, and other assorted mishaps. Severe bleeding from an open wound can actually endanger a dog's life, for example, a lacerated artery can result in life-threatening blood loss.

If your German Shepherd receives a wound and bleeds heavily (the blood gushes or spurts), you must first control the flow of blood. Using gauze or a clean cloth (a shirt will do in a pinch), apply pressure directly to the wound, holding the gauze or cloth firmly against the wound until the bleeding stops. Once you staunch the blood flow, take your dog to a veterinarian immediately. If you can't stop or slow the flow of blood, rush your dog to an emergency clinic right away, applying continual pressure to the wound while en route to the hospital.

If your dog is bleeding from an external wound but the blood oozes, rather than gushes or spurts, control the blood flow by applying pressure as you would for a more serious wound. If the wound is small, however, you don't need to rush your dog to the veterinarian. Once the wound has stopped bleeding, clean it with soap and water or hydrogen peroxide solution (3 percent). Gently dab the area with gauze and watch the wound closely over the next few days. Many wounds—especially deep puncture wounds—become infected easily. If any wound reddens and swells, seems very big or deep, or is any kind of puncture wound, take your dog to the veterinarian right away.

Internal Bleeding   Wounds sustained to the inside of a dog's body from a traumatic injury (such as being hit by a car) can cause internal bleeding. Depending on the location of the wound, internal bleeding can often be extremely serious or fatal. Internal bleeding requires immediate veterinary attention.

It's not always possible to tell when a dog is bleeding internally although pale gums can be an indicator of this. If you see blood coming from your dog's nose or mouth, he very likely has suffered internal damage to his lungs or abdomen. Keep him quiet and rush him to a veterinarian immediately.

Fractures

Broken bones are uncommon in dogs, but they do happen. Most canine fractures result from the dog falling or being hit by a car. The majority of fractures occur on the leg(s), although German Shepherds are susceptible to breaking their tails as well.

A dog can sustain either an open fracture, in which a wound results from the broken bone piercing the skin, or a closed fracture, in which the bone breaks without coming through the skin. Since open fractures easily become infected, they pose the greatest risk to the dog. Closed fractures can also turn into open fractures if the dog is not handled properly when the bone is broken.

With an open fracture, it is pretty obvious the dog has broken a bone. The bone will poke out of the dog's skin, and the dog will experience tremendous pain. It is somewhat more difficult to recognize a closed fracture, which some people can mistake for a muscle sprain. A cracking noise at the moment of the injury is one sign that the dog has suffered a bone fracture rather than a sprain. Swelling or a change in the shape of the leg or tail also indicates a bone fracture. Dogs with broken legs often will stand with the injured leg held up, dangling limply. Either way, a bone fracture requires emergency veterinary attention.

If your dog suffers extreme pain and acts out defensively, muzzle him for your safety. Although your dog wouldn't dream of biting you under ordinary circumstances, the pain involved with a fracture can make him behave aggressively. You can muzzle your dog by wrapping a piece of twine or a strip of cloth approximately two feet long around the base of his muzzle. Loop the twine or cloth around his muzzle twice, then tie it in a small knot under his jaw. Take the two ends of the twine or cloth, pull them behind the dog's neck, and tie the ends in a bow. Do not apply it so tightly that it obstructs your dog's breathing.

Cover your pet with a blanket to keep him warm, then get someone to help you lift your German Shepherd into a vehicle and transport him to the veterinarian for immediate treatment.

Heatstroke

Your German Shepherd's normal body temperature is approximately 102 degrees. If the air temperature exceeds 102 or if your dog exerts himself in hot weather, he will begin to have trouble cooling himself down. When a dog can't cool himself sufficiently, he becomes a candidate for heatstroke, which can seriously harm or kill a dog in a matter of minutes.

Many cases of heatstroke result from leaving a dog in a car on a hot day. Even with the windows open, the inside temperature of a vehicle parked in the sun can rise to as high as 130 degrees in a very short time. A dog can in no way cool himself under these conditions, and heatstroke results.

Dogs that are left outside in the sun with no shade on hot days also can fall victim to heatstroke, as can dogs that exercise hard in the heat. Likewise, dogs that are kept indoors in small areas with no ventilation also can become dangerously overheated. Older or overweight dogs or pets with heart conditions are more susceptible to heatstroke than are younger, healthier dogs. To keep your dog from suffering heatstroke, provide him with a cool environment and plenty of fresh water to drink. Since dogs cool themselves by panting, make sure your dog is able to breathe and pant freely in the heat.

Indications of heatstroke may include an elevated body temperature, an increased heart and respiratory rate, excessive panting or difficulty breathing, lethargy, anxiety, difficulty standing, and heavy salivating or drooling. The dog's mouth may also be completely dry. If untreated, heatstroke can quickly result in death.

> To keep your dog from suffering heatstroke, provide him with a cool environment and plenty of fresh water to drink. Since dogs cool themselves by panting, make sure your dog is able to breathe and pant freely in the heat.

If you suspect your dog is suffering from heatstroke, seek veterinary attention immediately. Do not waste time attempting to lower your dog's temperature on your own unless there is absolutely no chance of getting medical attention. Quickly soak him down with cold water using a hose or towels, place him in an air-conditioned car, and rush him to the animal hospital. The vet will carefully reduce his body temperature and will give him IV fluids to try to prevent organ damage. Complications from heatstroke, such as kidney failure and respiratory arrest, may not show up for hours or even days.

Seizures

Like humans and other animals, dogs, too, can develop epilepsy. In fact, German Shepherds are particularly prone to epileptic seizures.

Of course, epilepsy is not the only cause of seizures in canines. Brain seizures can also result from poisoning, head trauma (injury), brain tumors, hypoglycemia, and certain other illnesses and diseases like distemper.

Canine seizures are fairly easy to recognize. If your dog experiences a "general seizure," he probably will lay on his side, roll his eyes, and foam at the mouth. His jaw and legs will move somewhat rhythmically, and he may lose control of his bowels and/or bladder. General seizures can last for several minutes

A dog experiencing a "partial," or mild, seizure often will stare at nothing for minutes at a time, ignore your voice or presence, bump into things as if he's blind, twitch uncontrollably in certain areas of the body, or chase imaginary prey. Oftentimes, the symptoms of partial seizures are so mild that they often go unnoticed. Although partial seizures are usually brief, general seizures can sometimes follow them.

After a seizure stops, your dog may appear to fall asleep or to seem disoriented and possibly anxious.

If your dog starts to seizure, gently move him into a safe area where he can't hurt himself on walls or other objects. Place pillows around your pet, so his thrashing won't result in injury. Keep track of how long the seizure lasts. Do not put your hand or any other object in the dog's mouth during the seizure. It is a myth that a dog (or a human) will swallow his tongue if it is not depressed or held during a seizure.

If your dog's seizure lasts more than three minutes, rush him to a veterinarian right away. Although seizures of short duration typically are not life threatening, prolonged or repetitive seizures can kill your dog.

When your dog emerges from the seizure, confine him to a dark, quiet room to help reorient him. For several hours after the seizure, avoid feeding him any large meals or giving him too much water. Take the dog's temperature and make a note of it for the veterinarian.

Whenever your dog has a seizure, call your veterinarian right away to report and provide the doctor with details about the seizure. If your dog hasn't been previously diagnosed with a seizure disorder, the veterinarian will want to examine your pet to determine the cause of the seizure. If your dog had a seizure while on anti-seizure medication, notify your veterinarian.

Poisoning

Dogs are curious animals and can sometimes get themselves into trouble by putting strange things in their mouths. More than one overly inquisitive German Shepherd has put his life in serious danger by eating a highly toxic object or substance. Owners, too, have been known to poison their dogs by applying too much flea and tick killers and repellents.

It's often difficult to determine whether a dog has been poisoned and by what, because most canine poisonings occur when the dog eats something toxic, like a poisonous plant or antifreeze in their owner's absence.

If your German Shepherd has been out of your sight for a while and vomits severely; experiences terrible diarrhea; shakes or convulses; has a blue tongue;

Did You Know?

The tallest dog on record was 42 inches tall at the shoulders and weighed 238 pounds.

seems very weak; cannot stand; has trouble breathing; and/or drools excessively, he may have been poisoned. Look around your dog's mouth and head for signs of any toxic substance he may have ingested. (If you recently applied any kind of insecticide to the dog's coat, this could be the cause.)

An extreme emergency, poisoning requires an immediate call to a veterinarian. The doctor may give you instructions on what to do right then and there, particularly if you have an idea of what your dog has ingested.

If you know for certain that your dog has eaten something toxic, don't wait for him to develop symptoms of poisoning. Call your veterinarian immediately or rush him to the nearest emergency animal hospital.

> If you know for certain that your dog has eaten something toxic, don't wait for him to develop symptoms of poisoning. Call your veterinarian immediately or rush him to the nearest emergency animal hospital.

If you know what your dog ate, gather up a sample of it (along with the label, if there is one) to bring to the veterinarian. If not, collect some of the vomitus or diarrheal excrement.

If you suspect your dog has been poisoned by insecticide you applied to his skin or coat, wash him immediately with an abundance of water before rushing him to the veterinarian.

Fishhooks

German Shepherds that live or play near lakes or oceans are lucky pups, because this breed enjoys being in the water. Spending time in watery environments, however, puts your dog at risk of several hazards, among them being snared by a discarded fishhook.

Fishhooks that are left lying around by people who fish are a huge problem for both dogs and wildlife. Discarded fishhooks often end up lodged inside a dog's mouth or snagged in his paw or leg. Fishhooks, by design, are notoriously difficult to remove. The same barbs that keep a caught fish hooked also make it very hard to remove the hook from your dog.

The best person to remove a fishhook from your dog's body is your veterinarian. However, if you are in a remote area and don't have access to veterinary treatment, you can try to remove the hook yourself with a pair of wire cutters and pliers or tweezers.

Have a helper restrain your German Shepherd, so he will stay still while you work. Carefully examine the fishhook to determine which way the barb is pointing. Push the hook deeper into the skin until you expose the barb. Using the wire cutters, snip the fishhook right under the barb. Then, use the pliers or tweezers to gently remove each of the two pieces, pulling out one piece in one direction and the other piece in the opposite direction.

Keep an eye on the injured area for a few days after removing the hook. Swelling or discharge may indicate your dog has developed an infection. If this occurs, contact your veterinarian.

Burns

Since dogs are fairly astute about avoiding hot surfaces, canines rarely sustain burns. However, in their domestic life with humans, dogs sometimes are accidentally burned, whether by thermal, electrical, or chemical means.

Even the most minor burn can bring terrible pain and potential illness to your dog. Burns easily become infected, and if your dog receives burns to 15 percent or more of his body, it could jeopardize his life.

The nature and degree of the injury depend on the source of the burn. Thermal burns caused by an open flame, hot water, or a hot surface will cause the dog's skin to turn red. A severe burn will also singe off the dog's hair and blister his skin.

Electrical burns are one of the effects of electrocution. Dogs that have a tendency to chew on electrical wires are at serious risk for these kinds of burns. Most electrical burns appear on the dog's face or mouth, and are swollen and red with a light-colored middle.

Chemical burns usually result from a human-induced accident, for example, when someone inadvertently spills a caustic chemical on a dog's skin. Household chemicals containing alkali are the usual culprits of chemical burns. Chemical burns appear brown or whitish on the skin, and the burned skin will also appear slick. Acidic chemicals cause burns that dry out and darken the injured skin. (Use caution when handling chemical burns, because the chemical residue on your dog's skin could burn you if you touch it with your bare hands.)

If you are with your dog when a burn occurs, you will know what caused the burn and can inform your veterinarian. If you do not see the burn take place but instead find your dog in pain with a wound that fits one of the previous descriptions, you can assume your dog has come into contact with a heat or chemical source that has caused the problem.

You will need to take your dog to the veterinarian right away for immediate treatment of his burns. In the meantime, administer first aid to your dog to help with the pain, prevent infection, and ultimately speed recovery. If the burn is superficial, douse the burn with cold water, either by running water very slowly and gently over the area or by submersing the burned section of the dog's body in a bathtub. Then, place a cold compress on the area and hold it there while transporting your dog to the hospital.

If your dog suffers a severe burn, don't douse it with water, as that would cause extreme pain to your dog. Instead, cover the area with a soft, dry, clean cloth, being careful not to touch the burn, and take your German Shepherd to a vet right away.

Allergic Reactions

Dogs are very prone to allergies, just like humans. In most cases, allergic reactions among canines result in little more than sneezing, coughing, an aggravating itch, or hair loss. However, more serious allergic reactions can and do happen to dogs who are exposed to things to which they are particularly sensitive. Severe allergic reactions can sometimes endanger a dog's life.

Dogs typically develop allergic reactions to the same substances that trouble humans. Dust, mold, pollen, bug bites, and certain foods and drugs are the most common allergens for the canine species. Reactions vary from mild respiratory symptoms, such as sneezing and coughing, to diarrhea, vomiting, skin irritation, and anaphylactic shock.

Skin Irritations   Dogs that inhale or eat something they are allergic to often develop associated skin problems. Hives, itchy raised bumps spread around the skin, can afflict some dogs with internal or even external allergies, such as hypersensitivity to insect bites.

Another type of allergic skin reaction is canine atopic dermatitis, which causes severe itching after a dog inhales pollen or dust. As a result of the scratching and licking that goes on when a dog has atopic dermatitis, you may see patches of missing hair on his body and probably red, irritated skin.

Fleas are a common cause of allergic skin irritations in canines. Dogs that are allergic to these pesky parasites develop a condition known as flea allergy dermatitis, which results when saliva from the flea's mouth penetrates the dog's skin and generates a hypersensitivity reaction. The skin in the area of the flea bite becomes extremely itchy, and the itching is likely to spread throughout the dog's body. The most common spots for this condition include the base of the tail, the inside of the thighs, and the rear of the back legs.

Contact dermatitis is another allergic condition that affects a dog's skin. When a dog comes into contact with a chemical he is allergic to—such as a certain type of soap or insecticidal product—the dog's skin breaks out in red bumps that are very itchy. The skin becomes inflamed and irritated, and may even become crusty and ooze pus.

The treatment for allergic skin conditions depends on the type of allergy the dog has developed. You should also consult with your veterinarian to determine what your dog is allergic to, so that you can then remove the element from his environment, if possible, to prevent further attacks.

Stomach Troubles   Dogs can also react to eating something they are allergic to by vomiting and diarrhea. Some of the food items that typically cause allergic reactions in dogs include eggs, milk, cheese, horsemeat, wheat, and even beef. Different brands of commercial dog food can also induce allergic reactions in particular dogs, depending on the ingredients.

In most cases, it's difficult to figure out exactly what in a dog's diet is causing the allergic reaction. Your veterinarian is the best person to help you make this determination (and also to diagnose allergy-induced vomiting and diarrhea as opposed to other possible health conditions). If your vet believes your dog has a food allergy, you can try eliminating some of the previously mentioned ingredients in your dog's diet. An easy way to do this is to try feeding a commercially pre-pared diet without wheat (and no table scraps) as an experiment. If your dog's allergy-induced vomiting and diarrhea disappear on the new diet, the beef and/or wheat probably were the culprits.

Anaphylactic Shock   A severe and potentially fatal allergic reac-tion, called anaphylactic shock, can occur when a dog is exposed to an antigen, such as venom or a specific medication, to which the animal is extremely allergic. Anaphylactic shock usually re-sults when the allergen enters the dog's internal system, for exam-ple by being inhaled, ingested, or injected. However, it can also result from external exposure to the agent, as in the case of ani-mals that are hypersensitive and are exposed to high levels of poi-son oak oil. Dogs, like humans, typically are at risk of developing anaphylactic shock after becoming sensitized to the substance from previous severe allergic reactions.

Symptoms of anaphylactic shock include muscle weakness, welts or swelling on skin or mucous membranes, itchiness, ver-tigo, loss of consciousness, and difficulty breathing. Canine ana-phylactic shock requires emergency veterinary attention.

If your dog is allergic to penicillin or any other drugs, it's impor-tant that you notify all veterinarians, boarding kennels, and other caretakers of your pet's sensitivity. You should also make note of and inform caretakers of any severe allergic reactions your German Shepherd has experienced. If your dog ever goes into anaphylactic shock, take him to a veterinarian immediately.

Eye Injuries

When a dog injures one or both of his eyes, it can be a frightening situation for

Did You Know?

The average gesta-tion period for a dog is 63 days.

both the pet and his owner. The most common source of eye injuries is trauma caused by a blow or scratch to the eye or by a foreign object in the eye or under the lid. Dogs who ride with their heads sticking out of car windows are very susceptible to eye injuries resulting from foreign bodies blowing into their eyes.

You can detect eye injuries in your dog in one of several ways. The dog will probably squint in pain or blink excessively, and tears will stream from the injured eye. He may also paw at the eye. In severe cases, the dog's eye will actually bulge out of the socket. Bulging usually means the dog has sustained a blow to the head, and it is more common in breeds with round eyes than it is in German Shepherds, whose eyes are more almond shaped.

Regardless of how your dog has injured his eye, you must take him to a veterinarian immediately for special care. A long delay in treatment could actually result in the dog losing sight in the eye or the eye itself.

Electric Shock

Dogs that chew on electrical cords are susceptible to electric shock. This is especially true of teething puppies, since they tend to be much more vigorous chewers than adult dogs. Dogs also can be electrocuted if they are struck by lightning or make contact with a live power line.

When a dog receives an electric shock, the electricity can burn the skin and can often damage internal organs. While the burn will usually be obvious, it sometimes takes a day or two for the internal damage to become obvious.

If you think your dog has been electrocuted, check his head and body for electrical burns, which will be swollen and red, with a light-colored middle. He may also lay on his side and convulse, lose consciousness, and lose control of his bowel and bladder.

If you find your dog in this condition or actually see him receive an electrical shock, remove him from the source of the electricity right away—taking extreme caution to ensure the current has been broken. If your dog is still in contact with a live electrical current, you may electrocute yourself when you touch his body. Turn off the power source. If you are unable to do this, use a wooden stick to safely move the dog away from a live wire.

Next, cover your dog with a blanket and rush him to a veterinarian. If your dog stops breathing, perform CPR on him, if you know the technique. (Local dog clubs sometimes offer courses in canine CPR.)

If your dog appears to recover completely while en route to the hospital, don't abort your mission to get him immediate medical help. He may have damaged his internal organs, even though he seems okay.

Obesity

We often see overweight dogs in today's world. Human beings tend to equate food with love and, consequently, often give their dogs far too much to eat.

Maintaining a Healthy Weight

Obesity poses a serious health problem for dogs. Dogs that are too fat are prone to a variety of illnesses and conditions, including heat stroke, diabetes, heart problems, liver dysfunction, and joint pains. What's more, dogs of normal weight enjoy a longer life span than do overweight dogs.

The causes of obesity are much the same in dogs as they are in humans: too much food and too little exercise. Obese dogs consume more calories than they burn each day. Their bodies convert these excess calories into fat, which is stored in various places around the body. This stored fat causes stress on the joints and internal organs and makes it harder for the dog to exercise, resulting in a vicious cycle of continued weight gain.

> The causes of obesity are much the same in dogs as they are in humans: too much food and too little exercise.

You can tell whether your German Shepherd is overweight by feeling the area around his rib cage. You should be able to easily feel his ribs with your fingers. If you can't, your dog is packing too much poundage.

Another way to tell if your German Shepherd is too fat is to look at him from the side. You should see something called a "tuck up," or the waistline on a dog, which should appear behind his rib cage, just before his hind legs. If you don't see a distinct tuck up, but instead see a thick middle, your dog is overweight.

In the event your German Shepherd gradually develops a big round belly but appears thin elsewhere on his body, have him examined by a veterinarian. He may be suffering from another condition rather than weight gain.

Trimming Down a Chubby Dog

Some dogs put on too much weight because they are fed rich and fattening human foods on a regular basis. If you have been giving your dog table scraps every night, now is the time to stop. Limit his daily meals to dog food only and make sure to feed no more than the amount specified on the can or bag.

If your dog doesn't get table scraps but is overweight, he may be getting too much dog food. Check the feeding instructions on the can or bag. If you are feeding more than the specified amount, cut down on his portions. (When you scale back on the amount of food you feed your German Shepherd, continue to feed him at least twice a day, just in smaller portions.)

If your German Shepherd is overweight but eats only dog food and only the amount specified on the can or bag, you may need to switch him to a lower calorie dog food and/or provide him with more exercise. First, however, take the dog to your veterinarian to determine which diet to switch to and to ensure your pet is healthy enough to tolerate increased activity.

Health Concerns Specific to German Shepherds

Nearly every breed of purebred dog has some kind of illness that seems to afflict that breed more than it does others. Some of the diseases are genetically linked and result from decades of line breeding. Others derive from the particular breed's physical characteristics.

Consequently, German Shepherds are prone to a number of genetic and circumstantial illnesses and conditions. As a German Shepherd owner, it's important for you to understand these various problems, so you can come to recognize and cope with them should your dog develop any of these disorders.

Genetic illnesses common to German Shepherds are not unique to the breed but are frequently seen within it. When buying a puppy, it's very important to know who the dog's parents are and what kind of medical problems they might have. Chances are that whatever illness haunts your puppy's parents will also ultimately afflict your puppy.

Hip Dysplasia

Probably the most common genetic disorder afflicting German Shepherds is hip dysplasia. This disease affects the canine hip joint in varying degrees. It results when the head of the thighbone (the femur) doesn't fit correctly into the hip socket where it belongs. This poor fit results in inflammation to the joint and subsequent pain and lameness for the dog. A mild case of hip dysplasia can produce a slight limp, and may be unnoticable to the untrained eye, while a more severe case can cripple the dog to the point that he is literally unable to walk.

Hip dysplasia usually rears its ugly head by the time a dog reaches two years of age. The vet can confirm the illness by x-raying the dog's hip joints.

Since no real cure exists for hip dysplasia, treatment is aimed at relieving the dog's pain and helping the dog to remain as active as possible. Dogs with hip dysplasia are often reluctant to exercise, which weakens muscles and worsens the degeneration of the joints.

Dogs with mild to moderate hip dysplasia respond best to a variety of prescription pain relievers. Prescription anti-inflammatories, such as Rimadyl, offer the best pain relief. Avoid the temptation to use over-the-counter pain relievers without first checking with your vet. However, only surgery really helps dogs with severe hip dysplasia. The type of surgery performed depends on the dog's actual condition and sometimes requires the replacement of the dog's entire hip.

The good news about hip dysplasia is that two organizations called the Orthopedic Foundation for Animals (OFA) and PennHIP offer hip dysplasia screening for all German Shepherd dogs used in breeding programs. Before buying a puppy, make sure the dog's parents have received certification indicating they have healthy hips. Although having certified parents doesn't guarantee a puppy will not ultimately develop the disease, the chances of your pup developing hip dysplasia are reduced if his parents have healthy hips.

Elbow Dysplasia

A cousin to hip dysplasia, elbow dysplasia is also a joint problem frequently seen in German Shepherds. Elbow dysplasia affects the front legs of the dog, and results when the elbow joint doesn't fit properly into the socket. Eventually, this poor fit causes degenerative joint disease and lameness in the dog.

Dogs with elbow dysplasia show signs of the condition relatively early, usually at around six months of age. These dogs show a reluctance to put weight on their front legs when standing. You also may see a distinct limp when the dog trots.

Elbow dysplasia is diagnosed with x-rays. Surgery helps in some cases, and strides are being made to perfect a surgery that replaces the entire elbow. Most dogs with elbow dysplasia receive treatment in the form of prescription anti-inflammatory drugs, such as aspirin, which help relieve pain but don't cure the disease.

> **Did You Know?**
>
> Dogs have extremely sensitive hearing and a sense of smell up to 1,000 times better than humans to compensate for their relatively poor eyesight.

The Orthopedic Foundation for Animals screens dogs used for breeding for elbow dysplasia. Make sure the parents of any German Shepherd puppy you buy have been certified by the OFA's elbow registry. Having certified parents will not guarantee your puppy won't develop elbow dysplasia, but it reduces the possibility.

Degenerative Myelopathy

A suspected genetic disorder of the spine called degenerative myelopathy is also seen in the German Shepherd breed. This illness results in full or partial paralysis of the dog's limbs. Although all four limbs can be affected by the disease, paralysis usually occurs in the hind legs.

Degenerative myelopathy comes on slowly, and progressively gets worse until eventually the dog is unable to move his legs. Owners often notice a stiffness in the legs at first and assume the dog is developing arthritis. As the illness becomes worse, slight paralysis becomes apparent. Most German Shepherds affected by the disease are at least four years old. Male German Shepherds seem more prone to the illness than females.

To diagnose the disease, veterinarians perform laboratory tests to determine if the dog is indeed suffering from degenerative myelopathy. A diagnosis of degenerative myelopathy is bad news; the disease is untreatable and paralysis is inevitable. Owners of dogs suffering from this illness sometimes opt to provide a hind limb cart for their dogs, which can substitute for the dog's legs and provide the dog with mobility.

Aortic Stenosis

German Shepherds, along with a number of other large breeds, are prone to an illness of the heart called aortic

stenosis. The hearts of dogs affected with aortic stenosis show a narrow connection between the left ventricle and the aorta. This narrowing can result in an intolerance to exercise, or even sudden death.

Dogs with aortic stenosis are born with the disease, which is believed to be genetically acquired. Veterinarians diagnose the disease by listening to the dog's heart and sometimes by taking x-rays of the organ.

No cure for aortic stenosis exists, but dogs with the condition can be managed. Because exertion can cause collapse or even be fatal, dogs with aortic stenosis must have their exercise carefully controlled.

Exocrine Pancreatic Insufficiency

A genetic digestive disorder known as exocrine pancreatic insufficiency (EPI) affects many canine breeds, but it seems to occur more frequently in German Shepherds. In most German Shepherds, the disease becomes evident by the time the dog is two years old.

Exocrine pancreatic insufficiency results when the dog's pancreas fails to produce a number of the enzymes needed to break down certain nutrients. As a result, dogs with this condition receive less nutrition from their food than they should. Despite the fact that these dogs have very hearty appetites and consume a lot of food, they continuously lose weight and suffer from chronic borderline diarrhea.

In order to diagnose this disease, your veterinarian will need to perform a serum trypsin-like immunoreactivity (TLI) test, the most up-to-date and accurate of all the tests for exocrine pancreatic insufficiency. Dogs with the disease show low concentrations of serum TLI.

You can usually control EPI in your dog with little difficulty. Your veterinarian will give you a powdered pancreatic enzyme supplement to give to your dog with each of her meals.

Panosteitis

A genetic disease called panosteitis, believed to be hereditary in dogs, affects the leg bones of a number of breeds, including the German Shepherd. Panosteitis seems to afflict males dogs more often than females. The disease tends to show up in dogs younger than one year old, although adult dogs can also show first signs of the disease later in life.

Panosteitis is an inflammatory illness that causes lameness that usually starts in the front legs and can switch from one leg to another. Fever, loss of appetite, and depression also can accompany the leg pain.

Panosteitis is diagnosed by using x-rays. Your veterinarian will radiograph your dog's affected leg bones and then examine the x-ray for changes in density of the bone in certain critical areas.

No cure exists for panosteitis. The good news, however, is that the disease is not degenerative and the symptoms are intermittent. When the lameness shows up, the vet can treat the disease with anti-inflammatory drugs to reduce the dog's pain. A change in diet may also help control the disease.

Selective IgA Deficiency

A genetically transmitted immune system disorder known as selective IgA deficiency plagues German Shepherds, along with several other dog breeds. IgA derives from a lack of certain types of antibodies that help protect the dog's skin and other areas of the body.

Selective IgA deficiency shows up in the form of recurring infections, usually of the respiratory tract, the urinary tract, the ears, and the skin.

Veterinarians diagnose the disease by taking a blood sample and evaluating the immunoglobin levels in the dog's blood. Although no cure for selective IgA deficiency exists, veterinarians can provide supportive treatment for the symptoms accompanying the disease.

Chronic Superficial Keratitis

Some eye problems are genetic, which is thought to be the case with chronic superficial keratitis, also known as German Shepherd pannus. Chronic superficial keratitis was first discovered in, and is most commonly found in, the German Shepherd breed, but other breeds of dogs can and do get the disease.

With chronic superficial keratitis, blood vessels and pigment slowly spread across the dog's cornea (the outer layer of the eye), causing eventual blindness. Dogs with chronic superficial keratitis tend to show a dark film at the outer lower edge of the eye, which gradually moves inward and covers the cornea, making it impossible for the dog to see. Veterinarians diagnose the disease by examining the eye. Veterinary doctors specializing in ophthalmology are usually the best ones to make the diagnosis.

No cure for chronic superficial keratitis exists, but if the condition is caught early, corticosteriod drugs can halt the spread of pigment and blood vessels across the cornea. The drugs are given by injection under the eye's lining and by eye drops. Dogs with significant material

Did You Know?

An average of 800 dogs and cats are euthanized every hour in the United States.

already covering the cornea may possibly undergo a surgery called superficial keratectomy. However, the surgery is often only a temporary solution, since the symptoms can reoccur.

Demodicosis

German Shepherds are among several other breeds of dogs that are susceptible to demodicosis, a genetically linked immune system problem that affects the skin.

Demodicosis is caused by a microscopic organism called a demodex mite. This mite is always present on the skin of dogs in small numbers, but when a dog's immune system is defective, the mite gets out of control and multiplies to unmanageable levels, causing infection, redness, and loss of hair. The problem usually appears while the dog is a puppy.

Veterinarians diagnose demodicosis by taking a skin scraping and verifying the mite's presence under a microscope. If the mites are limited to only one area of the dog's body, many times the dog will eventually fight off the infection as he matures and will never again experience a problem with the condition. However, if large numbers of the mites cover the dog's entire body, he will require treatment to help get rid of the problem.

Veterinarians also treat dogs with demodicosis by trying to determine the cause of the dog's immune system problem and addressing that. They also kill the mite with insecticides that work to remove these creatures.

Primary Hyperparathyroidism

A disease affecting the parathyroid glands, primary hyperparathyroidism, has been seen in German Shepherds and a few other breeds.

Primary hyperparathyroidism is caused by a benign tumor lodged in the parathyroid glands, which rest right next to the thyroid glands in the neck. The tumor causes the parathyroid glands to produce too much of a substance called PTH, which regulates calcium throughout the dog's body. When the glands secrete too much PTH, the dog's body begins to break down calcium in his bones, and the bones grow weak and fragile.

Dogs suffering from primary hyperparathyroidism begin to show leg pain and a reluctance to play or move. Some have trouble eating, because their teeth loosen and sometimes fall out.

Veterinarians diagnose primary hyperparathyroidism through the use of blood tests that look for high calcium levels in the blood. They may also take X-rays to determine the extent to which the dog's bones have been damaged. Surgical removal of the tumor on the parathyroid gland is the only treatment for primary hyperparathyroidism.

Epilepsy

German Shepherds, along with a number of other dog breeds, are prone to inherited epilepsy. Unlike some other forms of epilepsy that are caused by head injuries, tumors, or other illnesses, inherited epilepsy has no known cause other than a simple genetic predisposition to seizures caused by abnormal electrical activity in the brain.

Dogs with inherited epilepsy sustain seizures on a recurrent basis. The seizures might occur as frequently as several times a day or only once in a while. The type of seizures may vary as well. Some dogs have partial seizures, which express themselves by the dog staring off at nothing for minutes at a time, bumping into things, twitching uncontrollably, or chasing imaginary prey. Partial seizures don't last longer than a few minutes.

General seizures, on the other hand, are more all-encompassing than partial seizures. When a dog experiences a general seizure, he will often lay on his side, roll his eyes, and froth at his mouth. The dog's jaw and legs will move spasmodically, and he may lose control of his bowels or bladder. General seizures can last for several minutes.

The seizures, whether partial or general, are not usually dangerous to the dog. (An exception to this is when seizures continue repeatedly for five minutes or longer without stopping, a condition called staticus epilepticus.) What is most dangerous about seizures for a dog is the loss of control the animal experiences and the possible physical harm that can result. A dog that has a seizure while walking up a flight of stairs, for instance, can fall and seriously injure himself.

Veterinarians diagnose inherited epilepsy by ruling out other possible sources for the seizures, such as brain tumors and infectious diseases. They treat the disorder with anti-convulsant drugs that suppress the seizure-causing electrical impulses in the dog's brain.

Medication does not control all cases of inherited epilepsy. Drug therapy may only reduce the number and/or severity of seizures a dog has.

Bloat

A strange disorder that primarily affects large breeds—the German Shepherd included—is gastric dilatation/volvulus, more commonly known as bloat. This dramatic condition occurs when the dog's stomach fills with air, at which point the air-filled stomach can twist inside the dog's abdominal cavity. This can impair the blood supply to the dog's stomach and release toxins into his bloodstream. Untreated, bloat can result in the dog's death within four to six hours.

Large-breed dogs with deep chests are most prone to bloat. The problem occurs when the dog swallows air while eating or drinking too quickly, from being stressed out, or due to unknown or undefined reasons. The dog will begin to act uncomfortable and will grow restless or depressed. The dog's abdominal area will start to protrude. He may try to vomit without being able to.

Bloat is an extreme emergency. If you suspect your dog is suffering from bloat, rush him to a veterinarian immediately. His chances of survival depend on surgery and other veterinary support.

To help prevent bloat from occurring, feed your dog at least two small meals a day rather than one. Don't allow free-choice feeding (allowing the dog to eat food whenever he wants). Also, avoid feeding your dog less than one hour before or after exercising.

Other ways to prevent bloat include dampening your dog's kibble before feeding it and removing his water bowl while he is eating. If your German Shepherd tends to gulp his food, put some of his larger toys in the dog bowl to force him to pick out his food more slowly.

Age-Related Disorders

Aging is inevitable for all of us, including German Shepherds. Although you cannot stop the process by which the body slows down and functions at a less efficient rate, you can help postpone your dog's aging and keep him relatively happy and healthy through his geriatric years.

A number of different diseases and conditions tend to come along with old age in dogs. Knowing how to recognize and manage these problems will help you give your German Shepherd a good quality of life long into his old age. Regular veterinary check ups every six months will also help increase your older dog's longevity.

Arthritis

Like humans, canines—especially large dogs like German Shepherds—tend to suffer from arthritis as they age. Arthritis is basically an inflammation of the bone and joint. The disease tends to appear gradually over a period of time. It may start out as a slight stiffness when the dog gets up from a nap and eventually become an all-out limp that doesn't go away. Other signs of arthritis include difficulty when walking, obvious discomfort when preparing to lie down, and a reluctance to run, play, and sometimes even walk.

Your veterinarian can do a lot to help your dog cope with his arthritis. The vet will probably prescribe an anti-inflammatory drug, to help control your dog's pain and stiffness. He or she may also recommend regular, gentle exercise to keep the dog's joints lubricated and blood flowing to his limbs.

At home, provide your arthritic German Shepherd with a soft bed to lay on. This will help keep his joints from getting too sore. If your dog experiences a lot of trouble walking and getting around, you may need to rearrange your home to make things easier for him. Eliminate the need for him to go up and down stairs. Keep his bed and his food and water bowls in an area that is easily accessible to him.

Bad Breath

The longer a dog is alive, the more likely he is to develop periodontal disease and other problems with his teeth. The bad breath people often associate with older dogs usually stems from gum and tooth problems.

Although many dog owners simply learn to live with their older dog's halitosis and accept it as part of the aging process, the problem is actually treatable.

If your German Shepherd has bad breath at any age, take him to your veterinarian for an examination and treatment. Not only is bad breath unpleasant to live with, it can also indicate something serious.

> If your German Shepherd has bad breath at any age, take him to your veterinarian for an examination and treatment. Not only is bad breath unpleasant to live with, it can also indicate something serious.

Cancer

With progressing age comes a greater chance of developing cancer, the dreaded illness that most of us consider fatal.

Although many cancers are difficult to treat, especially if they reach an advanced stage before they are discovered, a surprising number of cancerous conditions do respond to treatments such as surgery and chemotherapy.

If your veterinarian diagnoses your older dog with cancer, it's important to consider your pet's quality of life when discussing the treatment options. German Shepherds who are at an advanced age of 10 or more may not be good candidates for cancer treatment, because of the stress involved in the process. Your veterinarian should be able to help you make the best decision for your dog.

Cataracts

Older dogs tend to develop cataracts as time goes on. Senile cataracts, as they are known, consist of an opaque coloration that appears over the normally transparent part of the eye, interfering with the dog's sight. Some dogs can still see fairly well with cataracts—others are nearly blinded by them.

The vet can treat cataracts with surgery, which can restore much of the dog's sight. If your pet is diagnosed with senile cataracts, your veterinarian can discuss your dog's surgical options with you.

Heart Disease

Acquired valvular heart disease is very common in dogs that are in their geriatric years. This ailment results from age-related changes to the dog's heart valves. The valves literally start to wear out, causing blood to flow backward and putting strain on the heart.

Older dogs with acquired valvular heart disease first show signs of the disease by developing a dry cough that comes on after exercising and at night. If you notice your dog coughing under these conditions, take him to a veterinarian right away. Treatment for acquired valvular heart disease can slow the progression of the disease.

Incontinence

In their later years, dogs—especially older German Shepherds— tend to develop acquired non-neurogenic incontinence, which is basically a loss of bladder control. Dogs with this problem will dribble urine.

If your dog suffers from acquired non-neurogenic incontinence brought on by old age, your veterinarian can prescribe drugs that will help your pet regain control of his bladder.

Kidney Failure

One of the sad realities of old age for many dogs is kidney failure. As a dog ages, the kidneys often are the first organs to start giving out. If the problem is caught early, you can do much in the way of diet and medication to slow the process and prolong the life of the dog. Most dogs with kidney failure eventually succumb to the disease, although, when treated, some can live comfortably with it for several years.

Early signs of kidney failure include drinking more water than usual and an increased output of urine. Your dog also may start having accidents inside the house. If you notice a change in your dog's drinking and bathroom habits at any age, take him to your veterinarian right away.

Basic Training for German Shepherds

In This Chapter

○ When to Begin Training
○ Basic Dog Psychology
○ What Every Good Dog Needs to Know

If any breed of dog was created to serve humankind, it is the German Shepherd. From the breed's beginnings in the Old World until the present day, the German Shepherd has been the quintessential working dog. It is also a large dog, with a big body and an active mind.

Put these two factors together—a drive to work and a substantial bearing—and you have a dog who not only needs training to understand the rules of human society, but who craves it as well.

Basic training gives your German Shepherd a clear concept of how he should behave in the world, and it provides him with a job to occupy both his mind and his body. Some dog owners look at training as a chore, but it doesn't have to be that way. Training your German Shepherd can be a lot of fun for both you and your pet.

Why Train Your German Shepherd?

If you've ever met a dog who jumps up on people, runs wild through the house, ignores human commands, and is basically no fun to be around, you've encountered a dog with no training. Dogs are a lot like children: They instinctively react to their environment in ways that can be disruptive, and they need to learn the rules of society in order to behave properly. If you don't provide your dog with rules and the training he needs to obey them, you'll end up with an insecure creature who doesn't know his place and is unpleasant to be around.

Untrained German Shepherds are usually out of control, unsure, and difficult to handle. German Shepherds have been bred for generations to follow orders from their human handlers. Robbing a German Shepherd of the job he's been bred to perform will result in an unhappy and unruly dog. Because unhappy, unruly dogs are a pain in the neck to be around—and sometimes even dangerous—they end up banished to a yard or surrendered to an animal shelter.

Take Lotus, for example, a male German Shepherd owned by Carol and Jim Lee of Bakersfield, California. When Carol and Jim first got Lotus from a breeder, they thought he was

A well-trained dog will accept your guidance even when he would rather be doing something else.

the most adorable puppy they had ever seen. Their hectic work schedules and lack of knowledge of dog behavior resulted in Lotus going without much training for the first six months of his life.

"Basically, he was allowed to do whatever he wanted, as long as he didn't go to the bathroom in the house," says Carol. Consequently, by the time Lotus was six months old, he had become a holy terror. "We had a real problem on our hands," Carol adds. "Lotus was sweet but out of control. He would jump all over our guests and even knock down small children. When he was excited, he would run around the house like a banshee, knocking over things and ignoring our pleas to stop. When we took him to the park for a game of fetch, he'd play with us for a while but then would take off for parts unknown, completely ignoring us when we'd call him. We'd end up chasing him all over the place in a desperate attempt to catch him."

> Basic training gives your German Shepherd a clear concept of how he should behave in the world, and it provides him with a job to occupy both his mind and his body.

As a result of Lotus' misbehavior, the Lees soon greatly restricted what they allowed their dog to do. Because Lotus was destructive in the house, the Lees started keeping him by himself in the backyard for much of the time. They wouldn't allow him to make contact with any of their guests and stopped taking him to the park for playtime. Lotus became a lonely and unhappy dog, and started barking and whining all day long to express his misery.

"We were at our wits end," says Carol. "We were even thinking about getting rid of him. Instead, we decided to take him to a trainer."

Because Lotus is a German Shepherd and, therefore, highly trainable, he started to change dramatically within a matter of weeks. "He became so well behaved and obedient, we couldn't believe he was the same dog," says Carol. "The trainer not only taught Lotus how to act, but he also taught us how to handle Lotus. Now, we are one big happy family, and Lotus goes everywhere with us."

When to Begin Training

German Shepherds are naturals when it comes to training and can benefit from instruction at any time in their lives. However, the younger your Shepherd is when you start educating him, the better. Dogs who receive training at a young age tend to retain their instruction better than those who are trained as adults.

You can start informally training your German Shepherd when he is as young as eight weeks of age. However, eight weeks is too early to actually attend formal obedience classes, because puppies that young lack the attention span and mental capacity to learn formal obedience. In addition, because their immune systems are not quite up to speed, puppies under 12 weeks shouldn't be exposed to strange dogs. (Some vets think even 12 weeks is too young.) But you can prepare your young puppy for the lessons ahead by introducing him to basic training and socialization at home.

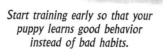

Start teaching your puppy some basic house rules when he is eight to nine weeks old. Let him know that it is not okay to bite and that he must go to the bathroom outdoors. Teach him to sit before he gets his meals.

Start training early so that your puppy learns good behavior instead of bad habits.

When your puppy reaches about 10 weeks of age, you can introduce him to the leash. Put the leash on his collar and let him pull it around the house for a short while, under supervision, so he can get the feel of it.

Remember that your puppy will retain as an adult any behavior that you allow when he is small. Although sleeping on your bed may seem cute when your dog weighs only a few pounds, you might not want him in bed with you in a few months when he's a lot bigger and still expects the same privileges. If you don't want your puppy to do something when he is fully grown, don't let him do it now.

Puppy Kindergarten

The best place for your puppy to learn the rules of domestic life is in puppy kindergarten class. Most kindergarten classes will accept your puppy after she's received two sets of vaccinations (generally around 12 weeks of age), although some veterinarians suggest you wait longer. Consult with your own vet to determine the best time to enroll your puppy in kindergarten.

In puppy kindergarten class, your little German Shepherd will be introduced to the basic obedience commands of sit, stay, down, and come. She also will get the chance to socialize with other puppies and humans. This environment provides an invaluable learning opportunity for puppies, who at that tender age are still forming a view of the world.

Basic Obedience Class

Puppies can move on to basic obedience class once they graduate from kindergarten or reach four months of age. Dogs who have never attended puppy kindergarten but are at least four months old also begin with basic obedience class. A basic obedience

Socializing Your Puppy

Dogs are very sociable creatures who are genetically wired to interact with members of their own species and even to ours. However, although German Shepherds are built for life in a social environment, they need help learning with whom and how to socialize.

A puppy's first lessons in socialization come from its mother. From birth, the puppy learns how to get along with other dogs through his interaction with both his mom and siblings.

When the puppy leaves his mother and littermates, the socialization process must continue. That is where you come in. Puppies must gain exposure at a young age to as many new and different things as possible in order to learn how to cope with the world around them.

Keep in mind that your pup's immune system takes six months to develop completely. For the first six months of your pup's life, therefore, arrange socialization situations that minimize or prevent his contact with strange or ill dogs. Healthy, vaccinated dogs are generally good playmates for your puppy and can help in the socialization process.

You may want to expose your puppy to and teach him to enjoy or respect the following creatures and situations:

Children. It's very important to give your puppy positive experiences with children of varying ages so he will grow up to be a dog with whom kids are safe.

Strangers. Introduce your puppy to many different kinds of people so he will learn to accept strangers that you have indicated are okay to be friendly to. Don't worry that this type of socialization might impair your German Shepherd's protective instincts. Dogs are very good at knowing the difference between a stranger you have accepted and an attacker or intruder.

Other dogs. Encourage your puppy to play with other dogs his own age.

This helps him learn to get along with members of his own species.

Other animals. Teach your puppy to respect cats and other animals by exposing him to them without allowing him to bother them. For his safety and theirs, don't allow your pup to chase or harass domestic or wild animals.

Special environments. If you plan to take your German Shepherd to the beach, on hikes, or to crowded areas when he is older, consider taking him to these places a few times while he is still a pup. This will get him used to the idea while he is still young and impressionable.

course will teach your dog the commands so important for every German Shepherd to know: sit, stay, down, come, and heel (walk beside you on leash). You will also have the opportunity to talk with your instructor about any behavior problems you may be experiencing with your dog, such as

Introduce your dog to other friendly, well-behaved, healthy dogs. Avoid rowdy, poorly behaved, aggressive dogs; they could scare your dog and ruin the socialization you've done so far.

jumping up, digging, chewing, or barking. Your instructor can help you solve these problems—or give you pointers on how to prevent them in the first place. You can also opt to hire a private trainer if your Shepherd doesn't respond well to group lessons or if you are having trouble learning to handle him.

Is It Ever Too Late?

If you have an adult German Shepherd, you may be wondering whether he is too old to train. Don't worry. German Shepherds are receptive to learning at nearly any age and are almost never too old to train.

Of course, you're better off training your Shepherd as a puppy, while he is still young and impressionable enough for the training to have the greatest impact on him. He won't have had time to develop bad habits, so you won't have to deal with the hassle of trying to re-train him. But that doesn't mean you can't teach an old dog new tricks. In fact, you can!

If you start working with your dog after puppyhood, will you be able to eliminate all of his misbehaviors? Probably not. But you'll be surprised at how much you can teach an older dog, especially a German Shepherd.

Basic Dog Psychology

In order to get along with your German Shepherd and appreciate him for all he's worth, you need to have a fundamental understanding of canine psychology. Knowing what motivates your dog—and doesn't motivate him—is key to your success in training and living with your German Shepherd.

Families and Packs

The single most important thing about dogs that every owner should know is that dogs are pack animals. The wild ancestors of today's German Shepherds lived in complex social groups called packs that consisted of members of varying rank. Modern domestic dogs share the same pack instincts that their ancestors lived by.

This pack instinct directly correlates to the fact that dogs and humans get along so well. In your dog's mind, you and the other members of your family are his pack members. That is why he is so happy to see you when you come home, why he is agreeable when you give him commands, and why he wants to be around you as much as possible.

> In your dog's mind, you and the other members of your family are his pack members.

The complex inner workings of canine hierarchy require that there be leaders and followers. One animal or one breeding pair reigns as the pack leader, a status that comes with responsiblility and privilege. The other members of the pack assume an order of increasing submissiveness, with the most submissive animal being the low man on the totem pole. In the wild, this arrangement is crucial to the survival of the pack.

What Does It Mean to Be Top Dog?

In pack social structure, the animals that make up the dominant breeding pair are referred to as the alpha male and the alpha female. The alphas make certain decisions for the group, such as when and where to hunt and where to locate the pack's den. The leaders eat before all other pack members, keeping the best part of the meal for themselves.

When dogs share their lives with people, a human member of the household must hold the alpha position. The dog should understand that his place is at the bottom of the pack order, beneath all adults and children. If humans do not assert themselves as the leaders, the dog often will take over the job himself—and that spells trouble, especially with a large and strong-willed breed like the German Shepherd.

Take, for example, Lucky, a German Shepherd owned by Jim and Debra Powell of Omaha, Nebraska. The Powells obtained Lucky from an animal shelter when he was eight months old and doted on their new dog. However, Jim and Debra neglected to take Lucky to obedience lessons, as the shelter workers had recommended when the Powells adopted him. Because Lucky had been born with a somewhat dominant personality, before long he became the top dog in the house.

"Lucky was a sweet dog, but he started to push us around a bit," says Jim. "When we took him for a walk, he would drag us. When we tried to take something out of his mouth, he wouldn't let go of it and would stare at us. Finally one day while Lucky was eating, Debra reached down to pick up his food bowl and Lucky growled at her."

Fortunately, at that point the Powells realized they had a problem and immediately contacted the shelter where they had adopted Lucky to ask for help.

"The shelter worker we spoke to recommended we take Lucky to training classes," says Jim. "She explained to us that Lucky was taking over the role of alpha in our family and that we needed to assert our leadership over him before things got out of control."

You must establish yourself as alpha with your German Shepherd when he first comes into your home. You can do this by teaching your dog to be obedient right away by house-training him, teaching him to come when called, and letting him know that biting is wrong. Training helps teach your dog that you are in charge.

Don't let your dog use his body language to show dominance. Your dog should recognize you (and your children) as above him in the family pack.

Reinforce your position of dominance by issuing commands to your dog on a regular basis and never doing anything that your dog could perceive as submissive. Things that mean nothing to you, such as allowing him to go through a doorway ahead of you, are signs of submissiveness in the eyes of your dog. Feed him only after you have eaten because dominant pack members always dine first. Allow him to go down stairs only after you, never ahead of you. Because an exposed belly indicates submission, have him lie down and roll over so you can rub his stomach. Also, never wrestle or play tug-of-war with your dog because these kinds of games encourage aggressive and dominant behavior.

Following these simple rules will help your dog view you as the alpha pack member. Accepting you as the pack leader will allow him to relax and take it easy, confident that you have things under control.

Getting Help

Never allow your German Shepherd to exhibit signs of aggressiveness toward you or anyone in your family. A Shepherd, or any other dog, who growls, bares teeth, or continually refuses to be submissive should be seen as a potential danger. If you are having trouble establishing dominance or find yourself facing a behavior problem with your German Shepherd that you are unable to correct on your own, it's time to seek assistance from a professional. You can hire a professional trainer or you may be able to find an animal behaviorist who can help you with the problem.

Professional dog trainers are abundant and relatively easy to find. Before you hire a trainer to help you with your dog, you need to do some homework to make certain that you are choosing the best individual for your situation.

Referrals from other dog owners are a good way to find a trainer. You can also contact a local dog obedience club or all-breed kennel club for a referral (contact the American Kennel Club for the names and numbers of dog clubs in your area). Organizations such as the Association of Pet Dog Trainers (APDT) and the National Association of Dog Obedience Instructors (NADOI) can also provide you with a list of members in your area.

> A Shepherd, or any other dog, who growls, bares teeth, or continually refuses to be submissive, should be seen as a potential danger.

An animal behaviorist can also help you deal with your dog's behavior problems. The best type of behaviorist to hire is a certified veterinary behaviorist, who will have a degree in veterinary medicine along with an advanced degree in animal behavior. Veterinary behaviorists are certified by the Animal Behavior Society, an organization that can provide you with a list of its members. However, individuals with these qualifications are few and far between. If you can't find a veterinary behaviorist in your area, contact your veterinarian for a referral to a recommended animal behaviorist or dog trainer.

Correction Versus Punishment

The best way to train any dog, regardless of breed, is through positive reinforcement. Instead of punishing your dog for bad behavior, focus on rewarding him when he behaves well. In times past, many people thought swatting a dog with a rolled-up newspaper was the way to teach a pet to behave properly. Today, trainers and behaviorists know that hitting a dog does nothing but cause pain, fear, and confusion, especially if the hitting occurs more than a few seconds after the animal commits the misdeed. After four or five seconds, dogs are unable to make the connection between what they did and the punishment they are receiving.

Although training a dog never involves punishment, it often requires correction. For example, when training your German Shepherd to come when you call him, you might need to jerk on his collar to let him know he must pay attention to you. When your German Shepherd commits other inappropriate acts—such as chewing on your shoes or going to the bathroom in the house—you will need to apply a correction to help teach the dog that his

Corrections should be given as the dog is making the mistake, not after the fact.

behaviors are inappropriate. Because corrections must be delivered during the misdeed or within only a few seconds after the action took place, you must be able to catch your dog in the act in order to correct him. If you come home and find the results of your dog's misbehavior but not the misbehavior itself, it's too late to correct the dog.

When correcting your dog, be sure to let him know that what he is doing is wrong by saying "No!" very loudly. Then, redirect the dog's actions to something positive. If you caught him chewing on your high heels, take the shoes away from him and give him a chew toy instead. If he was in the middle of piddling on the carpet, take him outside so he can finish his business in an appropriate place. When he replaces the misbehavior with appropriate behavior, praise him for doing the right thing.

How a Crate Can Help

One of the most useful of all training devices is a crate, a container designed to hold a pet during transport. Crates come in two basic styles. The most popular style, the airline crate, is essentially a plastic box with wire-mesh windows and door. With its solid sides and roof, a plastic crate gives dogs a sense of security. The other type of crate consists of wire on all four sides and the top, with a solid metal floor. Wire crates provide better

A crate helps your puppy develop bowel and bladder control, prevents accidents from happening, and becomes your puppy's special place.

ventilation but less security than an airline crate, and many are collapsible.

Crates are great for training dogs—especially puppies—because they give owners a way to confine their dogs and to control their actions. By using a crate, owners can teach their dogs the correct way to behave in many situations.

Crates come in especially handy for house-training a puppy. You can teach your puppy to eliminate only outdoors by restricting him to the crate while he is indoors and unsupervised. Dogs are born with a denning instinct that tells them not to go to the bathroom in the immediate area where they sleep. Confining your young puppy to a crate helps him learn to hold his urine and feces until he is taken outside.

Crates also serve as great tools for preventing your dog from getting into trouble when you aren't around to keep an eye on him. If left to wander at will when no one is home, puppies and even some older dogs will wreak havoc on your house. Boredom, and in many cases anxiety, during the owner's absence often result in a dog's misbehavior.

> Boredom, and in many cases anxiety, during the owner's absence often result in a dog's misbehavior.

Confining your dog to a crate not only will stop him from causing mischief, but also will help him feel more secure than if he had the run of the house. Again, because of their denning instinct, dogs tend to feel less anxious when they are enclosed in a small space.

Crate-Training Your Dog

It may seem cruel to confine your German Shepherd to what seems like a cage. In reality, your dog won't mind the crate at all—if you introduce him to it gradually, don't keep him in it for excessively long hours, and train him to understand that the crate is his safe place. Once he has learned to sleep in the crate, he will come to think of it as a place he can go for comfort and security.

Take Cody, for example, a German Shepherd owned by Carla Lorie of Syosset, New York. Carla bought Cody from a breeder when he was two years old and was reluctant to put him in the crate the breeder gave her, even though he'd been sleeping in one his whole life. "The first night I had Cody, I decided he should sleep in the bedroom with me and to heck with the crate. The crate seemed like a cage to me, and I didn't like the idea of putting him in it. So that night, I went to bed and left Cody loose in my bedroom. I got absolutely no sleep that night, because Cody was very restless and kept trying to crawl underneath the bed! I got the feeling he was feeling insecure. I got up and put his crate in the room. He immediately went inside, curled up, and went to sleep!"

To crate-train your German Shepherd, start by leaving the crate door open and encouraging him to go inside. You can do this by putting a treat inside the crate or by throwing in his favorite toy while he is watching. When he steps inside the crate to retrieve the treat or toy, tell him he's a good boy and do it again.

Once your dog comfortably goes into his crate when you toss something inside of it, you can start feeding him in the crate. Leave the crate door open and place your dog's food bowl deep inside. This will make your dog stand inside the crate while he eats and will help him associate the crate with something pleasant—namely, his dinner!

While teaching your German Shepherd to spend time in his crate, you may want to consider adding a verbal command, such as "crate." Whenever you put a treat or toy inside the crate, say the verbal command as your dog enters the crate. This will condition your dog to go to his crate when you tell him.

The best place to keep your dog's crate is in your bedroom or the bedroom of another family member. This enables your German Shepherd to spend time with you or another person while you are sleeping. If this arrangement doesn't work for you, make sure to put the dog's crate in an area of the house where you can hear him cry if he needs to go to the bathroom. It's important to keep the crate in an area where he can sense your presence nearby. Dogs get lonely and anxious if they are forced to spend long periods of time by themselves.

Do not confine your dog to his crate for longer than four hours at a time, except at night while he is sleeping. If you don't give your Shepherd ample time to exercise and to socialize with the family, he will grow to dislike his crate and think of it as an unpleasant place to go.

Selecting the Crate

In order for a crate to work effectively as a housetraining tool, it must be just the right size. A crate that is too big gives a dog the impression that he can go to the bathroom inside and still remain far enough away from the results for his comfort. By providing a crate that is small enough, you create an environment that feels more like a den to your dog—and not like a place to use as a toilet.

If your German Shepherd is a young puppy, you will probably need to start him off with one size of crate and then graduate to a bigger one as your dog grows older. Whether you are buying a crate for a puppy or an adult, the crate should be large enough for your dog to stand up, lie down, and turn around in comfortably.

Basic Obedience Commands

Every German Shepherd—in fact, every dog—should learn five basic obedience commands. These commands do more than just give you a way to control your dog with your voice. They also do wonders to bolster your dog's feelings of security within the family and to ensure he perceives you as a dominant pack member.

Sit

Teaching your German Shepherd to sit is not only easy, it is also useful. A dog who sits on command is usually a lot easier to control than one who doesn't. By telling your German Shepherd to sit, you can keep him from jumping up on guests, chasing small animals, and acting rambunctious.

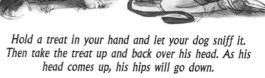

Hold a treat in your hand and let your dog sniff it. Then take the treat up and back over his head. As his head comes up, his hips will go down.

The sit command should be the first command you teach your dog. To train your German Shepherd to sit, hold a treat in your hand and let him sniff it. Tell him to sit as you take the treat away from his nose and back over his head. While you are doing this, say your dog's name and the sit command. As he watches the treat, his head should go up and back and his hips should go down.

With one hand on the front of the dog's chest under his neck, push gently up and back as you slide the other hand down his hips and tuck under. At the same time, tell your dog to sit. Praise him when he does.

If that doesn't work, try shaping him into a sitting position. Standing or sitting at your dog's side, place one hand on the front of your dog's neck between his throat and chin and push up and back. At the same time, slide your other hand down his back. As you are doing this, tell him to sit.

When your dog sits and his hips are on the ground, praise him.

When your dog sits, make him hold the position for several seconds, then release him by saying "okay" and touching him as you praise him and give him a treat. Practice this on a regular basis, and you'll be amazed to find that your German Shepherd will sit down with only a verbal command, within a few days.

Stay

The stay command—which means to sit or stand still—is one of the most important commands you can teach your German Shepherd. This handy command not only gives you basic control of your dog in normal situations, but it can also save her life at a critical moment. If your Shepherd is about to dart out of an open backyard gate, run into the path of an oncoming car, or do something else that could potentially harm her, the stay command can halt your dog in her tracks.

You can train your dog to stay in either a sitting or lying position. To teach your dog to stay on command, first put her on a leash and then tell her to sit. Stand in front of her and show her the signal for

The signal for stay is an open-palmed gesture right in front of the dog's face.

stay—your open, flat hand, palm side out, while you say her name and the word "stay." When you are fairly certain your dog isn't going to move, take one step away from her, wait 10 seconds, and then release her by saying "okay," as you praise and touch her. If she moves toward you when you step away, put her back in the sit position and repeat the process until she catches on that she is not supposed to move.

Repeat this several times over a few days. When your dog seems comfortable with sitting still for 10 seconds with you standing one step away, gradually increase the time you ask your dog to stay and the distance you stand away from her. Once your dog masters the command of staying in the sitting position, start to teach her to stay while lying down.

Down

The down command is most useful when used in connection with the stay command. Dogs will stay for longer periods when they are in a down position. Consequently, you can use this command to get your dog to remain still when company comes over for dinner so he won't annoy them. You can use this command for safety purposes as well—for example, if he is far away from you and you need time to catch up to him to put his leash on.

Have your dog sit and then show him a treat. Tell him to lie down as you take the treat from his nose down to the ground in front of his paws.

To teach your German Shepherd the down command, first put him in the sit position. Take one of his favorite treats and hold it in front of his nose. Then, say your dog's name followed by the down command as you move the treat to the floor. In trying to reach the treat in your hand, your dog will start to move the front part of his

body toward the floor. When he does this, put your left hand on his shoulder and gently help him go all the way down to the floor. If luring him with a treat doesn't work, gently scoop his front legs out from under him so he has to lie down. Use your left hand to gently keep him in the down position if he tries to get up. Make him stay down for several seconds and release him by saying "okay" and touching him as you praise him and give him the treat. Your dog will need several days of practice before he catches on completely and will reliably lie down upon command.

If your dog doesn't lie down for the treat, just scoop his front legs out from under him and gently lay him down. Praise him even though you're helping him do it.

As your dog lies down, praise him.

Walk Nicely on the Leash

Nothing is more exasperating than having a 75-pound German Shepherd drag you down the street while you try to walk him. Learning to behave on a leash is a fundamental lesson all dogs must learn—especially big ones like German Shepherds.

To teach your dog to walk nicely on the leash and to always pay attention to you, start by taking your Shepherd outdoors with his leash attached to his collar. Carry some of his favorite treats in your pocket. (If he's not big on treats, bring his favorite squeaky toy instead.) Choose an area with few distractions, because you'll want your dog to pay close attention to your instruction.

Holding the leash, stand in front of your dog and show him the treats. Back away and encourage him to follow you. If he follows you, praise him and give him a treat. If he doesn't follow you, try it again until you get his attention.

If your dog pulls on the leash and diverts his attention elsewhere, snap the leash to give a quick jerk on his collar. When your German Shepherd feels the jerk on his collar, he will turn his attention to you. When he does, tell him he's a good boy, show him you have treats or a toy, and ask him to follow you again.

Use a treat and your happy verbal praise to encourage the dog to follow you on the leash as you back away from him. Praise him when he follows you.

Your German Shepherd should eventually catch on and begin to follow you when you back away from him. Once he does, it's time to introduce a new move. This time, as he follows you, turn and walk forward with the dog at your left side. If he stays at your side, praise him and give him a treat. If he forges ahead of you, start to back up until he hits the end of the leash. When you feel that jerk on his collar, act surprised, and then start walking forward. Repeat this over and over, until he realizes that walking next to you means praise and treats and that pulling ahead means a jerk on his collar and a negative reaction from you.

When your dog is following you nicely, turn so that the both of you are walking forward together. Keep a treat handy to pop in front of his nose should he get distracted. Praise him.

Come

You've probably been to the park and seen it happen: A guy takes his dog off the leash so the dog can play, and then spends 10 minutes trying to catch the animal when it's time to go home. Few things cause more frustration than chasing a dog who will not come when called.

Teaching your dog the come command not only will spare you the aggravation and embarrassment of running after your pet, but it will also provide you with a valuable safety tool for protecting your dog. A well-trained German Shepherd named Wally, owned by Jack Brazak of Las Vegas, Nevada, avoided considerable pain and possible death during a hike in the desert when his owner yelled, "Wally, come," just as the dog prepared to pounce on a poisonous rattlesnake.

Wait until your dog reliably responds to the come command before trying it without a leash.

To teach your dog to come, you'll need a box of dog treats. Hopefully, your dog has already learned that the sound of this box shaking means a treat is forthcoming. If not, you'll first need to feed him treats from this box for a few days so he'll come to associate the sound of the box rattling with something good to eat.

Put your dog on his leash and keep the box of treats ready. Stand in front of your dog as you hold the leash, then shake the box and say your dog's name and the come command. When your dog comes toward you, back away. As he continues to follow you, tell him he's a good boy and give him a treat. Practice this over a period of time. Eventually your dog will start to respond to the come command without your needing to use treats.

What a Trained Dog Knows

Properly trained and socialized German Shepherds know and obey the following rules of conduct:

○ Behaves appropriately with humans—that is, no biting, no mouthing, no rough play, and no mounting

○ Requests and takes potty breaks outside

○ Greets people quietly and does not jump up on humans

○ Does not greet people and other animals without owner's permission

○ Walks through doorways only with permission and after people

○ Walks on leash quietly and obediently

○ Does not raid trash cans

○ Does not steal food from tabletops and counters

○ Does not beg

○ Chews only designated toys

○ Plays only with dog toys and leaves children's toys and human belongings alone

When you can depend on your German Shepherd to come toward you on command, switch to a very long leash, about 20 to 30 feet long. You can use a clothesline for this, or you can purchase something called a lunge line, which is made for horses and can be purchased from a tack and feed store.

Take your dog to a fenced outdoor area with few distractions. Let your Shepherd run loose with the long leash dragging. Shaking the box of treats, give him the come command. If he listens and comes to you, give him lots of praise and a treat. If he ignores you, pick up the end of the long leash and pull him toward you while you give the command again. Give him verbal praise when he reaches you, but no treat—he only gets a treat when he comes to you of his own free will.

It may take quite a lot of practice before your dog will consistently come to you without you having to pick up the leash and make him do it. When he does respond to you regularly, repeat the process outside in a secure area without a leash attached.

Once your dog learns the come command, reinforce it throughout his life by always insisting that he come to you when you call him—and by never punishing him or doing something unpleasant after he comes—as this will send him the wrong message. Don't ever let him get away with ignoring the command, or he will soon learn he doesn't have to pay attention when he hears it.

What Every Good Dog Needs to Know

In order to function well in human society, all German Shepherds need to learn the rules of good behavior. Your job is to teach your dog these rules and to make sure he consistently follows them.

No Jumping

Nothing will turn off guests to your home more than being assaulted by a massive German Shepherd the minute they walk through the door. It's important to teach your dog not to jump on people, not only because it is an annoying habit, but also because a dog the size of a German Shepherd could unintentionally hurt people by pouncing on them.

Rather than allowing your dog to jump up on people, instead teach him to sit when he greets them—including you and other members of your family.

First, train him to sit. Once he knows the sit command and performs it reliably, you can move on to training him not to jump up.

To teach your German Shepherd not to jump up on folks, you'll need to make sure your hands are free whenever you walk in the door during the training period. When you come in the house and your dog tries to jump up on you, grasp him by the collar and tell him "no jump." Then tell him to sit and hold him in this position while telling him what a good boy he is for sitting.

To train your dog not to jump up on company, you'll need your guests to help you. Tell your guests ahead of time not to pet or pay attention to your dog until he sits in front of them. Put a leash on your dog before your company arrives. As your company enters your home, hold the leash and tell your dog "sit." If he doesn't obey and instead tries to jump up on your visitors, hold him back with the leash and tell your guests to back away from him. They cannot pet him until he obediently sits and controls his impulse to jump up.

It's important to explain this procedure to your guests before they come over so they will cooperate in helping you train your dog. If your Shepherd finds out he can get away with jumping up on anybody, he'll have a very hard time learning to treat guests with respect.

Digging

The instinct to dig is strong in most dogs. If your dog is a digger, however, you must train him to channel his inborn need to excavate, unless you want your backyard to look like a mine field.

The best way to control your dog's digging urge is to give him a spot in the yard where he can dig to his heart's content. You might let him dig in a place where you've seen him working and you don't really mind that he digs. Alternatively, you may want to entice him to dig in an out-of-the-way area that is not visible from most parts of your yard.

If your dog shows no urge to dig, don't give him the idea! Wait until you notice him digging before you offer him a spot for this activity.

You can encourage your dog to dig in one particular area by partially burying some of his toys in that spot and guiding him to dig there. If you catch him digging in a forbidden spot, correct him by saying "no dig" and taking him to his allowed spot. If he digs in his designated digging area, praise him to let him know he has the right idea.

Allow Human Handling

Tasks like bathing, brushing, and nail clipping are a lot easier to perform on a dog who knows to stand still while being handled. The best way to teach a dog to tolerate different kinds of human handling is to start when he is a young puppy. Conduct practice sessions in which you have your pup stand still for a couple of minutes as you look in his ears and into his mouth, lift up his feet, and run your hands over his body. Do this several times a week for several months while your puppy is growing up to accustom him to such handling.

To Bark or Not to Bark

German Shepherds are natural guard dogs, so you can expect your dog to do some barking at strangers. However, you need to teach your German Shepherd that you will allow some barking, but not excessive barking. Allow your dog to bark two or three times when someone rings the doorbell, approaches your house, or walks past your yard. Do *not* let him bark frantically until the person eventually leaves the area.

Consistency is the key to training your German Shepherd not to bark excessively. Plan ahead and ask a friend to come to your home and ring the doorbell. When the bell rings, your dog will probably run toward the door and bark. Immediately grab your dog's collar, say his name, and then tell him "quiet." If he listens to you and ceases his barking, tell him he's a good boy. If he keeps on barking, wrap your hand around his muzzle to close it and repeat the quiet command. Once he stops barking, praise him.

After several practice sessions, your German Shepherd should start to catch on. If he doesn't, you'll have to resort to stronger tactics.

Fill a squirt bottle with a solution of water and a splash of vinegar—just enough to give the mixture a faint vinegar smell. When your dog runs to the door barking, grab his collar, say his name, and tell him "quiet." If he stops barking, praise him heartily. If he continues to bark, squirt the vinegar-and-water mixture toward his nose. The smell of the vinegar will distract his attention from the visitor at the door and he will stop barking. At this point, praise him for being quiet.

> Consistency is the key to training your German Shepherd not to bark excessively.

After your German Shepherd learns to respond reliably to the quiet command while inside your house, you can begin the training session outdoors in your yard. Ask friends and neighbors to help you with the training by walking past your property or doing whatever else it is that sets your dog off on a barking spree.

No Begging

Dogs seem to be born beggars, but you should discourage this behavior. Begging dogs not only annoy humans who are trying to eat, but these overindulged canines also can get rather pushy if their owners allow the begging to escalate. Most dogs find it pretty easy to graduate from begging to stealing, and small children are usually the victims of such dogs.

The best way to prevent your German Shepherd from begging is never to feed him from the table. Never feed him table scraps by hand; always place such treats you want to give him in his food bowl. Of course, this will only work if your dog hasn't already acquired this annoying habit. If he has, you'll have to do some work to retrain him.

Teach your dog to hold a down–stay while you're eating. He will learn that he gets to eat when you are finished so he must be patient.

First, make sure your dog reliably performs the down/stay command. Then, right before you sit down to eat, take your dog to a corner of the room, away from the table, and give him the command. Make your dog stay in this position until you release him with the okay signal.

If your dog gets up while you are still eating—and chances are he will during his re-training—tell him "no" and put him back in the corner where he is supposed to stay. Continue to do this until he learns he is not allowed to approach the table.

No Biting

If you teach your German Shepherd nothing else, you must teach him never, ever, to bite. Biting is a very serious misbehavior which can result in your dog being taken from you by authorities and euthanized.

Encouraging Appropriate Chewing

Puppies need to be taught what they can and cannot chew. Giving your puppy specially made commercial chew toys will help him learn that only certain items are acceptable for chewing.

Likewise, if you don't want your puppy to raid your closet and chew your shoes to ribbons, don't give him an old slipper to gnaw on. Puppies don't know the difference between a new shoe and an old one.

If you catch your puppy chewing on something he shouldn't, take the item away from him and give him an appropriate chew toy instead.

Also, keeping him confined to his crate when you can't supervise him directly will help prevent him from getting into the habit of chewing the wrong things.

The no-biting rule applies to any kind of biting—even gentle biting meant as play. Your dog must learn that his teeth must never make contact with human skin, even when he intends no aggression.

To teach your German Shepherd not to bite, start when he is a puppy. Whenever he tries to take your hand in his mouth, say "no bite" in a loud, firm voice and then walk away from him, ignoring him for a while so he gets the message. This method can also work with an adult dog who has learned to grab hands or other body parts in play. Remember to be consistent and to never allow your dog to get away with this kind of game.

If your puppy bites you hard in play, yell "ouch" in the loudest, most wounded, and highest-pitched voice you can muster, then say "no bite."

If your adult or adolescent German Shepherd bites you or anyone else—or threatens to bite—out of aggression, you have a

Games to Avoid

Certain games that people tend to play with their dogs can encourage aggressive behavior. As a German Shepherd owner, you should make a rule for yourself and everyone in your family to never play the following games with your dog:

Tug-of-war. This game teaches your dog to battle with you over a possession. Instead, you should train your German Shepherd to hand over any item you ask for and never encourage him to fight you for it.

Wrestling. If you get down on the floor and start wrestling with your dog, you are basically telling him that you and he share the same social ranking. Wrestling encourages a dog to challenge your authority.

Chase. Dogs think that games of chase are loads of fun—especially if they are the ones being chased. Unfortunately, engaging in this kind of activity encourages your dog to run away from you, which is exactly the opposite of what you want him to learn. It also encourages your dog to chase other people, bicycles, and even cars.

Play biting. Puppies naturally love to bite hands—as well as ears, noses, and toes—but they must learn that this is unacceptable behavior. You should discourage your dog from ever biting humans, even in play. When your puppy tries to play with you in this manner, correct him by saying "no bite" and ending the play session.

serious problem on your hands. Contact a trainer or a behaviorist right away for help before your dog injures someone.

House-Training Your German Shepherd

Luckily, it's pretty easy to teach a dog not to go to the bathroom in the house. By taking advantage of your dog's inborn denning instinct, you can get your German Shepherd into the habit of defecating and urinating outdoors, starting at an early age.

Using a Crate to Housebreak

All dogs are born with the knowledge that they should not eliminate waste in the same place where they sleep. The den—usually a small cave or hole in the ground—served as this sanitary place for our dogs' wild ancestors. Nature equipped dogs with this instinct for health reasons, because staying in close proximity to one's own waste can result in illness and disease. Domesticated dogs must learn to think of human dwellings as their dens and, therefore, as places where they cannot urinate or defecate.

You can start house-training lessons early, once your puppy has been weaned from his mother. The best way to teach a puppy not to go to the bathroom in the house is to use a crate. The puppy will instinctively think of the crate as his den and will automatically have an aversion to eliminating inside of it. This will give you the opportunity to teach him where he should go to the bathroom. It also will help him learn how to control his bladder and bowels. (An exception to this will be a puppy that comes from a pet shop. Because pet-shop pups are forced to eliminate in the same place where they sleep, they typically lose the instinct to get away from their waste. These puppies require a lot more work to housetrain.) You can also use a crate to housetrain an adult or adolescent dog who has already developed the habit of going to the bathroom indoors.

The principle behind housetraining with a crate is simple: Your dog will hold his waste while he's inside the crate, giving you the opportunity to condition him to go to the bathroom outside.

To house-train your German Shepherd using a crate, confine him to the crate whenever he is in the house and not under your direct supervision. If your puppy is young, take him out of the crate and outdoors every couple of hours since puppies can't hold their waste for long periods of time. (If your puppy is whimpering, it usually means he has to go.) Stay with him to make sure he eliminates while he is outside. As you see him begin his bathroom ritual of sniffing and looking for a spot, tell him "go potty." When he finishes his business, praise him heartily.

Immediately after your dog goes to the bathroom outside, you can give him a little more freedom by limiting him to one room of the house and keeping him under supervision. Don't allow him free run of the household until he has been reliably going to the bathroom outside for at least six to eight months. Many dog owners allow their dogs too much freedom too soon, which results in accidents indoors.

If you happen to catch your dog going to the bathroom in the house, give a loud verbal correction swiftly—either while the dog is eliminating or less than four seconds later. Your dog won't associate the act of elimination with any correction that comes later than that. If you see your dog circling around and sniffing, it is a clue he is about to go to the bathroom. Take him outside quickly and praise him when he relieves himself there. The praise is important in letting your dog know that going to the bathroom is a good thing, so long as it's outdoors. Dogs who misunderstand and think that the act of elimination is a bad thing will just become sneaky about doing it in the house when you aren't looking.

Asking for a Bathroom Break

If you like the idea of your dog asking to go outside when he needs to eliminate, you can train him to do so once he is completely house-trained.

Rather than encouraging him to bark when he needs to go the bathroom (you should discourage barking, which can easily be-

House-Training Timetable

Your puppy will need to relieve himself at the following times:

○ After every meal

○ After drinking water

○ After playing

○ After waking up from a nap

○ Every two or three hours

come a nuisance), you may want to teach your dog to ring a bell when he needs to use the outdoor facilities.

First, you need a set of bells that are about two inches across. You can purchase these at a craft store. Select the door you want your dog to use to go outside and hang the bells by a rope or ribbon from the doorknob at your dog's nose level. Get some cut-up pieces of hot dog and rub the hot dog on one of the bells. Show the bell to your dog. When he smells the hot dog juice on the bell, he will start licking it, and the bell will ring. This is when you open the door quickly and ask your dog to come outside with you. Once he follows you outside, give him a piece of hot dog and tell him he's a good boy.

Repeat this procedure four times a day for several days, and your dog will start to catch on that ringing the bell means you will open the door to let him outside. Use this method every time your dog acts as if he wants to go outside, making him ring the bells before you open the door and give him a piece of hot dog. Keep an ear out for those bells, because you'll want to respond quickly. When your dog rings the bell to go out, praise him heartily to let him know he's on the right track.

Training Is an Ongoing Process

As you have seen in this chapter, training your German Shepherd means you need to understand him. Why does he growl at other dogs? Why does he chew on things? Before you can deal with your dog's misbehavior, you need to understand why he does it.

A well-behaved dog is a joy to own and a pleasure to spend time with.

In addition, training is an ongoing process. There is no magic wand you can wave over your German Shepherd's head to make him into a perfectly well-behaved, fully grown dog. You must make training a part of your life and incorporate it into your dog's daily routine.

With understanding, training, and consistency, your German Shepherd will grow up to be a great friend who is a joy to have around.

7

Grooming

One of the things most German Shepherd owners appreciate about their dogs is that the breed requires minimal grooming. An occasional bath and regular brushing are all your German Shepherd really needs to look and smell his best. However, even though you'll enjoy your pet's relatively maintenance-free coat doesn't mean you should neglect his grooming needs. Good grooming is as important for your German Shepherd as it is for you.

German Shepherds are a lot easier to groom than are poodles, for example. Shepherds have a short, double coat of straight coarse hair on the top and soft undercoat below, which requires no special trimming or coifing. However, this double coat tends to retain oil and dirt and sheds almost constantly, which does necessitate consistent bathing and brushing. With his short and fairly easy-to-groom coat, your German Shepherd probably won't require the services of a professional groomer—unless, that is, you'd rather not bathe your dog and trim his nails yourself. Both of these tasks, particularly bathing if your dog spends a considerable amount of time outside, as many Shepherds do, must be done on a regular basis.

Home Grooming Versus Professional Grooming

It's important that you help your puppy or adult dog get used to being handled from the first day you bring him home. This will make him comfortable with the entire grooming process and will make grooming go smoothly in the future for you and/or a professional groomer. Take five minutes every day to sit on the floor with your German Shepherd to examine his entire body, while keeping up a running monologue of praise. Look in his eyes and check his ears. Open your dog's mouth and examine his teeth, lightly massaging your finger along his gum line. Next, run your hands along his body, giving extra attention to his feet. Pick up each paw and massage it, gently parting the toes and touching the nails. Many dogs grow anxious when their nails are trimmed, and some become so hysterical, their owners may be accused of dog abuse! Ease your dog's fears, and make your job easier, by introducing your pet to the procedure from the start. This daily "puppy pampering period" also will help you catch any coat or skin problems, such as fleas or suspicious lumps, early on.

If your puppy or adult dog was not handled often from birth (if he was a rescue dog, for example), you may need to work harder at getting him used to being touched. Gently manipulate any part of your Shepherd's body he seems sensitive about. The minute your dog calms down and stops resisting, verbally praise him. You can even reward him occasionally with a treat or a toy.

If you feel at ease grooming him on the floor, then stick with it. However, if you prefer to use a grooming table or plan on taking your dog to a professional (who will definitely use a table), you'll want to accustom him to being up off the ground. If you don't want to invest in a grooming table, you can put a rubber mat on top of a table that is an appropriate height or even on top of the clothes dryer. Of course, this latter option only works for puppies—it would be quite a feat to get an adult German Shepherd on your dryer!

> Although young puppies require little grooming, brushing for a few minutes each day will acquaint them with the process.

Simply hold out the brush and allow your pup to sniff it. If the puppy seems calm, you can try running the brush lightly through his fur. Although young puppies require little grooming, brushing for a few minutes each day will acquaint them with the process. Your puppy initially may react to this strange sensation by biting at the brush. If you realize you are pulling or tugging his fur, then, of course, you should stop what you're doing and proceed in a gentler manner. However, if you know you're not hurting the puppy and he's merely trying to assert himself, don't give in. Otherwise, he'll quickly learn that biting is a means of getting his own way. Instead, ignore the behavior and continue brushing.

If he continues to mouth the brush, calmly but firmly command "off!" or "leave it!" Don't shout: You don't want to scare the puppy into compliance. Although your puppy may be too young to know any commands yet, it is never too early to begin training. Your voice usually will distract him enough to stop what he's doing. As soon as he lets go of the brush, praise him. You also can offer him a treat for behaving, but don't over-reward, because that will create its own problems (he'll expect a treat every time he does what he's supposed to do).

Sometimes owners inadvertently make grooming difficult by trying too hard to make the experience fun for the dog. Although grooming should be enjoyable, some owners mistakenly turn it into a play session. Don't let your dog play with the grooming equipment, or he'll never hold still for future grooming sessions.

Even if you usually groom your dog yourself, a day may come when you want a professional to groom your German Shepherd. How do you go about finding a groomer?

Ask other dog owners or canine professionals for their recommendations. Your breeder, vet, or pet sitter might know of good groomers in the area. Once you have a few names, visit the shops personally. Ask what kind of training the groomers have received. Have they graduated from a grooming course and/or apprenticed with an experienced groomer? Pay attention to how the staff treats the dogs. Are they confident, yet gentle, when they're working with difficult dogs? Are they patient with puppies or dogs that have never been groomed? If the groomers enjoy their job, chances are their upbeat attitude will rub off on their clients' dogs.

Carefully check out the facility. Although you'll probably find that the reception area is neat and tidy, you'll also want to ensure the grooming area is clean and sterile. The staff should wash out and sanitize tubs after each dog's bath as well as sterilize crates between dogs.

What to Look for in a Groomer

The groomer you select for your German Shepherd should:

❍ Possess certifiable knowledge and hands-on experience

❍ Treat clients with courtesy and listen to their concerns

❍ Handle each dog firmly but gently

❍ Show a genuine love of dogs

❍ Never allow puppies that are not fully vaccinated to be around older dogs

The grooming facility should:

❍ Be sterile and clean

❍ Supply an adequate number of crates in all sizes to house its clients' dogs

❍ Provide a special outside area for potty breaks

If you must leave your dog for several hours beyond the time it takes to groom him (for example, if you leave him at the groomer's for the day, while you're at work), ask how often the groomer will take him out to relieve himself. A dog that is left in this new environment for hours on end may have an accident in his crate, making him more stressed and anxious.

Once you decide on a shop, take your pet for an introductory appointment. Inform the groomer that this is your Shepherd's first visit and spend a little extra time making sure your dog has a pleasant experience. If you've done your homework and spent time preparing your dog at home, this first grooming session and any to follow should go well for everyone. After all, what dog wouldn't like an occasional day at the spa?

Routine Care Every German Shepherd Needs

Let's get down to the basics. How often will your dog need to be groomed? What equipment do you need? And just how do you go about giving a 100-pound dog a bath?!

Brushing

German Shepherd coats require brushing only once or twice a week during most of the year. (You'll have to brush more often in the spring and fall, since German Shepherds shed the majority of their undercoat during those seasons.) Brushing your dog regularly is important, because German Shepherds shed continually. The more often you brush your dog, the less dog hair you will find around the house. You also should brush your dog before you bathe her. To brush your dog, you really need just two tools: a pin brush and a slicker brush. A pin brush is made of straight metal pins attached to a rubber base. This kind of brush is most suitable for the German Shepherd's double coat and does wonders for removing loose hair while also stimulating your dog's skin.

You can use a slicker brush, with its bent wire bristles, to give your Shepherd's coat a once over after you've used the pin brush. The slicker brush will pick up any remaining loose hairs and leave your dog with a shiny, pretty coat.

To brush your dog, first ask him to stand in front of you so you can groom him. Using your hand, separate a section of your dog's coat, making a visible part around the section you are holding. Brush outward from the part to give you access to your pet's under-

Removing Mats

If you brush your German Shepherd once or twice a week, you should experience few problems with mats in his coat. However, once in a while, a German Shepherd's double coat will mat up, especially in the areas where it is thickest, such as toward the back of the hind legs. Matting seems to occur most often on dogs who spend a lot of time in the water. If your German Shepherd swims frequently, you may need to remove mats from his coat on an occasional basis.

If you notice a mat in your dog's coat, do not bathe him. Wetting a dog with mats will only worsen the mats and make them even harder to remove. Get out those mats before you put your dog into the tub for a bath.

To clear a mat from your dog's coat, you will need two items: a slicker brush and a dematting tool. Carefully use the dematting tool to cut through the matted hair. You can then use the slicker brush to brush out the hairs that are still sticking together.

You should cut out a mat with scissors only as an absolute last resort, and be careful not to cut too close to the dog's skin. Before you get frustrated and start chopping with scissors, you may want to take your dog to a professional groomer. Most groomers are experts at mat removal and can often get rid of mats without resorting to cutting them.

coat. Repeat this sectioning and brushing all over the dog's body, one section at a time, removing accumulated hair from the brush as you go.

After you finish brushing the undercoat, use the pin brush to groom the topcoat. Brush the dog's entire body, moving in the same direction as the lay of the hair.

During the high shedding seasons of spring and fall, you may want to brush your German Shepherd with a shedding blade as well. Shedding blades, which are usually U-shaped and held in two hands, are designed to remove loose hair from a dog's coat. You simply run the blade along the dog's body in the direction the hair grows, and the loose hairs stick to the teeth on the blade. You then can give your dog's coat a final brushing with the slicker brush.

Bathing

You can have a lot of fun giving your dog a bath—if you enjoy getting wet! Because Shepherds are so big, they require plenty of water and elbow grease.

German Shepherds who spend a lot of time outdoors tend to get dirty faster than those who don't. You may need to bathe your dog as frequently as once a week, if your nose tells you her coat needs it. The coat of a dirty dog emits a distinctive odor that you will come to recognize, if you haven't already. Dogs that need baths often start scratching as well.

Before you start to bathe your German Shepherd, first gather up all the tools you will need. You can use either the bathtub in your bathroom or a portable dog bathtub that you can purchase at a pet supply store. The advantage of utilizing a commercially made dog tub is that you can put it wherever you want to give your dog a bath—even outside, if the weather is warm and you have access to warm water outdoors. Plus, you won't have to worry about dog hair clogging up your bathtub drain.

Place a bottle of shampoo with conditioner in a handy spot near the tub. Make sure the shampoo is specially made for dogs, since the pH level of a dog's skin differs from that of a human's. If you use a bathing mitt, which you can buy at a pet supply store, make sure it's handy. Otherwise, you can just work the shampoo (mixed with a little water) into your dog's coat with your bare hands.

Put a few towels nearby to dry off your dog. If you want to help dry her coat even faster, get the hair dryer ready (but make sure to keep it away from the water).

To bathe your dog, follow these steps:

○ Thoroughly brush your German Shepherd with a pin brush and slicker brush before you begin to bathe her. This removes any loose hairs and will enable you to more effectively clean his coat during bathing.

○ Put your dog in the bathtub. Soak her all over with lukewarm water, being careful not to get any water in her eyes, ears, or nose. Don't forget to wet her feet.

○ Pour some shampoo and water onto your hand or bath mitt, and work it into your dog's coat. Lather her body, taking care to avoid getting any soap around her eyes, ears, and nose.

○ If, at this time, your German Shepherd seems to be shedding heavily, brush hiherm with the pin brush while she is soaped up to remove a lot of the hair that is ready to fall out.

○ Rinse your dog thoroughly with lukewarm water, making sure not to get water in her eyes, ears, or nose. Rinse all of her body completely; any residual shampoo left on the dog will irritate her skin.

○ Stand back and let your dog shake the water from her coat. Then, towel-dry her to remove the excess water. You can blow dry his coat if you feel like it. If you do, don't let the hot air from the blow dryer burn her skin. If your dryer has a "warm" or "cool" setting, use one of those instead of the "hot" setting.

Remember: Don't allow your dog to go outside with a damp coat, unless the weather is warm.

Did You Know?

Unlike other breeds, the word "dog" is actually a part of the German Shepherd Dog's name.

Conquering Grooming Disasters

No matter how diligent you are about grooming your dog, there probably will come a time when she will get something nasty in her coat. Here are some tips for dealing with common grooming disasters.

Burrs Try to remove burrs, seeds, twigs, or other things sticking to your dog with a fine-toothed comb. Mink oil conditioners, available at grooming shops or supply stores, can make the coat sleek, which makes it easier to remove burrs.

Skunk Spray You may have heard that tomato juice takes out the smell of skunk. But before you douse your dog, I have to tell you that this is an old wives' tale. Not only will tomato juice not take the smell out, it will leave you with a pinkish, sticky dog! Instead, use a high-quality skunk shampoo; your pet supply store or groomer should be able to recommend one. Remember to brush your dog thoroughly before bathing her (plugging your nose, if need be), because any dead, loose fur will just retain the smell and prevent the shampoo from penetrating all the way down to the skin. No matter what you use, your dog may continue to smell slightly skunky every time she gets wet for a few weeks or months.

Paint Immediately wash out any latex paint your dog might brush against or roll in before it hardens. This paint, which is toxic, is, thankfully, water-soluble.

If your dog gets into oil-based paint, you'll have to cut away the fur with paint on it. Never use varsol or turpentine and never let your dog chew at the paint.

Gum Don't rush to get out the scissors yet. First, try rubbing the gum with ice cubes to make it brittle. If the gum is stuck only to the ends of the hairs, you should be able to break or lift it off. If it's down in the coat, however, try using peanut butter as a solvent.

If your dog steps in gum, try rubbing it with ice and then peeling it off the pads. If the gum is attached to the hair on the paw cut it away.

Tar If your pet comes in contact with hot tar, immediately apply cold water and see your veterinarian. If your Shepherd experiences a too-close encounter with sticky tar, apply ice cubes to harden the tar and then cut it away with scissors.

Nail Clipping

Canine toenails, just like human fingernails, grow continuously. As a result, you must trim your German Shepherd's toenails on a regular basis. Overgrown toenails can cause problems with the dog's foot, including foot deformities and torn nails.

The frequency with which your dog will need his toenails clipped depends on your dog and his activities. German Shepherds who spend a lot of time walking around on concrete seem to require toenail trims less frequently—maybe once every few weeks—than do dogs who spend most of their time on softer surfaces. The concrete wears down much of the excess nail growth. Conversely, dogs that play indoors and in grass-covered yards often need their toenails clipped about once a week.

You will need to clip your adult Shepherd's nails at least every few weeks or whenever you hear them clicking on hard surfaces, such as the kitchen floor. Puppies' nails grow even more quickly and need to be trimmed every week. Long nails are not only unsightly, they can actually interfere with your dog's movement. Nails that are allowed to grow unchecked can cause the toes to splay and can even begin to curl under and cut into a dog's pads. You should keep your dog's nails short, so that they rest just above the ground when he stands.

Most dog owners use one of two basic types of nail clippers: the scissors or the guillotine. You also can use a nail grinder, but it may take some time for your dog to get used to the noise. Grinding also is more time consuming, and the friction of the grinder can burn your dog's foot if you don't alternate between nails. However, the advantages of a nail grinder are that it

Did You Know?

German Shepherd Dog in German is "Deustche Schaferhund."

leaves the nails smoother and prevents you from cutting into the quick—the blood vessel that runs through your dog's nails.

If you use scissors or guillotine clippers, keep them sharp and clean. Dull clippers won't make a clean cut, and rusty, dirty ones can infect your dog if you cut the quick and your pet bleeds.

The objective when clipping nails is to trim as close to the quick as possible without accidentally nicking it. Dark nails are more difficult to cut than light-colored ones, since it is impossible to see the pink vein. Remove the dry-looking hook at the tip of the nail, cutting off small bits of nail at a time. As you cut the nail shorter, you'll notice the nail becomes softer and you'll see a small grayish-white dot under the nail, which is the end of the quick. When you reach this point, this nail is short enough; you can now move on to the next one. Keep in mind that the more often you trim, the shorter you can get the nail, since the quick actually recedes with frequent trimming. Cut each nail as quickly and cleanly as possible; cutting slowly tends to pinch the nail and may cause your dog discomfort.

> Don't stop and make a big fuss over your mistake, as it may make your dog even more apprehensive the next time you attempt to clip his nails.

If you accidentally cut the quick, don't panic. Apply a styptic powder to staunch the bleeding and continue clipping the other nails. Don't stop and make a big fuss over your mistake, as it may make your dog even more apprehensive the next time you attempt to clip his nails.

While trimming your dog's nails, use this time as an opportunity to inspect his paws for any problems. Look for objects lodged between the foot pads (foxtails are notorious for working their way into the skin of a dog's feet) as well as cuts, blisters, or swollen areas. If you find something lodged in your dog's paw, you can usually remove it yourself with tweezers. If the area appears red and swollen, it may mean an infection, in which case you should contact your veterinarian for help.

Ear and Eye Cleaning

German Shepherds have big ears, and you'll need to inspect them at least once a week and clean them when necessary in order to keep them in tip-top shape.

Tell your dog to sit or lie down. Look closely at each of his ears for any objects, such as foxtails, burrs, or even ticks, that may have lodged there. If you find something that doesn't belong in your dog's ear, remove it carefully with a pair of tweezers. (Safely removing ticks from your dog's skin is discussed in Chapter 5, Common Health Concerns.)

Clean dirty ears with a cotton ball swabbed in mineral oil or with ear cleaner purchased at a pet supply store. Don't overdo the ear cleaning, however, since the presence of some wax is necessary for the health of your dog's ears.

If you detect an unpleasant odor coming from your dog's ear canal, or if the ear seems excessively dirty, contact your veterinarian. Your dog may have an ear infection.

As for your dog's eyes, nature should do most of the work in keeping them clean. However, if your German Shepherd likes to play outside and get dirty, you may notice that dirt accumulates occasionally in the corners of her eyes. You can clean off this dirt with a cotton ball dampened with warm water. Be very gentle when you do this.

If your German Shepherd's eyes seem to need repeated cleaning because of a discharge, contact your veterinarian. Discharge is a sign that your dog has an eye problem, such as infection, requiring veterinary care.

Tooth Care

You should make brushing your German Shepherd's teeth a regular part of his grooming. Every so often your veterinarian will have to deep clean your dog's choppers to remove tartar that has gathered under the gum line. Brushing at home can do much to keep your dog's teeth in good health in between deep cleanings.

It is relatively easy to brush your dog's teeth. All you need is a commercial canine toothbrush, available at pet supply stores, or a simple piece of gauze wrapped around your index finger. You also need a tube of specially made dog toothpaste, because human toothpaste is unhealthy for dogs. (Unlike human toothpaste, dog toothpaste is meat flavored and digestible.)

To brush your German Shepherd's teeth, have your dog sit in front of you. (If your dog isn't cooperative, you may need someone to hold her while you perform the brushing.) Put some toothpaste on the toothbrush or on your gauze-wrapped finger, and lift her upper lip to expose the teeth on her upper jaw. Rub a couple of teeth at a time in a gentle, circular motion. Brush as close to the gum line as you can, because most of the tartar collects in that area. First, work around your dog's entire upper jaw, and then move down to the bottom teeth.

You should brush your German Shepherd's teeth as often as you can— as frequently as daily, if you have the time. The more often you brush her teeth, the healthier her mouth will be, and the less often she will need a veterinarian to clean her teeth.

Anal Glands

One of the most unpleasant aspects of grooming a dog is checking—and, if need be, expressing—the anal glands. These glands are found on each side of the anus. They produce a fluid that dogs use to mark their territory when they defecate. Although these sacs are supposed to empty out on a regular basis when your dog relieves himself, the sacs sometimes fail to completely excrete all of the fluid. Consequently, the fluid builds up, and the sacs become enlarged and painful.

If you see your dog scooting—dragging his hind end across the floor—or biting under his tail at his hind end, he may be experiencing trouble with his anal sacs. Take your dog to the veterinarian to determine whether this is, indeed, the problem.

If your dog's anal sacs are impacted, your veterinarian will empty your dog's anal glands. You can do this procedure at home as well. Most likely, though, you'll prefer to leave this stinky task to a professional.

8

Family Life

Although German Shepherds may be big, strong, and brave, they are also incredibly huggable. You will find that your German Shepherd will turn into your children's best friend, your closest confidant, and the protector and ally of everyone in the family.

From a German Shepherd's perspective, family life comprises many aspects. Both you and your dog will face numerous issues, everything from getting along with the kids to going on vacation.

Playing Nicely with Children

Because German Shepherds are such large dogs, it is especially important that they learn to play nicely with children. A frisky and rambunctious German Shepherd can easily knock down and frighten—or even injure—a child without meaning to. For this reason, you must teach your dog to treat children gently and with respect, especially at playtime.

The key to helping your German Shepherd play well with children is to make him understand that the children are above him in the social order of your family pack. (Packs and canine social structure are discussed in Chapter 6, Basic Training for German Shepherds.) That means the dog must learn never to steal food from a child, never to jump up on a child, and always to give way when a child wants to sit on a chair or a sofa occupied by the dog. (This assumes you allow your dog up on the furniture, which really isn't a good idea anyway.)

The best time to teach your German Shepherd to respect children is when he is a puppy. Whatever your dog learns at this young and impressionable age will stay with him throughout his life.

You will need to enlist the help of your children for this. You also will need to constantly supervise them while they are with the puppy to ensure the children, too, are behaving as they should.

Have your kids spend time with the puppy, playing with him and handling him. When handling the puppy, children should sit on the floor with the puppy in their laps. Wiggly puppies who kiss faces are fine; jumping, biting, roughhousing puppies are not. If the puppy gets unruly, say "no!" and have the child end the handling session by walking away.

Both kids and puppies love to play, and playing is a great way for the two to bond.

However, you must supervise the games to make sure they are appropriate. You should forbid any competitive games. Don't let the kids wrestle with the puppy or play tug-of-war. This only teaches the puppy to be rough with the kids and to not respect them.

Just as your German Shepherd has a responsibility to treat children gently and with respect, your children also share the same responsibility with your pet. Teach your kids to treat your dog kindly, and never allow them to tease him. You may then have a future aggression problem—and a bitten child—on your hands. Also, discourage your children from carrying the puppy around. They could drop him or injure him accidentally.

Times will likely come when your children are out in the backyard playing, and your German Shepherd puppy wants to be right in the midst of the ruckus. However, you need to keep watch on this scenario, because the puppy is very likely to get carried away. Two or more children screaming and running around can easily rile and excite your German Shepherd—and may result in some rowdy behavior from your dog. If your kids are getting wild, bring the dog in the house and keep him from getting involved in a situation in which he could lose control of his behavior, and he or the kids could get hurt. Also, you don't want him to learn that it's okay to play rough with children, since he'll be a lot bigger and, therefore, more likely to hurt one of them accidentally when he grows up.

Something like that happened to Cloe, a German Shepherd who lives with her family in Austin, Texas. "When Cloe was a puppy, she often roughhoused with the kids," says Carrie Wheaton, Cloe's owner. "Cloe was small then, and we all thought it was funny

> The best time to teach your German Shepherd to respect children is when he is a puppy. Whatever your dog learns at this young and impressionable age will stay with him throughout his life.

when she chased the kids around the backyard, jumping on their legs and nipping at their heels. However, when Cloe reached around five months old, she already weighed 60 pounds. She would try to play the same games she did as a puppy, but the kids would end up getting knocked down and crying. Pretty soon, they didn't want Cloe to play with them—and neither did I."

It's also important to make sure small children don't inadvertently hurt your dog while playing with him. Babies and toddlers often play too rough unintentionally. Young children will often get excited and throw themselves on top of a dog or pull his fur. If that were to happen, your German Shepherd could possibly bite the child in self-defense.

"I've had my Shepherd, Dusty, since he was a puppy, and he adores my three-year-old son, Michael," says Betty Sikes of Ithaca, New York. "But I never leave them alone together. Michael has occasionally pulled Dusty's ears and even stepped on his tail, and Dusty never lashes out. But it's just not a chance I want to take."

Remember to never leave your German Shepherd alone with a small child, no matter how much you trust the dog. If you can't supervise your baby or toddler while the dog is in the room, then take the dog with you.

Making Your German Shepherd a Good Neighbor

If you live in an urban or suburban neighborhood, then you already know the value of getting along well with your neighbors. If you own a German Shepherd, you'll need to take special care to ensure your dog is the kind of pooch people want to live near, so you can continue to get along well with others in your community.

Four Great Games Kids Can Play with a German Shepherd

Kids and dogs love to play together, but only certain games are appropriate for these fun-loving buddies. The following games are not only fun and safe, but they also actually teach your dog to respect your child.

Fetch. Using a ball, stick, or toy, have your child throw the object, so the dog can retrieve it. When the dog brings back the object to your child, have your child say, "drop it!" so the dog will turn over the object for your child to throw it again. (You can teach your dog to obey the drop-it command by practicing this game yourself. Simply offer a treat to the dog in exchange for the object as you say, "drop it!" The dog will learn to relinquish the object on command.)

Toy Chase. It is not a good idea to allow your child to play "chase me" with your dog, because this type of play can turn too rough and teaches the dog to run away from humans. However, since dogs love to chase things, you can still let your child play a chase game with your German Shepherd that is safe and appropriate. Do this by creating a lure of sorts, using a fishing pole and fishing line. Attach the fishing line to a light-colored plastic bag, then attach the line to the pole. Have your child whip the bag around on the ground, back and forth and in circles, so your dog can chase it.

Hide and Seek. Your child can play hide and seek with your German Shepherd, with you participating. Give your child one of your dog's favorite treats. Have your child show the treat to the dog, while you hold on to the dog's collar. Then, tell your child to hide somewhere in the house, as you keep your dog from following. Once your child has had time to hide, release your dog and tell him to go find your child. When the dog finds your child, give him a treat!

Water Games. Some German Shepherds love the water—others don't. If your German Shepherd likes to swim, you can let your child play fetch with the dog in the swimming pool or at a lake. Your child should stay out of the water while your dog is swimming, however, because your dog's paddling paws can easily scratch your child if the two get too close under water. Instead, have your child stand on the edge of the pool or lake, or on a pier, and throw an object into the water for your dog to retrieve.

Canine Rules of Conduct

Canine-related troubles are one of the greatest causes of poor relations among neighbors. Dogs that are not well trained, not well cared for, or not well controlled can wreak havoc in a neighborhood—and incur the wrath of the entire community upon the guilty dog owner.

To make sure your German Shepherd is a good neighbor, make certain he follows these rules of conduct:

No Barking   Dogs who spend a lot of time alone in the backyard often develop barking problems. These dogs bark out of boredom and loneliness, and their vocalizations can drive neighbors to distraction. Don't leave your German Shepherd out in the backyard for extended periods of time—especially during the day, when you are not home, or at night while you are sleeping. If you must leave your dog outside when you're away, check with your neighbors to find out whether your dog barks while you're gone. If he does, you'll need to either keep him indoors or work on correcting his nuisance barking. (Controlling excessive barking is discussed in Chapter 6, Basic Training for Your German Shepherd.)

> Dogs that are not well trained, not well cared for, or not well controlled can wreak havoc in a neighborhood—and incur the wrath of the entire community upon the guilty dog owner.

No Roaming   Nothing infuriates people more than dog owners who let their dogs run loose in the neighborhood. Loose dogs create all kinds of problems. They poop on the neighbors' lawns, terrorize other pets, scare children, and cause general mayhem.

Allowing your dog to run free in the neighborhood not only is inconsiderate to your neighbors, it is also dangerous for the dog and even illegal in many places.

Scoop the Poop   When you walk your dog around the neighborhood, diligently cleanup your dog's feces. This means not only deposits made directly on neighbors' lawns, but also his droppings on walking trails, gutters, and other common areas used by the people in your community. Your neighbors will respect you for it.

Train Your Dog   Obedience-trained dogs are good citizens in the community, because they are well behaved and easily controlled. Training will help prevent your dog from leaping at joggers passing by, jumping up on kids who stop to say hello, and lunging at other dogs you see on your walks. Teach your dog to walk quietly by your side and to respond to your commands of "sit" or "stay" when other people and animals pass by.

One way to ensure that your dog behaves the way he should in the community is to train him to earn a Canine Good Citizen title, offered by the American Kennel Club (AKC). Contact the AKC (see Resources) for information on a local dog club in your area that can help you train for this title.

License Your Dog   Most communities require that dog owners license their pets and inoculate them against rabies. Follow the licensing laws that apply to your dog within your community, and obey leash laws and other regulations pertaining to dogs and their owners.

Holiday Hazards

The holidays bring plenty of opportunity for fun for both dogs and humans. However, you need to keep a close eye on your German Shepherd during this festive time of year. Dogs can get into trouble during the holidays in an assortment of ways. Learn the potential dangers to your dog, so you can protect her and make sure both she and you have a good time.

Festive Foods   Holidays are a big time for indulging in culinary delights. Your German Shepherd, too, will be tempted to partake in this food fest, but you need to vigilantly keep her away from holiday treats. Rich foods can make your dog sick. Poultry containing bones can harm her digestive system. One particular human treat—chocolate—can even prove fatal to your dog, if she eats a large enough quantity. Most canine chocolate poisonings occur at Halloween, Christmas, Thanksgiving, and Valentine's Day holidays.

Some holiday items no human would consider edible end up being consumed by dogs, often to their detriment. These dangerous-to-canine festive items include holiday plants, such as mistletoe and poinsettia, which are toxic to dogs. Overzealous dogs (especially puppies) can also sometimes swallow the ribbon used to wrap gifts, and even small parts from new Christmas toys can end up in your dog's stomach and result in an intestinal obstruction. Resist the temptation to feed your dog leftovers or holiday treats during festive times of the year—and tell your guests to do the same. Although you'll find it hard to deny those pleading eyes, your dog will be much better off eating only his dog food, since an overindulgence in rich human food can result in digestive problems and even pancreatitis.

Comings and Goings   Holiday time means visits from friends and family—and that means plenty of comings and goings through your house. During this time keep a close eye on your German Shepherd to make sure she doesn't slip out an open door or get herself into some other kind of trouble as a result of visiting house guests. Educate your guests on the house rules regarding your dog (no feeding from the table, no roaming around outdoors, no jumping up on people) and make sure they enforce your rules, for both your dog's safety and theirs.

When you are expecting company for the holidays, it's best to keep your dog in her crate or in an out-of-the-way room until all your guests have arrived. That way, she won't become overexcited as each person rings the doorbell and makes an entrance into your home.

If your German Shepherd is a young puppy, it's best to keep her confined to her crate for the entire time your guests are present. Although the fun and laughter of the holidays can be a blast for participating humans, it can sometimes over-stimulate young puppies. If you want your guests to meet your new family member, bring her out on a leash for introductions and then put her back in her quiet place after she has had a chance to meet everyone.

Loud Noise   One particular holiday, Independence Day, can be a tremendous nightmare for many dogs. The sound of fireworks going off around the neighborhood can drive many noise-sensitive dogs to distraction. In fact, immediately after the Fourth of July, animal shelters around the country find themselves filled to the brim with dogs who got lost while trying to escape the noise.

If your dog is afraid of the sound of fireworks, do not leave her out in your backyard on Independence Day while you go off to your friend's barbecue. Your dog will either find a way out of your yard or will destroy everything in it in an attempt to escape.

The kindest thing to do for your dog on Independence Day is to stay at home with her. Then, reassure her everything is okay by trying to distract her during the fireworks with an indoor game of fetch or by simply sitting in the room with her while she hides under the bed. Keep your mood upbeat and even offer your dog a treat if she ventures out from her hiding place. (Avoid cooing to her and trying to soothe her with sympathetic words since she may interpret this as praise for her cowardly behavior.) If you must leave your dog alone on the Fourth of July, put her inside the house in her crate, with a radio or TV on in the same room to help drown out the noise from outside.

Decorative Dangers   One of the best things about the Christmas holiday are the decorations. However, live trees, blinking lights, and strings of electrical cords can all pose problems, if you have a dog in the house. Because of their propensity to chew, puppies are especially prone to getting into trouble around a Christmas tree. Gnawing on a light cord can result in a fatal electric shock . A puppy who swallows tinsel or pine needles can end up with an intestinal blockage. Use extreme caution if you have both a puppy and a Christmas tree. Don't allow the puppy to stay in the same room with the tree without supervision.

Fully grown dogs also can get into trouble around Christmas trees. Some male dogs think they can use the tree as a bathroom and will urinate on it, just as they do with trees outdoors. To remedy this problem, spray a dog repellent, available at pet supply stores, on the dog-level parts of the tree.

Because German Shepherds are big dogs, their very presence creates a hazard around a Christmas tree. Take Tim, for example, a German Shepherd owned by Karen Walters of Brooklyn, New York. "I always put my Christmas tree up right in front of the bay windows in my living room, so passersby can see the tree from outside," says Karen. "One year, Tim apparently decided on the first day the tree was up that he wanted to look out the bay window, something he did all the time. I was in the kitchen when I heard a crash. I ran into the living room and found Tim looking out the window, with the tree laying on its side on the floor!"

The moral of the story: Put your tree in a part of the room where your German Shepherd isn't likely to brush past it.

Traveling with and Boarding Your Dog

When vacation time rolls around, you will need to give some thought to what you are going to do with your German Shepherd. Will you take him along with you on your trip? Or would he do better staying home? These are decisions you will have to make, based on what is best for your dog and your family.

To Board or Not to Board?

Certain types of vacations are just perfect for dogs. Trips in which you will drive to your destination and then camp or stay in a pet friendly motel, for example, are great for including your dog. You might also want to take your dog with you on visits to relatives within driving distance provided your relatives have no problem with your dog coming to stay with them.

Gypsy, a German Shepherd owned by Steve and Claire Stern of Georgetown, Maryland, goes everywhere with her owners. "We take Gypsy every place we go," says Claire. "Whenever we go on a vacation that we drive to, she comes along. When we stay with family, she is always invited, because she is well behaved and never causes a problem."

Some vacations, however, are best left to the humans. Any trip that requires you to fly to your destination is not a good vacation on which to bring your dog. Flying is stressful to dogs and even risky at times of the year when the weather is hot. If you need to fly in order to get where you are going, leave your dog at a boarding kennel. Also, if you plan to drive to your vacation spot but want to sightsee along the way at places that don't allow dogs, it's probably not a good idea to take your dog on the trip. Leaving your dog alone in the car is very dangerous, because the temperature inside a vehicle in hot weather can quickly climb to dangerous highs and kill a dog, even with the windows open. Plus, dogs left alone in cars are vulnerable to theft.

Road Trips with Your German Shepherd

Before embarking on a vacation-destination car trip with your German Shepherd, you should first make some preparations. You'll need to get your dog ready for the trip and to make sure you have the proper equipment and accommodations for him.

A few weeks before your trip, figure out if your dog is likely to encounter anything new to him while on your vacation. For example, if you live out in the country and plan to drive a few hundred miles to spend a week in the big city, you should start getting your dog used to crowds and different types of people. Take him to the park a few times and ask people to come up to him and pet him. Try to walk him through an area where there are lots of people walking around too. He will then feel more comfortable when he encounters the bustling city streets where you are going, because he's already tackled crowds at home.

The Sterns practiced this routine with Gypsy before taking her on vacation with them for the first time. "We were going on vacation to a beach resort, but Gypsy had never seen the beach. In fact, she had never even walked on sand," says Claire. "So we took her to a park and made her walk around in the sand box to get the feel of sand on her paws. At first, she seemed a bit unnerved when she sunk in the sand, but after a while she started to dig in it and have a good time with it. When we eventually took her to the beach on vacation, she had a blast playing in the sand.

Because you will be driving to your destination, you should start getting your dog ready for long hours spent in the car. Place your dog's crate in your vehicle (or, if your car can't accommodate your German Shepherd's crate, purchase a canine seat belt at a pet supply store) and take your dog on short rides in the car at least every other day. Take him somewhere fun or just for a drive around the block. Don't take him to a place he doesn't like (like the vet's office), because he will come to associate riding in the car with something unpleasant.

Gradually increase the length of time your dog must spend in the car until he is finally comfortable with being in the vehicle for long periods of time. You'll

Did You Know?

According to the American Animal Hospital Association, more than 40 percent of pet owners talk to their pets on the phone or through the answering machine.

appreciate this preparation when you are tooling down the highway for hours at a time with a sleeping dog in the back seat—rather than an anxious pet who is panting, pacing, and whining.

When preparing your dog for his long car trip, you should pay special attention to whether your dog seems to suffer from car sickness. A dog with car sickness will act distressed and eventually vomit. If you suspect your dog has a problem with motion sickness, or if you just want to take precautions, line the back seat with plastic (a large plastic garbage bag will do). If your car is large enough to accommodate your dog's crate, you won't need to worry about covering up your seats. If your dog vomits in her crate, you can easily clean it up.

If it turns out your dog does get motion sickness, talk to your veterinarian about the kinds of medications you can give him before the trip to keep him from getting ill. Meanwhile, avoid feeding her large meals before taking her in the car and withhold water for a couple of hours before the trip.

If your dog becomes car sick while on your journey, stop frequently to take her on short walks. Also, drive with the windows open, if the weather permits (but don't let your dog hang her head out the window). You can offer her ice to chew on too.

If you are traveling out of state, your dog may be exposed to regional parasites and diseases to which she is unaccustomed. Before you embark on your trek, make a call to the state veterinarian of your destination site to inquire about which kinds of health problems your dog may encounter and how you can guard against them. (You can get the number of the state veterinary office from directory assistance in the state's capitol city. The number may be listed under the State Department of Agriculture.) For example, dogs traveling to the Northeast in the spring, summer, and fall are at risk for Lyme disease. States with heavy mosquito populations put your dog in danger of infection with heartworm. In parts of the Southwest, a fungus called coccidioidomycosis lives in the soil and causes bone and breathing problems in dogs who have no immunity to the disease.

If you are taking your dog camping or hiking on your vacation, you also should be aware of the risks of your canine companion becoming infected with giardia, a protozoa that lives in many fresh water sources in the United States. (Protecting and treating your dog for infections such as giardia and other ailments is discussed in Chapter 5, Common Health Concerns.).

If you need overnight accommodations on your drive to your final destination, it's a good idea to make reservations in pet-friendly motels and hotels before you actually leave on your trip. Because many motels and hotels do not allow dogs, if you don't have a reservation in one that does, you could end up with nowhere to spend the night with your pet.

You also should make sure you have the right equipment for a vacation with your dog. Outfit your German Shepherd with a secure collar and identification tags that cite the name and phone number of someone who can reach you while you are on your trip. That way, if your dog becomes lost on your vacation, whoever finds her can call a person who knows how to contact you.

> Outfit your German Shepherd with a secure collar and identification tags that cite the name and phone number of someone who can reach you while you are on your trip.

Your dog will also need a leash to keep her secure during driving stops and when you get to where you are ultimately going. It's unsafe to allow your dog to run loose without a leash, no matter how obedient she is.

What to Pack

Remember to bring the following items for your dog when you go on vacation:

- ❍ Enough dog food and familiar water to get you to your destination (don't forget the can opener)
- ❍ Toys and treats
- ❍ A collar fitted with identification tags giving the name and phone number of someone who knows how to reach you while you are away

- ❍ A leash
- ❍ A crate or seat belt harness for the car
- ❍ Medication, if your dog is taking any
- ❍ Grooming supplies
- ❍ Repellent for fleas and ticks
- ❍ A pooper scooper or plastic bags for waste removal

Don't forget to bring your dog's food and water bowls as well as a supply of his regular dog food. Make sure you have enough food to last during the entire vacation, unless you are certain you can buy more of the exact brand once you get to where you're going. Changing your dog's diet on a vacation is sure to make him ill with a bad case of diarrhea.

Speaking of diarrhea, you should consider bringing several jugs of the same water you give your German Shepherd at home. An abrupt change in your dog's water can give him the runs—the last thing you need on a long car trip! While driving, you should give him only the water you brought with you. Once you get to your destination spot, you can gradually mix the familiar water with the new water there. (If your dog drinks bottled water, then you should continue to give it to him for the entire trip.)

Rules of the Road   In order to have a safe and fun journey with your dog, you need to set some in-the-car rules for your pooch.

First, your dog must be restrained at all times while you are driving—either in her crate or buckled to a seat with a special seat belt harness made for dogs (available from pet supply stores). If you have a station wagon or sports utility vehicle, you can instead use a specially made metal mesh barrier to section off the back end of your car and confine your dog there.

The reason for all this is pure and simple: safety, both yours and your dog's. If your dog is loose in the car, she can distract you as you drive and cause you to get into an accident. Likewise, if you are in an accident and your dog is unrestrained, she may suffer serious injuries or even death. Many tragically true stories exist of unrestrained dogs who died in auto accidents after hurtling into the windshield during collisions.

Second, never allow your German Shepherd to ride with her head sticking out of the car window, even though she may want to do just that. Although this is a favorite canine pastime, it is actually very dangerous. The majority of eye injuries in dogs result from dogs riding with their heads out the car window. With the wind blowing in the dog's face, all kinds of debris can end up lodged in her eyes. The wind also can dry out your dog's eyes, causing them to become irritated. Roll up your windows high enough to keep your dog's head in the car. If you want to roll down your windows completely while your dog is in the car with you, you can purchase wire mesh window guards to place in the open window frames. These will allow air in but will prevent your dog from sticking out her head.

If you plan to travel with your German Shepherd in the bed of a pickup truck, think again. This is not the safest place for your pet to ride for several reasons. Your dog can easily jump or fall out of the back of the truck while you are on the road. If the weather is hot, your dog can suffer from heatstroke in the back of an open pickup or injure her paws on the hot surface. She also is vulnerable to flying debris when in the back of an open truck bed, and she's at high risk of death or injury should you get into an accident.

If you must travel with your dog in your truck bed, keep the dog inside a crate. In the event of an accident, the crate will help protect your dog from injury. It also will provide her with shade and secure footing. Make sure to carefully secure the crate to the truck bed, so it won't fly out if your vehicle is struck.

If you do not want to keep your dog in a crate, at the very least use a truck restraint with your dog. This is a cable tie-out that is much safer than simply tying your dog with a rope. It attaches to the front and sides of your truck bed and allows you to secure your dog to the cable with a nylon collar. Using this method, your dog is less likely to fall out of or be thrown from your truck during an accident.

Once you're on the road driving to your destination, make sure to stop every four to six hours to give your dog a chance to go to the bathroom and stretch her legs. Taking breaks even more often will keep your dog from going stir crazy in the car and will help prevent you from becoming fatigued from too much driving.

Traveling by Air

If you are flying to your destination and absolutely must take your dog with you, you'll need to make certain advance preparations.

The first requirement of canine air travel is that your German Shepherd must be crate trained, because he will spend several hours in a plastic airline crate in the luggage compartment of the aircraft. If your dog isn't already crate trained, begin working on this several months before your trip. (Crate training is discussed in Chapter 6, Basic Training for German Shepherds.) For your dog's comfort, place a crate pad or blanket in the crate and leave it there during your dog's flight. (Do this only if your dog is unlikely to chew up the bedding. Chronic chewers must travel without bedding.)

Next, take your dog to the veterinarian for an examination within 30 days of your trip to ensure he is in good health. You will need to obtain a health certificate from the vet indicating the dog is current on his inoculations. All airlines require health certificates for dogs traveling by air. If you are flying to an international destination, check with that country's consulate to determine which inoculations are required and how many days before the trip the health certificate should be issued.

You also can discuss with your veterinarian the possibility of giving your dog a tranquilizer for the trip. While some veterinarians recommend tranquilizers for dogs who become anxious when traveling, many do not, because the medication can impair the dog's ability to cope with the physiological stresses of air travel.

When planning your trip, you'll need to make a reservation for your dog as well as for yourself. If you are traveling during the summer or through a part of the country with a warm climate, schedule your flight so your dog will not be traveling in the heat of the day. The cargo hold of an aircraft is not temperature controlled, and flying during periods of extreme heat can be very dangerous for your dog. Nighttime travel is the safest for your pet during the summer and in warmer climates. You should also avoid layovers, when the plane will sit on the runway during stops, with the dog left in the cargo hold. If possible, avoid flights that require you to change planes, since your dog can also be at risk in these situations.

Did You Know?

Millie, President Bush's English springer spaniel, earned over four times as much as her owner in 1991.

Whatever you do, make sure your dog travels on the same plane you do, so you can watch out for her. If the plane gets held up on the runway and the weather is warm, you must demand that the airline personnel remove your dog from the cargo hold, so she won't suffer heatstroke. If personnel resist, be persistant. Your dog's life is at stake. Another reason to be on the plane is to ensure that your Shepherd gets unloaded and loaded onto the correct plane, when flights require that you switch planes. Otherwise, your dog could mistakenly be sent on to another destination.

On the day of your flight, do not allow your dog to eat anything for eight hours before take-off time or drink anything for a couple of hours beforehand. This will help prevent him from having to eliminate during the flight. (If the flight is long, you can put a few ice cubes in his dish inside the crate.) Before you put your dog in the crate for loading on the plane, encourage him to relieve himself somewhere outside the terminal.

When traveling with a German Shepherd, you'll need to arrive at the airport two hours before your flight. Make sure your name and address are clearly marked on the crate, using a label that can't fall off. Check to ensure the crate is tagged with the proper destination sticker when you check in your dog.

When you board the plane, let the flight attendant know you have a dog on the plane. Ask the attendant to inform the pilot of your dog's presence, so if the plane is delayed on the runway, the pilot can have the dog temporarily removed from the cargo hold for the animal's safety. If your plane is delayed after your dog has been loaded, ask a flight attendant to make sure airline personnel take care of your dog. Remember, you are your dog's number one advocate in the air.

Where to Stay

Although many hotels around the country don't allow dogs as guests, plenty of them do. Most campgrounds also permit dogs, as long as they are kept on leashes and do not roam.

Hotels and Motels   Before you embark on a trip with your dog in tow, it is wise to make reservations in advance. Book your stay in a place that allows pets. You can find pet-friendly motels and hotels in nearly every city in the country with the help of automobile clubs and books that list only "pets allowed" lodging. You will discover that some of these establishments do more than allow dogs—they also welcome them with open arms, providing treats and special amenities to accommodate them.

> You can find pet-friendly motels and hotels in nearly every city in the country with the help of automobile clubs and books that list only "pets allowed" lodging.

Once you arrive at the hotel or motel you have booked, encourage the establishment to continue allowing dogs by being a good guest. Don't leave your German Shepherd unsupervised in the room unless you have him in a crate. Even then, don't leave him alone for long periods of time. (If your dog isn't reliably housebroken, you should never let him run loose in the room, even when you are with him.) Unrestrained dogs can cause a lot of damage to hotel rooms, and even crated dogs can cause trouble with nuisance barking. In fact, if your dog has a tendency to bark at passersby even when you are present, request a room that is somewhat off the beaten path, so he'll have less to bark at.

If your dog likes to sleep on the bed with you or lounge around on the furniture, bring a sheet from home to place on the bed or couch to protect the furnishings from dog hair.

Cleanup after your dog when you walk him around the hotel or motel grounds. Also, refrain from bathing your dog in the hotel or motel bathtub, because dog hair is notorious for clogging up bathtub drains.

Camping with Your German Shepherd

Taking your German Shepherd along on a camping trip can be loads of fun. To make the most of your outing, it's important to prepare ahead of time.

Before you start off on your journey to the campsite, make certain your camping destination allows dogs. National forests usually allow dogs at campsites, as do a smaller number of national parks and state parks. However, you won't know for sure unless you call first. Also, some parks allow dogs in the campsites but not on hiking trails.

If you will be tent camping with your dog, first make sure there is room in the tent for your German Shepherd, you, and whomever else you'll be bunking with. Remember how big German Shepherds are! You will need as much room for your dog inside your tent as you would for another person.

To ensure your dog has everything he needs while away from home on a camping trip, you should pack the following items:

○ Dog food (and a can opener, if your dog eats canned food)
○ Food and water bowls
○ Bottled water or containers filled with the water your dog is used to drinking
○ Leash and collar with identification tags
○ Tie-out to stake your dog at the campsite (available at pet supply stores)
○ First aid kit
○ Flea and tick repellent

○ Plastic bags with which to cleanup after your dog

○ Canine backpack, where you can keep some lightweight items for the dog, if you intend to go hiking (have your dog practice wearing his backpack for a few weeks before the trip)

If you plan to hike with your dog, you must follow some basic rules of safety and courtesy. Do not allow your dog to hike off leash. Off-leash hiking is not allowed on most trails, anyway, but even in places where it is not forbidden, it is never a good idea. Your German Shepherd can get into way too much trouble if left to his own devices on the trail. He may come into contact with a poisonous snake or insect, or he may run off and get lost in the middle of nowhere.

That is what happened to a German Shepherd named Jake, who was hiking with his owner in a wilderness park when the dog saw a rabbit and took off after it. "I yelled to him, but he was so focused on the rabbit, he didn't even seem to hear me," said Jake's owner, Bill Rush. "He just disappeared into the brush. It took three hours of constant searching by my whole family before we finally found him, wandering around in the woods."

Others dogs provide another reason to keep your dog on a leash while on the trail. If you encounter a fellow hiker with a dog, a fight between the two animals could ensue if your dog is off leash. Your off-leash German Shepherd also could frighten horses being ridden on the trail or scare hikers who are uncomfortable around big dogs.

When hiking on trails, show courtesy to fellow trail users, such as horseback riders, other hikers, and mountain bikers. Remember that horses have the right of way on trails, which means you should pull off to the side of the trail and let riders pass. Don't allow your dog to lunge at the horses or chase after them, because this could spook the horse and cause a serious accident.

Mountain bikers are supposed to yield to hikers and most do. However, if you are hiking with your dog in an area with a lot of mountain bikers, stay alert, especially on narrow, winding wooded trails where visibility is limited. Bikers coming around sharp turns at high speeds sometimes don't see hikers.

For your dog's comfort on the trail, bring water with you, so he can have an occasional drink. You may even want to purchase a lightweight, portable water bowl for your dog from a pet supply store before you leave on your trip. That way, you won't have to carry around your dog's regular water bowl with you when you are hiking. (If your dog wears a backpack, you can keep the portable water bowl, along with a few dog treats and plastic bags for scooping poop, in the pack.)

If you apply flea and tick repellent to your dog's coat before your hike, it should protect your dog well against these parasites. However, it still wouldn't hurt to check your dog's coat after your hike to make certain he hasn't picked up any unwelcome hitchhikers. (Dealing with unwanted fleas and other pests is discussed in Chapter 5, Common Health Concerns.)

Don't forget to check your dog's paws after your hike as well. Look for thorns or other debris that may have lodged between his paw pads.

If your dog isn't used to hiking or strenuous activity, don't take him on excessively long trips down the trail. Remember, you will need to condition your German Shepherd in advance for long, serious hikes that last the whole day.

Boarding Your German Shepherd

For trips that require flying or for destinations that are unsuitable for dogs, boarding your dog while you are away is the best way to go. A good boarding kennel will give your dog consistent care and companionship as well as exercise and play time, if you so desire.

You may wonder why you should pay a boarding kennel to house your dog while you are away, instead of just leaving her behind in your home with daily visits from a friend or relative. The reason is that dogs are very social creatures and suffer terribly when left alone for long periods of time. If you leave your dog in the house or yard for days on end with only a once or twice daily visit from a caretaker, your dog will grow lonely and anxious. She may then destroy your property or bark and howl incessantly, driving your neighbors crazy. Dogs left alone for days on end can also get themselves into trouble, because they are bored and unsupervised.

A German Shepherd named Lydia did just that when her owners, Richard and Kathy Markman of Dallas, Texas, decided to leave her alone at home for a long weekend. "We had a friend come by every day to feed Lydia, and we left her out in the backyard with her doghouse, thinking she would be safe there," says Richard. "Instead, she somehow managed to get out of the yard, probably by jumping the fence, and was found wandering around several miles from our home. It's a good thing she was wearing ID tags, or we never would have gotten her back."

Finding a Good Kennel   Before leaving your dog behind when you go on a trip, you must make sure he will be staying at the best boarding kennel you can afford. Finding a good kennel requires some research on your part.

The best way to locate a good boarding kennel in your area is to ask other

Did You Know?

Forty percent of dog and cat owners carry pictures of their pets in their wallets.

dog owners for referrals. Check with your friends and neighbors to find out which facility they use and why they like it. Once you've obtained one or two kennel names, contact your local Better Business Bureau to make certain no complaints have been lodged against the facilities.

Before you leave your dog at any boarding kennel, visit the facility. Ask for a tour of the kennel. Check to ensure the runs look and smell clean, and are secure and well maintained. The kennel fences should be high enough so your German Shepherd can't climb or jump out. A visual barrier should exist between each run to prevent your dog from having face-to-face contact with the dog next door. Make sure the runs are well constructed and in good condition.

Key Questions to Ask   When you visit the kennel, ask questions about the kind of care the facility offers. Do not even consider leaving your Shepherd at a boarding kennel that can't guarantee someone who is trained to recognize illness in dogs will check your pet several times each day. If you can, hold out for a kennel that provides 24-hour supervision.

Ask the kennel staff how and when dogs are fed and watered at the facility. Your dog should have fresh water available at all times. You should also have the option of bringing your dog's usual food when you board him, which the staff will then feed to him instead of whatever food the kennel feeds on its own. Suddenly changing your dog's diet can wreak havoc with his digestive system. The manager at a good kennel will know this and will allow owners to provide food for their dogs.

Find out as much as you can about kennel policies. Determine whether a veterinarian is on call 24 hours a day who can tend to your dog should he become ill while being boarded. Also ask if the boarding kennel has more than one facility in the area. Some kennels will transport your dog to another location if they find themselves running out of room at busy times of the year. You should know this in advance, because you may not want your dog moved from one facility to another.

Finally, the boarding kennel should require that your dog be immunized against distemper, rabies, parvovirus, parainfluenza, and tracheobronchitis before they allow the animal to board. If the kennel does not require any or all of these immunizations, do not board your dog there. If you do, your pet may be exposed to sick animals.

Hiring a Pet Sitter

If you can't take your German Shepherd with you when you travel away from home, the best thing to do is leave him at a reputable boarding kennel. However, if you're going away for only the day and would rather not board your pet, consider getting a pet sitter to come in your home to take care of your dog during your absence. Most experts do not recommend leaving a dog home alone for any extended period of time, so a housesitter who will stay overnight in your home and care for your dog is the best option, if you'll be gone overnight. But for times when you will be gone all day long and need someone to care for your dog during that time, a professional pet sitter is a great idea.

A professional pet sitter will come to your home and take care of your dog while you are away. That means he or she will feed and water your dog, walk him, give him any medications he may require, and even brush him, if you so desire.

To find a reputable pet sitter, try to get a referral from another dog owner or from your veterinarian. If you are unable to get the name of a pet sitter in your area from either of these sources, contact Pet Sitters International (listed in Appendix A) for a listing of pet sitters near you.

Before you hire any pet sitter, ask the individual some important questions. Find out how much the person charges to care for a large dog. Ask how many times a day the pet sitter will come to see your dog, at what times of the day he or she will come, and what services are available. For example, in addition to feeding and walking, will the pet sitter play with your dog or groom him? How much extra will he or she charge for these additional services?

Ask the pet sitter for several references and call each of these people to find out whether they were happy with the pet sitter's work. Ask if the pet sitter is responsible, if the pet sitter took good care of the animals in question, and if they would recommend this pet sitter to others.

Most professional pet sitters are bonded and will ask you to sign an agreement for the services that they will render. The agreement also may include a liability waiver that holds the pet sitter free from certain responsibilities if anything should happen to your pet or your home while the pet sitter is in charge. Read any agreement carefully before you sign it and make sure you have no problem with the stipulations the pet sitter has put forth.

Similar to the pet sitter is the dog walker, a person whose job is to come to your home and take your dog out on a walk while you are away. Dog walkers do not feed or perform other services—they simply take dogs out on walks. This is an excellent option for dog owners who will be home to feed and water their pets in the morning and night, but won't be around in the middle of the day to take their dogs out for bathroom breaks and exercise.

Finding a dog walker is a lot like finding a pet sitter. Since this person will have the keys to your house and will be responsible for caring for your dog, you should do your homework before choosing this individual. Ask your veterinarian and other dog owners for the names of dog walkers in your area and make sure to get—and call—references from the dog walkers you are considering. Ask the dog walkers you interview questions about how much they charge, what time of the day they plan to walk your dog, the length of time they will walk your pet, and where they intend to take the dog during walks.

Many dog walkers walk more than one dog at a time, which can also give your dog a chance to interact with other canines. If the dog walker you choose takes more than one dog on a walk, find out if the dog walker requires that dogs be immunized against common canine illnesses. If he or she doesn't require immunizations, or if you'd simply prefer that he or she walk your dog alone, you will need to specify this to the dog walker. You may be asked to pay extra for this individual service.

> Doggy day care centers are springing up all over the country and are designed to give dogs the social interaction and exercise they need while their owners are away for the day.

Other Services

If you are only going to be gone from your home for one day, an alternative to hiring a pet sitter is day care. Doggy day care centers are springing up all over the country and are designed to give dogs the social interaction and exercise they need while their owners are away for the day.

Doggy day care works like this: You drop off your German Shepherd in the morning before you leave for the day. The center will feed and water your dog, and he will get the opportunity to play with other dogs, go on walks, and do other activities during the day while you are away. At the end of the day, you pick up your dog and take him home—it's that simple.

You can find a doggy day care center in your area by asking your veterinarian or other dog owners. You can also try looking in the telephone book under "dogs."

Before you leave your dog at a doggy day care center, find out exactly what services the center offers. Also, determine whether a veterinarian is on call during the hours your dog will be there and how many other dogs will be cared for on the day of your dog's visit. Make sure they require proof of immunization for all dogs and screen dogs for good temperament before allowing them to interact with other animals. The management should also have a policy of putting only compatible dogs together in day care groups.

Take a trip to the facility and observe the workers and how they interact with their canine clients. Make sure the facility is clean, professional, and staffed with people who understand dogs. Check the play areas to make sure they are secure enough to keep dogs from getting loose or being stolen.

Finally, ask the day care center for the names of clients you can contact. Call these references and ask them questions about the kind of care their dogs received. Ask them whether they recommend you send your dog to this particular facility—and heed their advice.

9

A Lifetime of Love and Good Health

In This Chapter

○ Your Aging German Shepherd—What to Expect
○ How to Keep Your Older Dog Comfortable
○ Saying Goodbye

When you own a dog, the years seem to fly by in the blink of an eye. One day, your little German Shepherd puppy is running around the house, playing with her toys and eliciting laughter from everyone in the family; then, in a seemingly short time, you realize your dog has grown old. You notice she is showing the signs of age and even beginning to look and act like a senior citizen.

Your Aging German Shepherd— What to Expect

When your German Shepherd reaches her golden years, she will develop special needs. She will no longer be able to keep up with the kids as they run and play in your yard. It will take her longer to stand up in the morning, and she may need more frequent bathroom breaks than ever before.

Your German Shepherd has provided you with years of loyalty and companionship. The senior years of your dog's life are your opportunity to repay all that love and devotion she has given you. By tending to your aging dog's special needs, you can make life easier and more comfortable for your senior canine.

> The senior years of your dog's life are your opportunity to repay all that love and devotion she has given you.

Almost everyone is familiar with the affects of old age on human beings. People who have reached their senior years usually tend to move a little slower than they did in their youth. They sometimes are less quick to react to things as they once were. And a host of physical problems may plague them.

Dogs experience very similar effects of aging. A German Shepherd who once romped tirelessly becomes reluctant to play. She'll likely get out of the way more slowly and may even develop a few health problems that weren't there in her youth.

You may see various signs of old age in your German Shepherd once she starts moving up in years. These problems may include the following:

○ **Arthritis.** As your dog ages, her joints will start to lose their lubrication and become inflamed, causing pain and stiffness. A condition called degenerative joint disease, or osteoarthritis, is by far the most common form of arthritis affecting aging dogs.

You can tell that your German Shepherd suffers from arthritis if you see her getting up and lying down a lot more slowly than she did in the past. She also will walk with stiffness in her legs that you never noticed when she was younger. She will do a lot less running around than she did in the past, and if the condition is severe, she won't even be able to walk up stairs or jump into the car like she once did. (A diagnosis of arthritis—or any other ailment that can cause these symptoms—must be made by your veterinarian.)

○ **Slowing Down.** Older dogs have a lot less energy than they did when they were young, which you can readily detect by the activities they choose to participate in. When young, your German Shepherd may have greeted a new dog in the neighborhood with extreme excitement, complete with barking and all kinds of animated greeting behaviors. Your older dog, on the other hand, will most likely react with a lot less physical activity, choosing instead to nonchalantly gaze in the newcomer's direction and to simply sniff and wag her tail when the two meet.

This was the change that Mike Laslow of Boise, Idaho, saw in his German Shepherd, Casey. "In his youth, Casey considered himself the master of the block," says Mike. "He would bark and carry on whenever he saw a strange dog in the neighborhood. But now that he is older, it seems as if he could care less. It's almost like it's not worth the effort." If your German Shepherd seems to slow down very suddenly and show no interest in anything, she may have more than just normal age-related slow-down. Take her to a vet for a checkup.

○ **Personality Changes.** Because your older dog won't feel as energetic and athletic as she did in her youth, she may lose her desire to play, run, and perform other activities that require physical exertion. She also may become a bit of a grouch in her old age and less tolerant of playing children, rambunctious puppies, and other things that never bothered her when she was young. Some older dogs even go so far as to growl and threaten to bite anyone who disturbs them while they're resting or trying to eat. If the personality change goes that far, discuss the problem with a veterinarian, since the change could be the result of a medical condition. If your dog checks out healthy, consult a trainer for help.

Older dogs sometimes become anxious when they are left home alone, despite the fact that they may have been okay with staying on their own in their youth. This newfound anxiety probably results from the dog's feelings of vulnerability. Older dogs often don't feel as confident as they did in their youth, which leads to separation anxiety when they are left alone by their human family.

○ **Bathroom Breaks.** In most cases, older dogs need more frequent bathroom breaks, because the muscles surrounding their bladders and bowels become weaker, making them unable to hold urine and feces for extended periods of time. When some dogs get older, they become completely incontinent, which means they are unable to hold their urine and bowel movements at all.

○ **Assorted Ailments.** Older dogs are prone to a number of maladies that are related to the body's weakening and aging process. Among the most common of these problems are kidney disease, heart problems, digestive difficulties, and cataracts. (Health problems of aging dogs are discussed in Chapter 5, Common Health Concerns.) Your dog's veterinarian can help you manage these conditions.

○ **Loss of Senses.** Old age brings with it a reduction in the senses for many dogs, particularly hearing and sight. Old dogs often become increasingly deaf as times goes on and sometimes lose their sight partially or completely. A common cause of blindness in dogs is cataracts. Another common condition of aging canine eyes called nuclear sclerosis, a hardening of the lens protein, makes the dog's eye appear cloudy. Unlike with cataracts, dogs with nuclear sclerosis can still see.

○ **Bad Breath.** Older dogs tend to develop bad breath, usually in large part because their teeth have not been well cared for throughout their life. Without regular brushing and periodic deep cleaning by a veterinarian, plaque can build up to dangerous levels in a canine's mouth by the time the dog reaches old age. Other things that can cause bad breath in older dogs include dental problems, such as abscesses and infected gums, as well as kidney failure and diabetes. Don't just live with your older dog's bad breath—take her to a veterinarian to determine the cause of the problem.

○ **Weight Gain.** Just as with aging humans, dogs who are getting up in years tend to put on weight. In the case of both dogs and humans, this weight gain results from slowing metabolisms. You should help your dog combat this effect of aging, because excess weight can reduce your dog's life span and make getting around uncomfortable for her.

○ **Graying Muzzle.** When humans age, their hair turns gray. When German Shepherds get old, their muzzles become peppered with white hairs. This phenomenon doesn't happen only to German

Shepherds, of course. You've no doubt seen black Labrador Retrievers and other darkly colored dogs with salt-and-pepper muzzles. A graying muzzle is a classic sign of old age in a dog.

How to Keep Your Older Dog Comfortable

Because old age can challenge your German Shepherd, you undoubtedly will want to help your dog get through this time in her life with minimal discomfort. You can do plenty to keep your pet as happy and well off as possible.

The nature of your older dog's problems will determine the course of action you should take to make her life easier. Keeping a close eye on your aging pet and understanding the variety of things that plague older Shepherds will enable you to give her the kind of support she needs to live as long and as enjoyable a life as possible.

Although certain physical problems inevitably come as your dog grows older, that does not mean your pet must suffer helplessly with whatever difficulties nature deals her. Advances in veterinary medicine in the area of geriatric medicine make it possible to successfully treat many of the conditions commonly associated with canine old age.

As your German Shepherd's owner, it's important to develop a partnership with your veterinarian. You should watch for changes that may signal serious disease such as increased or decreased thirst, a change in bladder or bowel movements, increased or decreased appetite, grumpiness, or depression.

Lifestyle Changes

One of the kindest things you can do for your older dog is to make her life easier and less stressful. Exactly what that will entail depends on your dog, the kinds of problems she encounters late in her life, and your lifestyle.

You can start out by taking your dog to the veterinarian for checkups more frequently than you did when she was younger. Instead of having her checked over once a year, take her every six months. This will help your veterinarian spot any problems that are brewing before they get too out of hand—and before your dog starts to experience discomfort.

Arthritic Dogs

If your older German Shepherd starts showing signs of stiffness and pain when she walks, talk to your veterinarian about this problem. In recent years, veterinarians have gained access to a number of new medications that can help older dogs to deal with arthritis. These drugs seem to slow down the degeneration that comes with arthritis and to reduce the pain, making it easier for your dog to get around.

Since dogs with arthritis tend to become stiff when they don't move around for a period of time, create a regular exercise regimen for your dog. Most arthritic dogs benefit from a half-hour walk on soft ground twice a day, which also helps keep them fit and mentally stimulated. (Before you begin any exercise program for an older dog, discuss it with your veterinarian to make sure you are not asking your dog to do more than she is able.)

Arthritic dogs also appreciate a soft, warm bed to sleep in. Buy your dog an orthopedic dog bed, available in pet supply stores. This will help cushion her joints and help her awaken

> One of the kindest things you can do for your older dog is to make her life easier and less stressful.

from her naps less stiff and sore. Keep the bed in an area of your home that stays warm in cold weather and is free of drafts, because cold temperatures can aggravate the symptoms of arthritis.

Impaired Sight

If you believe your older dog may not see as well as she used to, take her to the veterinarian for an eye exam. If it turns out your dog is losing her sight and the condition is not curable, you can help her out in a number of ways. First, avoid any temptations to rearrange your furniture. Dogs are good at coping with blindness, provided they are kept in familiar surroundings. Your dog will learn the exact location of the coffee table, the couch, and the end table. She will learn to walk around objects that she cannot see, simply because she knows they are there. If you move things around or one day leave a big box in the middle of the living room in the area where she normally walks, it will likely confuse your dog and make her start running into things. Keep her familiar surroundings as unaltered as you possibly can.

If you must rearrange the furniture in your house, put your dog on a leash, and lead her around slowly so she can learn where things are now being kept. Help guide her around objects while still allowing her to realize that things have changed.

Once your Shepherd's sight wanes, certain areas in your home might prove to be dangerous to your dog. For example, the top of a stairway can create a hazard for a dog who cannot see. Likewise, an open trap door leading to a basement also can be extremely dangerous if your dog can't see it is open. You can protect your dog from such perils by being aware of them and by putting up baby gates to keep her from stepping some place where she shouldn't.

You should help your blind dog in and out of the car when you take her on trips. If your German Shepherd can't see, she is likely to step out of the car without realizing how high up she is. Carefully guide her out of the vehicle so she doesn't get hurt.

Dogs who have lost their sight still need exercise and mental stimulation. Take your dog on walks and on outings with you, so she continues to feel like part of the family. The sounds and smells your dog encounters while out in the world will help keep your pet interested in what is going on around her. Just remember to keep a close watch on your dog, if she is unable to see hazards coming. Don't allow strangers to pet her or to approach her with other dogs, because these types of situations could unnerve her and cause her to behave aggressively in self-defense.

You will interact with your sightless dog differently than you did when her eyes worked properly. Since your dog can't see you coming, always speak to her before you begin to approach, especially if you sense she really has no idea you are there. You also will need to help your dog to rely more heavily on her other senses. With your help, your German Shepherd can learn to locate objects using her senses of smell and hearing. Call her to her food bowl at dinnertime (she won't see you are about to put it down). Let her know the back door is open for her to go out. Place her toys close to her nose at playtime, so she can smell them.

Impaired Hearing

Many older dogs gradually lose their hearing, just as elderly humans tend to

> ## Did You Know?
> The old rule of multiplying a dog's age by seven to find the equivalent human age is inaccurate. A better measure is to count the first year as 15, the second year as 10, and each year after that as 5.

do. Hearing loss in a dog is not a terrible handicap, because dogs seem to use hearing the least of all their senses; the senses of sight and smell are far more important to dogs. However, hearing loss can present a problem for older dogs in that it makes it more difficult for their owners to communicate with them. Deaf dogs are easily startled as well and can react unpredictably when this occurs.

If you suspect your older dog may be losing her hearing, you can do a simple test to determine whether her ears are not what they used to be. Stand behind your German Shepherd and wait until her attention is focused on something other than you. Speak your dog's name or say "cookie" or some other word that usually gets her attention quickly. Pay heed to whether your dog's ears move backward in response to your word. If you see no ear movement, your dog may have hearing loss.

If the results of this simple at-home test indicate your Shepherd is having trouble hearing, take her to the veterinarian for an examination. Your vet can help you determine whether the dog is deaf or going deaf, and will let you know if you can do anything to help her. If nothing can be done to restore or improve your pet's hearing, you will need to adjust the way you interact with your dog to accommodate her hearing impairment.

When your German Shepherd was young, you taught her to respond to verbal commands, like "sit," "down," and "stay." When your dog can no longer hear your commands, you'll have to teach her a sign language version of these edicts.

You can teach your dog sign language using methods similar to those you originally employed in training her to obey basic obedience commands. (Obedience training is discussed further in Chapter 6, Basic Training for German Shepherds.) First, develop hand signals for four basic commands: sit, stay, down, and come. You can represent "sit" with a sweeping arc of your hand, for example. "Stay" should be a flat palm held up in front of the dog's nose, and "down" should be a flat palm pressing toward the ground. "Come" can consist of the traditional motion to come toward you that you would use for a person who is out of earshot. Choose distinct signals that you are comfortable with, because these gestures must remain the same throughout your dog's training.

Because your dog already knows the basic commands and just needs to learn to associate the act of performing the command with the hand signal, it should be easy to teach her this new form of communication. Use treats to get her to perform each of the commands, as you did early on in her training. However, this time use your hand signals, rather than the verbal commands, in conjunction with her actions. Your German Shepherd will catch on in no time.

A disadvantage to living with a deaf dog is that the animal cannot hear you coming. If your dog is asleep and you approach her, she may not know you are there until you are right on top of her. At that point, your close presence—or the presence of a child or a stranger—may startle your Shepherd and cause her to react with fear and possibly with aggression. That is why it is important to alert your dog of your presence. As you approach your dog while she is sleeping or doesn't see you, stop and stamp your feet on the floor so the dog will feel the vibrations. You can also try using a very high pitched whistle, since many older dogs don't completely lose their hearing and remain sensitive to certain pitches.

Weight Gain

As your dog ages, her metabolism starts to slow down. At the same time, her energy level decreases, and she becomes less active. The result of this reality is that your older dog may start to gain weight. Although some older dogs actually become thinner as they reach their senior years, the majority of older dogs tend to gain weight.

An overweight dog is an unhealthy dog, and this is particularly true for the older canine. The internal organs of aging dogs often function less efficiently than they once did, and the added strain of excess weight on the body can drastically shorten the life of dogs whose hearts and other organs are no longer at their peak. Excess weight can also make it harder for your older dog to get around with arthritic joints and weakening muscles.

If you have noticed that your older dog is starting to gain weight, don't wait until she is obese before you take action. First, try weighing her once a week for a period of a month or so. If this confirms your suspicions and your dog is indeed putting on the pounds, contact your veterinarian and explain your concerns. Your vet may recommend that you decrease the amount of food your dog is eating in order to help her lose weight. The vet also or instead may suggest that you switch your dog to a lower-calorie food. If your dog is dangerously overweight, your vet may recommend that you temporarily place your Shepherd on a prescription food designed to help dogs shed pounds. Once your dog gets down to the desired weight, your vet will then suggest that you switch to a moderate-calorie maintenance diet.

If you want to head off possible weight gain in your older dog before it happens, consider switching her to a special "senior diet," available in many premium dog food brands, once she gets to be around six or seven years old.

Be aware that a sudden weight gain around the belly could indicate heart failure or liver disease. If your dog suddenly develops a pot belly, contact your veterinarian right away.

If you want to head off possible weight gain in your older dog before it happens, consider switching her to a special "senior diet," available in many premium dog food brands, once she gets to be around six or seven years old. These types of foods are usually lower in fat and calories and higher in fiber than regular dog foods. (If your dog has a health problem like kidney disease or diabetes, first check with your veterinarian before switching to a senior food.)

Another way to help your older dog from putting on weight is to give her adequate exercise on a daily basis. Talk to your veterinarian to determine what is the best amount of exercise for your particular German Shepherd. Her exercise regimen will depend on her age and general health.

Temperament Changes

Many people notice that their older dogs are not quite as energetic and agreeable as they once were. Dogs who once couldn't wait to play avoid activities that would have been nearly impossible to keep them from in their youth.

"When he was young, Roger loved to play with kids," says Ron Johnson of Santa Ana, California. "The children would play in our yard, and Roger was always in the middle of everything, bounding around and wanting to get in on the fun. Now that he is older, though, when kids come over, he just lies there and is content to watch them from afar. All his interest in playing with them seems to have vanished."

Did You Know?

The oldest dog ever documented was an Australian cattle dog named Bluey, who was put to sleep at the age of 29 years and 5 months.

Seeing your once exuberant German Shepherd become more of an observer than a participant can make you feel sad. Many dog owners tend to interpret this behavior as a decreased interest in life and worry that their dogs seem to be "checking out." However, although your German Shepherd may no longer want to chase butterflies, that doesn't mean that she is losing interest in the world around her. Rather, it means she has matured and now looks at life through wiser, more dignified eyes.

To help your older dog continue to enjoy life from her new perspective, continue to provide her with new experiences that she will find pleasant. Take her out for daily walks and on trips to the beach or park. Give your aging Shepherd short training sessions, teaching her new commands or even tricks you may have seen your friends' dogs perform. Don't assume your old dog isn't still able to learn new tricks. At the very least, she will truly appreciate the time you are spending with her.

Conversely, don't ask your older dog to put up with situations that he obviously finds unpleasant. If you are having guests for dinner who include one or two small children, put your German Shepherd in her crate or confine her to another part of the house. Don't subject your pet to the antics of small children at her age, especially kids who haven't been taught how to behave around dogs.

Some dog owners think that adding a puppy to the household is a good idea, because it will help breathe new life into an older dog. The reality, however, is that the puppy will most likely pester your geriatric canine, leaving your older dog wishing she was anywhere but in the same house with the rambunctious youngster. Also, it forces your older dog to adjust to life with a newcomer around and to getting by with less attention from you, since the puppy will take up much of your time. If your dog is getting up there in years and seems to be noticeably slowing down, think long and hard about how she will react to having a puppy around the house.

Puppies can be particularly stressful for an older dog to cope with, but just about any big change in the dog's household or routine can cause her suffering. Any situation that causes a disruption in your German Shepherd's life—moving around the furniture, changing your work schedule, moving someone new into the house—makes things that much harder for her. Before you make changes in your situation, first give your older dog some thought. Don't make changes just for the sake of them. Stick to only those modifications that are necessary, because they will affect your dog.

Although personality changes are natural for a German Shepherd who is growing older, take care not to assume that old age is the cause of any sudden lethargy or depression on your dog's part. Normal age-related changes in your pet's personality will be subtle, appearing gradually over time. If your German Shepherd suddenly becomes reluctant to move or eat, or doesn't respond to you the way he normally does, contact your veterinarian immediately.

Bathroom Habits

Older dogs often have trouble holding their urine and feces as well as they did when they were younger. The reason for this is that the muscles in this area of the dog's body just aren't as strong as they used to be. Sometimes, the muscles become so weak that the dog is completely incontinent, meaning she can't hold her feces or urine at all.

If your older dog starts asking to go outside a lot more frequently than she used to or to have accidents in the house when

How to Remove Stains and Odors

Living with an older dog around the house can sometimes mean having to cleanup accidents on the carpet. Although medication can help many older dogs who are suffering from incontinence, one of the realities of owning an older dog is that mistakes will occasionally happen around the house.

You should cleanup your dog's accidents as quickly and as thoroughly as possible. Not only do you want to get rid of any evidence of the event left in your carpet, but you also want to eliminate even the faintest odor. A lingering scent from a previous accident will encourage your dog to go to the bathroom in this same spot again.

You can take one of two approaches to cleaning up an area where your dog has made a mess. You can go to a pet supply store and purchase one of several products on the market designed specifically for the very purpose of cleaning up such accidents. These products are meant to remove stains and to eliminate any trace of odor that might entice your dog into a repeat offense.

If you prefer to try a home remedy for the problem, mix two tablespoons of white vinegar and three tablespoons of mild dishwashing soap in a quart-sized container of warm water. Mix it well and apply it to the soiled carpet with a sprayer bottle. Wait a few minutes and then blot the area with a towel or with paper towels or napkins.

Whatever you do, resist cleaning up messes on the floor with ammonia-based cleaners. The ammonia in these products can smell like urine to your dog and invite her to again use that spot.

you aren't home, she is probably having trouble holding her urine and feces. If the problem occurs only occasionally, you can make your dog's life more comfortable by simply giving her more opportunities to go to the bathroom. Let her out or take her on walks every few hours, instead of only a few times during the day. If this solves the problem, then you can be relatively certain your dog simply needed an increase in the number of potty breaks she gets per day. You should also contact your veterinarian, because incontinence that is the result of lost muscle tone can often be treated with medication.

If your dog's inability to hold her waste seems more severe—that is, she can't seem to hold it for even a couple of hours—she may be experiencing an incontinence problem with a distinct medical cause, such as a bladder infection or other disease. Take your dog to the veterinarian for an examination to determine the exact cause of the incontinence.

If the problem turns out to be simply a result from old age and your dog is unable to hold her waste at all, consider giving her free access to your yard so she can take a potty break whenever she needs one. In situations where she messes on herself or on her bedding, make sure to clean the dog and soiled bedding right away to prevent skin irritation and disease.

Saying Goodbye

The hardest aspect to owning a German Shepherd is saying goodbye to her. By the time your dog reaches old age, you will have grown incredibly attached to her. She will have become a member of your family whom you can't even imagine living without. Yet, for most people, the reality is that they will outlive their German Shepherds and must endure the painful task of grieving for their dogs.

Euthanasia

One of the most difficult things about having a dog is having to make the decision to put the animal to sleep, or euthanize, as veterinarians refer to the procedure. Dog owners often find

themselves in this incredibly arduous situation, in which they must decide whether to let their pet go on suffering or instead choose a humane death for the animal.

Understanding what euthanasia is all about can assist you in trying to make this painful decision. Knowing how the procedure works and what the dog feels during the process can help you make this difficult choice more easily.

Basically, euthanasia is the process of injecting a large dose of barbiturates into a dog's bloodstream. The drug stops the functioning of the animal's brain, which in turn causes the dog to lose consciousness almost immediately after the injection. Respiration ceases, and the dog's heart stops beating.

This type of euthanasia is completely painless for the dog, and offers a calm and gentle way for the animal to die. The dog doesn't know what is happening to her. One minute she is conscious; the next minute she is not. She experiences no fear or sense of what is about to occur. Few decisions in life are as difficult as the one that determines whether your dog will die of her own accord or through euthanasia. Although dogs are fortunate in that they have us to make this decision for them and, thereby, to reduce their suffering considerably, we humans face the unfortunate responsibility of having to be the ones to decide if and when this humane death will take place.

Euthanasia often becomes a very real consideration for a pet when the animal becomes terminally ill and/or is suffering terribly. Most veterinarians present euthanasia as an option when the animal's prognosis is poor and the suffering is great.

Linda Eastley of Woodland Hills, California, went through this with her German Shepherd, Kiley. The dog was diagnosed with kidney failure at eight years of age. "Kiley had suddenly stopped eating, so I took him to the vet," she says. "The diagnosis was kidney failure. The vet recommended that we feed Kiley special food and do a few other things for him. This helped for a while, but soon Kiley wouldn't eat and was back in the vet's office. At that point, our vet said there wasn't much else we could do for Kiley. I realized then that the best thing for the dog was to put him down so he wouldn't suffer anymore."

Even though the decision to euthanize a dog may seem clear-cut, as in Kiley's case, it can still be a hard choice to make.

"I knew Kiley was going to die either way," says Linda. "Yet, it was really, really hard to give the vet the go-ahead to make it happen right then and there. In fact, it was probably the hardest decision I've ever had to make. But I did it, because I couldn't bear the idea that Kiley was going to suffer even more than he already had if I let him die on his own."

Sometimes, the situation is not as obvious as the one encountered by Linda. Sometimes a dog is plagued by an incurable condition that will not result in certain death, but will result in lifelong pain. For example, surgery may help a German Shepherd with severe hip dysplasia—or he may continue to have considerable difficulty getting around, even after getting veterinary help.

> Even though the decision to euthanize a dog may seem clear-cut, it can still be a hard choice to make.

Situations like these are the toughest of all for dog owners. Should you let your dog live out her life in obvious pain and misery? Or should you have her euthanized to end her suffering? Euthanasia may seem like the rational choice in these dire situations, yet actually making the decision to end your dog's life is not even close to being easy.

Under such circumstances, all you can do is think long and hard about your German Shepherd's quality of life—and to put yourself in your dog's place. If you would choose a quiet, peaceful death over a lifetime of suffering, then perhaps this is the choice you should make for your dog.

One thing that makes the decision to euthanize particularly hard is the owner's reluctance to let go. If you love your dog, you don't want to lose her, period. You want her to stay with you. You don't want her to die. These are natural feelings that all dog owners experience when trying to make this agonizing decision. However, it's important not to allow your own feelings to get in the way of your dog's well being. Although saying good-bye to your dog will be horribly painful for you, letting her suffer just to spare yourself this trauma simply isn't right.

When trying to determine whether euthanasia is the best choice for your dog, make sure to engage your veterinarian in the decision. A good vet will take the time to discuss the decision with you and will give you information that will help you put your dog's situation clearly in perspective. Your vet may even go so far as to recommend euthanasia, if further treatments are unavailable or impractical. Listen carefully to what your veterinarian has to say, letting him or her be a partner in your decision.

Your Dog's Remains

The owners of euthanized dogs have several options when it comes to dealing with their pet's remains. Burial on your own property is a possibility, if your municipality allows this and you have the room for a large dog. Alternately, you could opt to have your dog buried at a commercial pet cemetery for a fee.

Cremation provides another option after a pet's death. Most veterinary hospitals provide this service, and will return your pet's remains to you for safekeeping or burial or will dispose of them on their own. If you decide to cremate your dog and to keep or bury the ashes, tell the hospital staff that you want your pet cremated separately (rather than with other pets). This will cost you more money, but it ensures that the ashes you get back are those of your pet and your pet alone.

Grieving

People who have never before loved and lost a dog are often shocked at how devastated they feel when their pets die. They hadn't imagined in their wildest

> **M**any people who have lost pets say the level of their sadness matches feelings they've had when they've lost a beloved person.

dreams they could feel such grief over an animal. Many people who have lost pets say the level of their sadness matches feelings they've had when they've lost a beloved person. This does not diminish the value of the beloved person, but instead makes a dog owner realize just how much attachment he had to his dog.

Sometimes pet owners have trouble finding a sympathetic shoulder to cry on when they are grieving for an animal they love. Friends and relatives who don't have pets will often say things like, "Why are you so upset? It was just a dog!" or "Why don't you just go out and get another one?" Because they do not share your love of animals, they do not understand how devastating the loss of a pet can be.

Grieving pet owners do best when they limit their discussions of sadness over their pet's loss to friends and family members who can relate to what they are feeling. For those who can't find anyone sympathetic to talk to during these moments of sorrow, help is available. A number of veterinary schools around the country have set up grief counseling hotlines to help pet owners endure their losses. (A listing of these hotlines appears in Appendix A.)

The day will come when you will lose your German Shepherd, probably to old age. When that day arrives, remember that grief is a natural process. The pain is strong, but time heals the wound. Although you will never forget your beloved pet, eventually thoughts of her will change from waves of anguish to those of happiness in the knowledge you were fortunate enough to have shared the life of such a magnificent animal.

Appendix A: Resources

Boarding, Pet Sitting, Traveling

books
Dog Lover's Companion series
Guides on traveling with dogs for
    several states and cities
Foghorn Press
P.O. Box 2036, Santa Rosa, CA
    95405-0036
(800) FOGHORN

*Take Your Pet Too!: Fun Things
    to Do!*, Heather MacLean
    Walters
M.C.E. Publishing
 P.O. Box 84
Chester, NJ 07930-0084

Take Your Pet USA, Arthur Frank
Artco Publishing
12 Channel St.
Boston, MA 02210

*Traveling with Your Pet 1999:
    The AAA Petbook*, Greg
    Weeks, Editor
Guide to pet-friendly lodging in
    the U.S. and Canada

Vacationing With Your Pet!,
    Eileen Barish
Pet-Friendly Publications
P.O. Box 8459
Scottsdale, AZ 85252
(800) 496-2665

...other resources
The American Boarding Kennels
    Association
4575 Galley Road, Suite 400-A
Colorado Springs, CO 80915
(719) 591-1113
www.abka.com

Independent Pet and Animal
    Transportation Association
5521 Greenville Ave., Ste 104-310
Dallas, TX 75206
(903) 769-2267
www.ipata.com

National Association of Professional
  Pet Sitters
1200 G St. N.W., Suite 760
Washington, DC 20005
(800) 286-PETS
www.petsitters.org

Pet Sitters International
418 East King Street
King, NC 27021-9163
(336)-983-9222
www.petsit.com

Breed Information, Clubs, Registries

American Kennel Club
260 Madison Avenue
New York, NY 10016
(212) 696-8800
Customer Service (919) 233-9767
www.akc.org/

Canadian Kennel Club
Commerce Park
89 Skyway Ave., Suite 100
Etobicoke, Ontario, Canada M9W
  6R4
(416) 675-5511
www.ckc.ca/

German Shepherd Dog Club of
  America, Inc.
Corresponding Secretary, Eleanor A.
  Goede
P.O. Box 237
Monmouth, OR 97361
www.gsdca.org/

InfoPet
P.O. Box 716
Agoura Hills, CA 91376
(800) 858-0248

The Kennel Club
(British equivalent to the American
  Kennel Club)
1-5 Clarges Street
Piccadilly
London W1Y 8AB
ENGLAND
http://www.the-kennel-club.org.uk/

National Dog Registry
Box 116
Woodstock, NY 12498
(800) 637-3647
www.natldogregistry.com/

Tatoo-A-Pet
6571 S.W. 20th Court
Ft. Lauderdale, FL 33317
(800) 828-8667
www.tattoo-a-pet.com

United Kennel Club
100 East Kilgore Rd.
Kalamazoo, MI 49001-5598
(616) 343-9020
http://ukcdogs.com

Dog Publications

AKC Gazette and AKC Events Calendar
American Kennel Club
51 Madison Avenue
New York, NY 10010
Subscriptions: (919) 233-9767
www.akc.org/gazet.htm
www.akc.org/event.htm

Direct Book Service
(800) 776-2665
www2.dogandcatbooks.com/direct-book

Dog Fancy
P.O. Box 6050
Mission Viejo, CA 92690
(714) 855-8822
www.dogfancy.com/

Dog World
500 N. Dearborn, Suite 1100
Chicago, IL 60610
(312) 396-0600
www.dogworldmag.com/

Fun, Grooming, Obedience, and Training

American Dog Trainers Network
(212) 727-7257
www.inch.com/~dogs/index.html

American Grooming Shop Association
(719) 570-7788

American Kennel Club (tracking, agility, obedience, herding)
Performance Events Dept.
5580 Centerview Drive
Raleigh, NC 27606
(919) 854-0199
www.akc.org

Animal Behavior Society
Susan Foster
Department of Biology
Clark University
950 Main Street
Worcester, MA 01610-1477

Association of Pet Dog Trainers
P.O. Box 385
Davis, CA 95617
(800) PET-DOGS
www.apdt.com/

The Dog Agility Page
http://www.dogpatch.org/agility/

Intergroom
76 Carol Drive
Dedham, MA 02026
www.intergroom.com

National Association of Dog Obedience Instructors
729 Grapevine Highway, #369
Hurst, TX 76054-2085
http://www.nadoi.org/

National Dog Groomers Association
of America
P.O. Box 101
Clark, PA 16113
(724) 962-2711

North American Dog Agility Council
HCR 2 Box 277
St. Maries, ID 83861
www.nadac.com

North American Flyball Association
1400 W. Devon Ave, #512
Chicago, IL 60660
(309) 688-9840
http://muskie.fishnet.com/~flyball/

Grooming supplies
Pet Warehouse
P.O. Box 752138
Dayton, OH 45475-2138
(800) 443-1160

United States Canine Combined
Training Association
2755 Old Thompson Mill Road
Buford, GA 30519
(770) 932-8604
http://www.siriusweb.com/USCCTA/

United States Dog Agility Association, Inc.
P.O. Box 850955
Richardson, Texas 75085-0955
(972) 231-9700
www.usdaa.com/

Grief Hotlines

Chicago Veterinary Medical Association
(630) 603-3994

Cornell University
(607) 253-3932

Michigan State University
College of Veterinary Medicine
(517) 432-2696

Tufts University (Massachusetts)
School of Veterinary Medicine
(508) 839-7966

University of California, Davis
(530) 752-4200

University of Florida at Gainesville
College of Veterinary Medicine
(352) 392- 4700

Virginia-Maryland Regional College
of Veterinary Medicine
(540) 231-8038

Washington State University
College of Veterinary Medicine
(509) 335-5704

Humane Organizations and Rescue Groups

American Humane Association
63 Inverness Drive E
Englewood CO   80112-5117
(800) 227-4645
www.americanhumane.org

American Society for the Prevention
    of Cruelty to Animals (ASPCA)
424 East 92nd Street
New York, NY 10128-6804
(212) 876-7700
www.aspca.org

Animal Protection Institute of Amer-
    ica
P.O. Box 22505
Sacramento, CA 95822
(916) 731-5521

Humane Society of the United States
2100 L Street, NW
Washington, DC 20037
(301) 258-3072, (202) 452-1100
www.hsus.org/

Massachusetts Society for the Pre-
    vention of Cruelty to Animals
350 South Huntington Avenue
Boston, MA 02130
(617) 522-7400
http://www.mspca.org/

SPAY/USA
14 Vanderventer Avenue
Port Washington, NY 11050
(516) 944-5025, (203) 377-1116 in
    Connecticut
(800) 248-SPAY
www.spayusa.org/

Medical and Emergency Information

American Animal Hospital Associa-
    tion
P.O. Box 150899
Denver, CO 80215-0899
(800) 252-2242
www.healthypet.com

American Holistic Veterinary Medi-
    cine Association
2214 Old Emmorton Road
Bel Air, MD 21015
(410) 569-2346

American Kennel Club Canine
    Health Foundation
251 West Garfield Road, Suite 160
Aurora, OH 44202
(888) 682-9696
www.akcchf.org/main.htm

American Veterinary Medical Association
1931 North Meacham Road, Suite 100
Schaumburg, IL 60173-4360
(847) 925-8070
http://www.avma.org/

Canine Eye Registration Foundation
   (CERF)
Veterinary Medical Data Program
South Campus Courts, Building C
Purdue University
West Lafayette, IN 47907
(765) 494-8179
www.vet.purdue.edu/~yshen/cerf.html

Centers for Disease Control and Prevention
1600 Clifton Road NE
Atlanta, GA 30333
(404) 639-3311 (CEC Operator)
(800) 311-3435 (CEC Public Inquiries)
www.cdc.gov

Complementary and Alternative Veterinary Medicine
www.altvetmed.com

Infectious Diseases of the Dog and Cat,
   Craig E. Greene, Editor
W B Saunders Company

National Animal Poison Control Center
1717 S. Philo, Suite 36
Urbana, IL 61802
(888) 426 4435, $45 per case, with as
   many follow-up calls as necessary included. Have name, address, phone
   number, dog's breed, age, sex, and
   type of poison ingested, if known,
   available
www.napcc.aspca.org

Orthopedic Foundation for Animals
   (OFA)
2300 E. Nifong Blvd.
Columbia, MO 65201-3856
(573) 442-0418
www.offa.org/

PennHIP
c/o Synbiotics
11011 Via Frontera
San Diego, CA 92127
(800) 228-4305

Pet First Aid: Cats and Dogs, by Bobbi
   Mammato, D.V.M.
Mosby Year Book

*Skin Diseases of Dogs and Cats: A Guide
   for Pet Owners and Professionals,* Dr.
   Steven A. Melman
Dermapet, Inc.
P.O. Box 59713
Potomac, MD 20859

U.S. Pharmacopeia
vaccine reactions: (800) 487-7776
customer service: (800) 487-7776
www.usp.org

Veterinary Medical Database/
    Canine Eye Registration Foun-
    dation
Department of Veterinary Clinical
    Science
School of Veterinary Medicine
Purdue University
West Lafayette, IN 47907
(765) 494-8179
http://www.vet.purdue.edu/~yshen/

Veterinary Pet Insurance (VPI)
4175 E. La Palma Ave., #100
Anaheim, CA 92807-1846
(714) 996-2311
www.petplan.net/

Nutrition and Natural Foods

California Natural, Natural Pet Prod-
    ucts
P.O. Box 271
Santa Clara, CA 95052
(800) 532-7261
www.naturapet.com

Home Prepared Dog and Cat Diets,
    Donald R. Strombeck
Iowa State University Press
(515) 292-0140

PHD Products Inc.
P.O. Box 8313
White Plains, NY 10602
(800) 863-3403
www.phdproducts.net/

Sensible Choice, Pet Products Plus
5600 Mexico Road
St. Peters, MO 63376
(800) 592-6687
www.sensiblechoice.com/

Search and Rescue Dogs

National Association for Search and
    Rescue
4500 Southgate Place, Suite 100
Chantilly, VA 20151-1714
(703) 622-6283
http://www.nasar.org/

National Disaster Search Dog Foun-
    dation
323 East Matilija Avenue, #110-245
Ojai, CA 93023-2740
http://www.west.net/~rescue/

Service and Working Dogs

Canine Companions for Indepen-
    dence
P.O. Box 446
Santa Rosa, CA 95402-0446
(800) 572-2275
http://www.caninecompanions.org/

Delta Society National Service Dog
Center
289 Perimeter Road East
Renton, WA 98055-1329
(800) 869-6898
http://petsforum.com/deltasociety/ds
b000.htm

Guiding Eyes for the Blind
611 Granite Springs Road
Yorktown Heights, NY 10598
http://www.guiding-eyes.org/

The National Education for Assistance Dog Services, Inc.
P.O. Box 213
West Boylston, MA 01583
(508) 422-9064
http://chamber.worcester.ma.us/nead
s/INDEX.HTM

North American Working Dog Asso-
ciation
Southeast Kreisgruppe
P.O. Box 833
Brunswick, GA 31521

The Seeing Eye
P.O. Box 375
Morristown, NJ 07963-0375
(973) 539-4425
http://www.seeingeye.org/

Therapy Dogs Incorporated
2416 E. Fox Farm Road
Cheyenne, WY 82007
(877) 843-7364
www.therapydogs.com

Therapy Dogs International
6 Hilltop Road
Mendham, NJ 07945
(973) 252-9800
http://www.tdi-dog.org/

Appendix B:
Official Standard for the German Shepherd Dog

General Appearance

The first impression of a good German Shepherd Dog is that of a strong, agile, well muscled animal, alert and full of life. It is well balanced, with harmonious development of the forequarter and hindquarter. The dog is longer than tall, deep-bodied, and presents an outline of smooth curves rather than angles. It looks substantial and not spindly, giving the impression, both at rest and in motion, of muscular fitness and nimbleness without any look of clumsiness or soft living. The ideal dog is stamped with a look of quality and nobility difficult to define, but unmistakable when present. Secondary sex characteristics are strongly marked, and every animal gives a definite impression of masculinity or femininity, according to its sex.

Temperament

The breed has a distinct personality marked by direct and fearless, but not hostile, expression, self-confidence and a certain aloofness that does not lend itself to immediate and indiscriminate friendships. The dog must be approachable, quietly standing its ground and showing confidence and willingness to meet overtures without itself making them.

It is poised, but when the occasion demands, eager and alert; both fit and willing to serve in its capacity as companion, watchdog, blind leader, herding dog, or guardian, whichever the circumstances may demand. The dog must not be timid, shrinking behind its master or handler; it should not be nervous, looking about or upward with anxious expression or showing nervous reactions, such as tucking of tail, to strange sounds or sights. Lack of confidence under any surroundings is not typical of good character. Any of the above deficiencies in character which indicate shyness must be penalized as very **serious faults** and any dog exhibiting pronounced indications of these must be excused from the ring. It must be possible for the judge to observe the teeth and to determine that both testicles are descended. Any dog that attempts to bite the judge must be **disqualified.** The ideal dog is a working animal with an incorruptible character combined with body and gait suitable for the arduous work that constitutes its primary purpose.

Size, Proportion, Substance

The desired **height** for males at the top of the highest point of the shoulder blade is 24 to 26 inches; and for bitches, 22 to 24 inches.

The German Shepherd Dog is longer than tall, with the most desirable **proportion** as 10 to 8½. The length is measured from the point of the prosternum or breastbone to the rear edge of the pelvis, the ischial tuberosity. The desirable long proportion is not derived from a long back, but from overall length with relation to height, which is achieved by length of forequarter and length of withers and hindquarter, viewed from the side.

Head

The **head** is noble, cleanly chiseled, strong without coarseness, but above all not fine, and in proportion to the body. The head of the male is distinctly masculine, and that of the bitch distinctly feminine.

The **expression** keen, intelligent and composed. **Eyes** of medium size, almond shaped, set a little obliquely and not protruding. The color is as dark as possible. **Ears** are moderately pointed, in proportion to the skull, open toward the front, and carried erect when at attention, the ideal carriage being one in which the center lines of the ears, viewed from the front, are parallel to each other and perpendicular to the ground. A dog with cropped or hanging ears must be **disqualified.**

Seen from the front the forehead is only moderately arched, and the skull slopes into the long, wedge-shaped muzzle without abrupt stop. The **muzzle** is long and strong, and its topline is parallel to the topline of the skull. **Nose** black. A dog with a nose that is not predominantly black must be **disqualified.** The lips are firmly fitted. Jaws are strongly developed. **Teeth**—42 in number—20 upper and 22 lower—are strongly developed and meet in a scissors bite in which part of the inner surface of the upper incisors meet and engage part of the outer surface of the lower incisors. An overshot jaw or a level bite is undesirable. An undershot jaw is a **disqualifying fault.** Complete dentition is to be preferred. Any missing teeth other than first premolars is a **serious fault.**

Neck, Topline, Body

The **neck** is strong and muscular, clean-cut and relatively long, proportionate in size to the head and without loose folds of skin. When the dog is at attention or excited, the head is raised and the neck carried high; otherwise typical carriage of the head is forward rather than up and but little higher than the top of the shoulders, particularly in motion.

Topline—The **withers** are higher than and sloping into the level back. The **back** is straight, very strongly developed without sag or roach, and relatively short.

The whole structure of the **body** gives an impression of depth and solidity without bulkiness.

Chest—Commencing at the prosternum, it is well filled and carried well down between the legs. It is deep and capacious, never shallow, with ample room for lungs and heart, carried well forward, with the prosternum showing ahead of the shoulder in profile. **Ribs** well sprung and long, neither barrel-shaped nor too flat, and carried down to a sternum which reaches to the elbows. Correct ribbing allows the elbows to move back freely when the dog is at a trot. Too round causes interference and throws the elbows out; too flat or short causes pinched elbows. Ribbing is carried well back so that the loin is relatively short. **Abdomen** firmly held and not paunchy. The bottom line is only moderately tucked up in the loin.

Loin—Viewed from the top, broad and strong. Undue length between the last rib and the thigh, when viewed from the side, is undesirable. **Croup** long and gradually sloping. **Tail** bushy, with the last vertebra extended at least to the hock joint. It is set smoothly into the croup and low rather than high. At rest, the tail hangs in a slight curve like a saber. A slight hook- sometimes carried to one side-is faulty only to the extent that it mars general appearance. When the dog is excited or in motion, the curve is accentuated and the tail raised, but it should never be curled forward beyond a vertical line. Tails too short, or with clumpy ends due to ankylosis, are **serious faults**. A dog with a docked tail must be **disqualified.**

Forequarters

The shoulder blades are long and obliquely angled, laid on flat and not placed forward. The upper arm joins the shoulder blade at about a right angle. Both the upper arm and the shoulder blade are well muscled. The forelegs, viewed from all sides, are straight and the bone oval rather than round. The pasterns are strong and springy and angulated at approximately a 25-degree angle from the vertical. Dewclaws on the forelegs may be removed, but are normally left on. The feet are short, compact with toes well arched, pads thick and firm, nails short and dark.

Hindquarters

The whole assembly of the thigh, viewed from the side, is broad, with both upper and lower thigh well muscled, forming as nearly as possible a right angle. The upper thigh bone parallels the shoulder blade while the lower thigh bone parallels the upper arm. The metatarsus (the unit between the hock joint and the foot) is short, strong and tightly articulated. The dewclaws, if any, should be removed from the hind legs. Feet as in front.

Coat

The ideal dog has a double coat of medium length. The outer coat should be as dense as possible, hair straight, harsh and lying close to the body. A slightly wavy outer coat, often of wiry texture, is permissible. The head, including the inner ear and foreface, and the legs and paws are covered with short hair, and the neck with longer and thicker hair. The rear of the forelegs and hind legs has somewhat longer hair extending to the pastern and hock, respectively. **Faults** in coat include soft, silky, too long outer coat, woolly, curly, and open coat.

Color

The German Shepherd Dog varies in color, and most colors are permissible. Strong rich colors are preferred. Pale, washed-out colors and blues or livers are **serious faults.** A white dog must be **disqualified.**

Gait

A German Shepherd Dog is a trotting dog, and its structure has been developed to meet the requirements of its work. **General Impression**—The gait is outreaching, elastic, seemingly without effort, smooth and rhythmic, covering the maximum amount of ground with the minimum number of steps. At a walk it covers a great deal of ground, with long stride of both hind legs and forelegs. At a trot the dog covers still more ground with even longer stride, and moves powerfully but easily, with coordination and balance so that the gait appears to be the steady motion of a well-lubricated machine. The feet travel close to the ground on both forward reach and backward push. In order to achieve ideal movement of this kind, there must be good muscular development and ligamentation. The hindquarters deliver, through the back, a powerful forward thrust which slightly lifts the whole animal and drives the body forward. Reaching far under, and passing the imprint left by the front foot, the hind foot takes hold of the ground; then hock, stifle and upper thigh come into play and sweep back, the stroke of the hind leg finishing with the foot still close to the ground in a smooth follow-through. The overreach of the hindquarter usually necessitates one hind foot passing outside and the other hind foot passing inside the track of the forefeet, and such action is not faulty unless the locomotion is crabwise with the dog's body sideways out of the normal straight line.

Transmission—The typical smooth, flowing gait is maintained with great strength and firmness of back. The whole effort of the hindquarter is transmitted to the forequarter through the loin, back and withers. At full trot, the back must remain firm and level without sway, roll, whip or roach. Unlevel topline with withers lower than the hip is a **fault**. To compensate for the forward motion imparted by the hindquarters, the shoulder should open to its full extent. The forelegs should reach out close to the ground in a long stride in harmony with that of the hindquarters. The dog does not track on widely separated parallel lines, but brings the feet inward toward the middle line of the body when trotting, in order to maintain balance. The feet track closely but do not strike or cross over. Viewed from the front, the front legs function from the shoulder joint to the pad in a straight line. Viewed from the rear, the hind legs function from the hip joint to the pad in a straight line. Faults of gait, whether from front, rear or side, are to be considered very **serious faults.**

DISQUALIFICATIONS

Cropped or hanging ears. Dogs with noses not predominantly black. Undershot jaw. Docked tail. White dogs. Any dog that attempts to bite the judge.

Approved February 11, 1978
Reformatted July 11, 1994

© 1994 German Shepherd Dog Club of America, Inc.

Index